ND/001

SPORT FANS

THE PSYCHOLOGY
AND SOCIAL IMPACT
OF SPECTATORS

SPORT FANS

THE PSYCHOLOGY
AND SOCIAL IMPACT
OF SPECTATORS

Daniel L. Wann

Merrill J. Melnick

Gordon W. Russell

Dale G. Pease

ROUTLEDGE   NEW YORK ■ LONDON

"Sports Fans: Measuring Degree of Identification with Their Team," by Wann and Branscombe. *International Journal of Sport Psychology:* 24 (1), 1993, p. 5 Reprinted with permission.

"Preliminary Validation of the Sport Fan Motivation Scale," *Journal of Sport & Social Issues:* 19 (4), pp. 382–383. Reprinted with permission of Sage Publication, Inc.

"Assessing the Psychological Well-being of Sport Fans Using the Profiles of Mood States: The Importance of Team Identification," by Wann, et al. *International Sport Journal:* 3 (1), p. 84. Reprinted with permission.

"We Believe . . . ," by Spink, C.C. *The Sporting News:* June 10, 1978, p. 2. Reprinted with permission.

Published in 2001 by
Routledge
29 West 35th Street
New York, NY 10001

Published in Great Britain by
Routledge
11 New Fetter Lane
London EC4P 4EE

Rouledge is an imprint of the Taylor & Francis Group.

Library of Congress Cataloging-in-Publishing Data

Sports fans : the psychological and social impact of spectators / Daniel L. Wann ... [et. al.].
    p. cm.
  Includes bibliographical references and index.
  ISBN 0-415-92463-4 — ISBN 0-415-92464-2 (pbk.)
    1. Sports spectators—Psychology. 2. Sports—Social aspects. 3. Sports spectators—Social conditions. I. Wann, Daniel L.

GV 715 ,S655 2000
306.4'83'0973—dc21

00-032821

To Eric and Kevin, from Dan

To Dad, from Merrill

To Private H. E. Cummer, First Canadian Parachute Battalion
        Killed in action, March 24, 1945, age 21, from Gordon

To Patricia, from Dale

We are your biggest fans.

CONTENTS

ACKNOWLEDGMENTS

The authors wish to acknowledge the following individuals for their invaluable assistance throughout the writing of this book. First, we would like to thank Publishing Director of Behavioral Sciences Heidi A. Freund and her staff at Routledge Press for their tireless efforts throughout the various phases of this project.

Second, a special note of thanks must be given to Lawrence A. Wenner, Ph.D, University of San Francisco and Beth Dietz-Uhler, Ph.D, University of Miami, Ohio, for their efforts as reviewers on earlier versions of this book. Your insights and suggestions were most useful and informative and served to strengthen this book.

Third, we would like to express our gratitude to Dr. Beth Dietz-Uhler and Christian End of the University of Miami, Ohio, and to Dr. Dawn Stephens, Jay Pacelli, Cheryl Kelly, and Jaime Schulz of the University of Iowa for their assistance in the data collection phase of this project. Your efforts were truly beyond the call of duty.

Fourth, we would like to thank Sherry Fortner, secretary in the Department of Psychology at Murray State University, for all of her patience and assistance with the "technical" aspects of this project.

And finally, a special note of thanks goes to Christi L. Ensor. Simply stated, without your work as graduate assistant for Daniel L. Wann, this project could not have been completed. Thank you.

Chapter One | AN INTRODUCTION TO THE STUDY OF SPORT FANS

When individuals are asked to imagine a typical "sport fan" or "sport spectator," their images can vastly differ. Some describe both as happy, psychologically stable persons who are participating in a pastime that is important and beneficial to the structure of modern society. They imagine the strong social bonds that form among spectators—families coming together around a sporting event, groups of joyous fans storming onto the field to congratulate the victorious players. Others, however, hold a negative view of sport fans and spectators. They perceive them as beer-drinking couch potatoes with a pathological obsession with a trivial and socially disruptive activity. They imagine the violent outbursts of sport fans, the strained marital relationships between fans and their spouses, the lives that have been ruined because of sport-related gambling, and the ways that sport directs attention away from life's more important concerns, such as religion, politics, education, and the betterment of humanity.

Thus, while some perceive sport fandom as a positive force for both individuals and society, others view it as having a predominantly negative impact. Which of these divergent perspectives is correct? Is sport beneficial or harmful for society and its members? Are sport fans psychologically healthy or disturbed? Are fan behaviors harmless or harmful? To answer these questions fully, one must conduct a careful and thorough investigation of the personalities and characteristics of sport fans, the reasons underlying their decision to participate in the activity, and the relationship between sport fans and society. Such an investigation is the aim of this text. We attempt to answer these and similar questions by discussing and critiquing the current state of psychological and sociological research and theory on sport fandom. The desired result is a better understanding of sport fans, the meaning of sport in their lives, and the place of sport in contemporary society.

In this first chapter, we examine several basic topics relevant to the scientific exploration of sport fandom, thereby setting the stage for the remainder of the text. We begin by clearly defining, comparing, and contrasting sport fans, sport spectators, sport consumers, and highly identified fans. We then paint a picture of the typical sport fan by examining research on his/her demographic and personality characteristics. Next, we present data revealing the pervasiveness and impact of sport in contemporary society. In conclusion, we preview subsequent chapters.

DEFINING AND CLASSIFYING SPORT FANS

An important first step in understanding sport fandom is to define and classify those persons involved in the consumption of sport. In the following paragraphs, we will distinguish between sport fans and spectators, direct and indirect sport consumers, and lowly and highly identified sport fans.

Distinguishing between Sport Fans and Sport Spectators

The first important distinction to be made involves differentiating between sport *fans* and sport *spectators* (Wann, 1995, 1997). Sport fans are individuals who are interested in and follow a sport, team, and/or athlete. Sport spectators (also called sport consumers) are those individuals who actively witness a sporting event in person or through some form of media (radio, television, etc.). Unfortunately, even among sport scientists the terms sport fan and sport spectator are often used interchangeably. However, they should not be confused because some sport fans rarely witness sporting events in person, while some spectators have little interest in identifying with a favorite sport team or player. For instance, consider a person who attends a college basketball game simply because he was given a free ticket. This person may attend the contest even though he has no interest in the event itself; he simply wishes to be with his friends who are attending the game. Although this person would be classified as a sport spectator, he should not be classified as a sport fan. Consequently, to keep the distinction between fandom and spectating clear, we will use "sport fans" as a generic term to describe individuals with an abiding interest in sport. We will reserve the use of "sport spectators" for descriptions of those persons who actually witness an event. Of course, the terms "fan" and "spectator" are not mutually exclusive. Certainly, the majority of persons who witness a particular sporting event are also fans of that sport or one of the teams or players involved, while most fans do, at least on occasion, spectate sporting events.

Distinguishing between Direct and Indirect Sport Consumers

Another important distinction involves the classification of sport consumers (i.e., spectators) into two groups: direct sport consumers and indirect sport consumers (Kenyon, 1969; McPherson, 1975). Direct sport consumption involves one's personal attendance at a sporting event. Indirect sport consumption involves one's exposure to sport through some form of mass media, such as television, radio, or the Internet. According to Kenyon (1969), the key distinction between direct and indirect sport consumption is that with the former, the spectator becomes a part of the sporting environment and has the opportunity to impact the event. Thus, an individual who attends the Super Bowl in person would be classified as a direct sport consumer, while someone watching the same contest on television would be classified as an indirect sport consumer. This distinction is important because the situational context in which a spectator witnesses an event may impact his or her response to the event (Brummett & Duncan, 1990; Duncan & Brummett, 1989; Gantz, 1981; Hemphill, 1995; Wenner & Gantz, 1989).

Distinguishing between Lowly and Highly Identified Sport Fans

The next time you attend a sporting event, take a moment to watch the other spectators. As you do this, one fact will become very clear—spectators exhibit wide variations in their level of involvement with, and interest in, the contest. Some appear rather disinterested. They do not wear apparel that signifies their allegiance to a particular team, they rarely yell or clap in response to the actions of the athletes, and they seem more interested in talking to their friends than watching the game. Others, however, appear to be immersed in the contest. They are dressed (and maybe even painted) in their team's colors, actively root and yell for their team, attempt to distract the opposing players, and boo loudly when an official's call goes against their team. These examples contrast the various levels of team identification found among sport fans. Team identification refers to the extent to which a fan feels psychologically connected to a team (Guttmann, 1986; Hirt, Zillmann, Erickson, & Kennedy, 1992; M. R.

Real & Mechikoff, 1992; Sloan, 1989; Wann, 1997; Wann & Branscombe, 1993). This term is also used to describe a fan's loyalty to a specific player (e.g., Rinehart, 1998; Wann, 1997). Research indicates that team identification is not a function of the location or outcome of a team's most recent game (Wann, 1996, 2000; Wann, Dolan, McGeorge, & Allison, 1994; Wann & Schrader, 1996). Rather, fans tend to report highly consistent levels of identification from game to game and from season to season. Thus, one's level of identification with a particular team appears to be relatively stable.

For fans with a low level of team identification, the role of team follower is merely a peripheral component of their self-concept. As a result, these persons tend to exhibit only mild reactions to the team's performances. However, for fans with a high level of team identification, the role of team follower is a central component of their identity. In fact, they will readily present themselves as a fan of their team to others (Wann, Royalty, & Roberts, 1999). Because of their close association with a team, highly identified fans often view it as a reflection of themselves. That is, the team becomes an extension of the individual (E. R. Smith & Henry, 1996; Tajfel, 1981; Tajfel & Turner, 1979). The team's successes become the fan's successes and the team's failures become the fan's failures. The NCAA attempted to market this phenomenon during the 1999 men's basketball championship tournament with the slogan, "When it happens to my team, it happens to me."

Because of the increased importance highly identified fans place on their team's performances, their affective, cognitive, and behavioral reactions tend to be quite extreme. For instance, research indicates that compared to lowly identified fans, those high in team identification are more likely to attempt to influence the outcome of a sporting event (Wann et al., 1994), experience greater levels of anxiety and arousal watching their team compete (Branscombe & Wann, 1992a; Wann, Schrader, & Adamson, 1998), feel that sport spectating is a more enjoyable activity (Madrigal, 1995; Wann & Schrader, 1997), and possess a greater level of knowledge about their team and about sport in general (Wann & Branscombe, 1995a; Wann et al., 1997). Further, level of team identification is related to several topics examined in this text, including the motives of fans (see chapter 2), attendance decisions (chapter 3), sport hero worship (chapter 4), spectator aggression (chapter 5), and the psychological benefits of fandom (chapter 7).

The Measurement of Team Identification To assist in the accurate assessment of team identification, Wann and Branscombe (1993) developed the Sport Spectator Identification Scale (SSIS). Investigators from several countries have successfully used the SSIS in their work, including researchers in the United States (Gayton, Coffin, & Hearns, 1998; see Wann, 1997, for a review), Germany (Straub, 1995), and Japan (Uemukai, Takenouchi, Okuda, Matsumoto, & Yamanaka, 1995). The items comprising the SSIS are presented in table 1.1. The SSIS contains seven items with response options ranging from 1 to 8. Higher numbers represent greater levels of team identification. To determine your level of identification for your favorite team, simply answer the items listed in table 1.1. Then sum your responses to all seven. In general, scores less than 18 indicate a low level of identification, while scores greater than 35 suggest a high level of identification. Individuals scoring between 18 and 35 are classified as moderately identified.

The Origin of Team Identification Think for a moment about your favorite sport team. Now think back to when you first started supporting this team. This may be a somewhat difficult task because you probably have been a supporter of this team for a number of years (Wann & Branscombe, 1993). Can you recall the reasons for your initial decision to follow this team? Recent work by Wann, Tucker, and Schrader (1996) indicates that although there are dozens of reasons underlying an individual's decision to first identify with a particular team, a few reasons are particularly prominent. The authors asked ninety-one college students to state why they originally began and continued to follow their current favorite sport team. In addition, the respondents were asked to list the reasons why they stopped following a formerly favorite team. The most common reason listed for originally identifying with a team was that one's parents were supporters of the team. The second greatest influence was the talent and characteristics of the players. Geographical reasons (i.e., following the local team) and the influence of one's friends and peers tied for the third most prominent reason. Surprisingly, the success of the team was only the fifth most commonly mentioned reason for originally identifying with a team. However, when the same fans were asked to state why they continued to support the team, the success of the team was the number one reason (see also End, Dietz-Uhler, Harrick, & Jacquemotte, 1999). Similarly, a lack of team success was the most commonly cited reason for discontinuing one's identification with a formerly favorite team.

Research by I. Jones (1997) found a different pattern of identification decisions. This investigator asked English professional football (i.e., soccer) fans to state the reasons for their continued identification with their favorite team. Contrary to Wann et al. (1996), team

TABLE 1.1

The Sport Spectator Identification Scale

Instructions: Please list your favorite sport team. _____

Now answer each of the following questions with this team in mind by circling the most accurate number (i.e., response) to each item.

1. How important is it to you that the team listed above wins?
   Not Important 1   2   3   4   5   6   7   8   Very Important

2. How strongly do you see yourself as a fan of the team listed above?
   Not at All a Fan 1   2   3   4   5   6   7   8   Very Much a Fan

3. How strongly do your friends see you as a fan of the team listed above?
   Not at All a Fan 1   2   3   4   5   6   7   8   Very Much a Fan

4. During the season, how closely do you follow the team listed above via ANY of the following: in person or on television, on the radio, or televised news or a newspaper?
   Never 1   2   3   4   5   6   7   8   Almost Every Day

5. How important is being a fan of the team listed above to you?
   Not Important 1   2   3   4   5   6   7   8   Very Important

6. How much to you dislike the greatest rivals of the team listed above?
   Do Not Dislike 1   2   3   4   5   6   7   8   Dislike Very Much

7. How often do you display the above team's name or insignia at your place of work, where you live, or on your clothing?
   Never 1   2   3   4   5   6   7   8   Always

Reprinted with permission from Wann and Branscombe, "Sports Fans: Measuring Degree of Identification with Their Team." *International Journal of Sport Psychology*, 24 (1), 1993, p. 5.

success was not the greatest influence on the respondents' decisions to continue following a sport team. Rather, Jones found that geographical reasons were by far the most prominent ones listed. The success of the team was the fourteenth ranked reason given. Research by Uemukai et al. (1995) on Japanese football also found that geographical reasons topped the list of reasons for currently identifying with a team (see also Eastman & Riggs, 1994).

Research by Branscombe and Wann (1991) suggests that the contradictory findings described here may be due to a complex interaction among geography, team success, and team identification. These investigators asked several hundred college students to list their favorite Major League Baseball (MLB) team and to complete the SSIS for that team. The authors then correlated the subjects' identification scores with the success of their favorite team (success was operationally defined as the team's win/loss record over the previous five seasons). When all twenty-six teams were included in the analysis, the results failed to reveal a significant relationship between identification and team success. However, when the data for subjects identifying with the geographically closest team were removed from the analysis, a statistically significant relationship emerged in which "displaced" fans (fans of a geographically distant team) reported higher levels of identification for more successful teams. Therefore, one can conclude that team success is more closely related to the current identification of displaced fans than of local fans. This fact may help explain why Wann et al. (1996) found that team success was the most important determinant of current level of identification, while I. Jones (1997) and Uemukai et al. (1995) found that geographical reasons were most prominent. In the Wann et al. research, the participants were asked to list their favorite sport team from any sport and to report their reasons for continuing to identify with that team. Because participants could choose any team from any sport, it is likely that a number of respondents would have been classified as displaced fans (i.e., their favorite teams were geographically distant). However, participants in the Jones and Uemukai et al. studies were asked about specific teams. This may have resulted in very few displaced fans being included in their sample. Because most of the fans identified with a geographically close team, the teams' performances were less relevant than their geographical nearness.

DEMOGRAPHIC AND PERSONALITY TRAITS OF SPORT FANS

Now that we have classified the various types of sport fans and spectators, it is appropriate to discuss the demographic and personality patterns of these persons. A number of researchers have attempted to establish a demographic and personality profile of sport fans. Table 1.2 summarizes this literature.

Several points regarding this research warrant mention. First, researchers have been inconsistent in their operational definitions of sport fandom. Some researchers have compared the characteristics of persons with a stated interest in fandom with those without such an interest. In this instance, the researcher is clearly contrasting the profiles of fans and nonfans. However, other investigators have compared individuals who attended a specific athletic event with individuals who chose not to attend. Unfortunately, there is no way of knowing how many persons in the nonattendance group were sport fans who simply did not attend that particular game. This shortcoming limits the generalizability of the findings.

To aid researchers in acquiring a consistent and reliable assessment of sport fandom, Wann (in press) recently developed and validated the Sport Fandom Questionnaire (SFQ). The SFQ includes five items that are designed to measure level of identification with the role of sport fan. Hopefully, future researchers will employ the SFQ when assessing level of sport fandom, resulting in a clearer and more consistent operational definition of the construct.

A second important point that should be noted is that much of the research on the personality patterns of sport fans has been atheoretical. That is, similar to personality work on athletes (Martens, 1981; Morgan, 1980; Silva, 1984), investigations of the personality profile of sport fans have not been guided by a theoretical rationale. Without theory, investigators are often left "fishing" for significant differences between fans and nonfans. Such findings are often difficult to replicate because they are the artifactual result of a single, unpredicted observation. A more appropriate line of research would be to use relevant theory to predict specific differences between fans and nonfans, and then test those predictions.

Third, some of the findings outlined in table 1.2 have been contradicted by other research. For instance, although Murrell and Dietz (1992) and B. A. Lee and Zeiss (1980) found that age and sport fandom are positively correlated, recent work by Wann (in press) failed to replicate this relationship (see also Lieberman, 1991). Similarly, although some researchers have found a positive relationship between socioeconomic status and sport fandom (Mashiach, 1980; Pan, Gabert, McGaugh, & Branvold, 1997; Prisuta, 1979; Yergin, 1986), others have not (Freischlag & Hardin, 1975; S. J. Grove, Pickett, & Dodder, 1982). These contradictions are most likely due to the inconsistent methodologies employed by the researchers, the aforementioned inconsistencies in operationally defining sport fandom, and the atheoretical nature of the research.

Thus, it is readily apparent that there is much work to be done before we have a complete profile of the typical sport fan and sport spectator. The information presented in table 1.2 is simply a summary of current research on the demographic and personality characteristics of these people. Hopefully, future researchers will be able to expand and improve on this literature, the result being more accurate and complete profiles of the sport fan and sport consumer.

TABLE 1.2

Demographic and Personality Characteristics Associated with Sport Fandom

CHARACTERISTIC	REFERENCE(S)
1. Disproportionately likely to be African American	Schurr et al. (1985); Schurr et al. (1988)
2. Disproportionately likely to be male	Anderson & Stone (1981); Bloss (1970); Dietz-Uhler et al. (1999); Doyle et al. (1980); Grove et al. (1982); Lieberman (1991); McPherson (1975); Murrell & Dietz (1992); Prisuta (1979); Roloff & Solomon (1989); Sargent et al. (1998); Schurr et al. (1985); Schurr et al. (1988); Wann (1998b); Yergin (1986); Zuckerman et al. (1980)
3. Positively correlated with socioeconomic status	Lieberman (1991); Mashiach (1980); McPherson (1975); Pan et al. (1997); Prisuta (1979); Yergin (1986)
4. Positively correlated with age	Lee & Zeiss (1980); Murrell & Dietz (1992)
5. Positively correlated with involvement in sport as a participant	Bloss (1970); Freischlag & Hardin (1975); Grove et al. (1982); Prisuta (1979); Schurr et al. (1985); Shank & Beasley (1998); Smith et al. (1981)
6. Positively correlated with active vocational interests*	Schurr et al. (1985); Schurr et al. (1988)
7. Spectators at college sporting events likely to have a distant home town	Schurr et al. (1985); Schurr et al. (1988)
8. Spectators at college sporting events likely to live in a residence hall	McPherson (1975); Schurr et al. (1985); Schurr et al. (1988)
9. No correlation with introversion-extroversion	Lane & Lester (1995); Schurr et al. (1985); Schurr et al. (1988)

continued on the next page

CHARACTERISTIC	REFERENCE(S)
10. No correlation with tobacco use	Wann (1998b)
11. No correlation with alcohol use	Wann (1998a)
12. No correlation with internal/external locus of control	Miller (1976)

* Operationally defined as interest in vocations such as physical education, business, and radio/television, rather than vocations such as arts, humanities, and architecture.

THE PERVASIVENESS AND IMPACT OF SPORT IN TODAY'S SOCIETY

Now that we have established clear definitions and classifications of the various types of sport fans and have an understanding of who these persons are (at least a basic understanding), one important question remains: Why should we bother to study these persons? Perhaps the best justification for an empirical examination of sport fans lies in the pervasiveness of sport fandom in modern society (as well as ancient civilizations; see Guttmann, 1986). Simply put, sport has had and continues to have a tremendous impact on society and its members. Several lines of evidence lead to this conclusion. For instance, studies conducted in the 1970s (D. Anderson & Stone, 1981), 1980s (Thomas, 1986), and again in the early 1990s (Lieberman, 1991) revealed that at least two-thirds of Americans considered themselves to be a sport fan.

Data collected by the authors of this text during the late 1990s also indicate the pervasiveness of sport in contemporary society (the authors express their gratitude to Dr. Beth Dietz-Uhler and Christian End of the University of Miami, Ohio, and to Dr. Dawn Stephens, Jay Pacelli, Cheryl Kelly, and Jaime Schulz of the University of Iowa, for their assistance in gathering the data for this study). We asked slightly over one thousand college students to complete a questionnaire assessing a variety of behaviors related to sport fandom (students from five different universities participated in the study: Murray State University, the University of Houston, the State University of New York, College at Brockport, the University of Miami, Ohio, and the University of Iowa). The participants were asked to report how often they (1) attended sporting events in person, (2) watched sporting events on television (including sport news programs), (3) listened to sporting events on the radio, and (4) discussed sport with their friends or relatives. The participants were asked to choose from one of the following eight response options: never, about once a year, about twice a year, about once a month, about twice a month, about once a week, about twice a week, or about once a day. The results are shown in table 1.3. The vast majority of subjects participated regularly in sport fandom behaviors. For instance, over 69 percent of the participants watched a televised sporting event at least once a week, while almost 67 percent discussed sports on a weekly basis. Further, very few participants stated that they never attended sporting events (8 percent), watched sport on television (3.8 percent), or discussed sport with their friends or relatives (4.2 percent). While these data clearly indicate the strong place of sport in the lives of the respondents, it is important to remember that all were college students. Consequently, one must be cautious when generalizing the aforementioned results to noncollege populations.

TABLE 1.3

University Students' Level of Involvement with Sport Fandom

FREQUENCY ITEM	NEVER	ABOUT ONCE A YEAR	ABOUT TWICE A YEAR	ABOUT ONCE A MONTH	ABOUT TWICE A MONTH	ABOUT ONCE A WEEK	ABOUT TWICE A WEEK	ABOUT ONCE A DAY
Attend sporting events in person	8.0	9.2	22.8	22.4	17.6	13.4	5.9	0.7
Watch sporting events on television	3.8	2.1	5.1	11.2	8.7	16.6	18.7	33.9
Listen to sporting events on the radio	29.2	12.7	14.9	17.0	9.8	7.0	5.1	4.0
Discuss sports with friends or relatives	4.2	4.0	6.4	10.1	8.4	16.5	16.0	34.4

Note: Numbers listed above are percentages. Numbers may not sum to 100 because of missing responses and rounding.

The pervasiveness of sport in contemporary society is not simply reflected in the number of persons who report an interest in sport. Rather, one can also document this pervasiveness through attendance figures, the amount of sport coverage on television and radio, the large number of sport-related movies and videos, the impact of sport on the print media (i.e., books, magazines, and newspapers), and the emergence of sport on the Internet.

The Pervasiveness of Sport as Revealed through Attendance Data

Perhaps no other set of statistics reveals the pervasiveness of sport more than attendance figures. For instance, in 1998, attendance at MLB games topped 64 million. Attendance figures for the other major sports are equally impressive: NCAA men's basketball—28.2 million (1996 season), National Basketball Association (NBA)—21.8 million (1997–98 season), NCAA football—37.5 million (1998 season), National Football League (NFL)—19.7 million (1998 season), and National Hockey League (NHL)—17.3 million (1997–98 season). Professional auto racing—perhaps the fastest growing spectator sport in the United States—also draws large crowds. For instance, 2.1 million spectators attended the 1998 Busch series, while 6.4 million attended the 1998 Winston Cup series. In fact, events such as the Daytona 500 and the Indianapolis 500 typically draw more than 100,000 spectators every year. Interestingly, spectators are attending these sporting events in record numbers even though ticket prices have risen an average of 7.2 percent annually since 1991, compared to an annual inflation rate of only 2.8 percent during the same time period (McCallum & O'Brien, 1998d).

However, the major colleges and the professional sport leagues do not hold a monopoly on the interest of sport spectators. Attendance data from several less visible sports also indicate that an astounding number of persons attend sporting events each year. For instance, consider the following:

1. Many NCAA Division I women's basketball teams average several thousand spectators per contest (e.g., the Tennessee University Volunteers routinely draw more than 12,000 spectators per game). In fact, attendance at NCAA women's basketball contests topped 5 million spectators in 1996.
2. Most Arena Football League teams average in excess of 10,000 spectators per contest.
3. Crowds at Major League Soccer games totaled over 2.7 million in 1998.

4. In 1995 the St. Paul Saints of the independent Northern League (minor league baseball) attracted over 250,000 fans to their forty-one home games.
5. The Women's National Basketball Association established attendance records in 1999 as more than 1.7 million spectators attended the contests.

Examples such as these suggest that sport fans are willing to purchase tickets to watch almost any sport played at almost any level.

Although each of these examples involves North American sports, sport is highly relevant in most other societies as well. For instance, soccer is the national pastime of many countries and an obsession for hundreds of millions of spectators worldwide. As proof of this, consider that when 160,000 1998 World Cup tickets went on sale in France, the sponsoring organization received four million phone calls requesting tickets *in the first hour* (McCallum & O'Brien, 1998b).

The Pervasiveness of Sport as Revealed through Television and Radio Coverage

The pervasiveness of sport in the lives of fans and its important place in society are also evident in the extensive coverage of sport on television and radio. With respect to television coverage, one need only turn on the television set and channel surf to document the pervasiveness of sport. For each of the three major networks in the United States (ABC, CBS, and NBC) sport is a major component of their overall programming schedule, particularly during weekends. In fact, Madrigal (1995) reports that these networks broadcast over 1,800 hours of sport programming in 1988, a 500 percent increase over the 300 hours broadcast in 1960. When one considers the addition of Fox (NFL football, MLB, and NHL hockey), the Fox Sports Network (Fox Sports Rocky Mountain, Fox Sports South, Fox Sports Bay Area, and so on), the ESPN Network (ESPN, ESPN2, ESPN News, ESPN Classic), the Golf Channel, WGN (Chicago Cubs and Chicago White Sox baseball, Chicago Bulls basketball), TBS (NBA basketball, Atlanta Braves baseball, the Goodwill Games), TNN (motor sports), TNT (NBA basketball), HBO and Showtime (boxing and *Inside the NFL*), and the coverage of sport news on CNN and Headline News, two things become abundantly clear: (1) network executives desperately want a piece of the sport programming pie, and (2) sport fans are rarely, if ever, deprived of sport on television.

How many viewers tune in to these various sport programs? Consider that in 1997, NFL games or highlights were broadcast in 190 different countries and territories (O'Brien & Hersch, 1997b), resulting in well over 100 million viewers each week (O'Brien & Hersch, 1997a). An estimated 133 million individuals watched Super Bowl XXXIII (West, 1998). During the 1999 season, NBA games were broadcast to 650 million households in 190 countries (from A, Afghanistan, to Z, Zimbabwe). The Canadian Television Network (CTV) estimated that 2 billion viewers were tuned in to at least a portion of their broadcast of the 1988 Calgary Olympics (CTV controlled the broadcast feeds sent to the networks in other nations; see MacNeill, 1996). The ratings of sport programs are equally impressive. In fact, the fourth, fifth, sixth, and seventh highest rated television shows of all time are sport programs (fourth—Super Bowl XVI, 40.0 million viewers; fifth—Super Bowl XVII, 40.5 million; sixth—second Wednesday of the XVII Winter Olympics, 45.7 million; seventh—Super Bowl XX, 41.5 million). Of the 43 highest rated television shows of all time, twenty-one are sporting events (Famighetti, 1998).

The networks are well aware of the ratings potential of major sport programs and are willing to pay extraordinary sums of money for the broadcast rights. For instance, in 1998, CBS, ABC, and ESPN paid a combined $17.6 billion to the NFL in order to telecast football games through the year 2005 (McCallum & O'Brien, 1998a). CBS president Leslie Moonves was especially excited about the return of NFL football to CBS (CBS had lost the NFL broadcast rights during the previous contract). During a 1998 interview, Moonves stated, "Young men had deserted us. Now there are signs of life here [at CBS]." CBS also paid $350 million for the rights to broadcast the 1998 Nagano Olympics (MacNeill, 1996). This figure was 7,500 times greater than the $50,000 CBS paid for the broadcast rights to the 1960 Squaw Valley Olympics only thirty-eight years earlier. Even more impressive was the $3.5 billion NBC paid for the broadcast rights for the 2000 to 2008 Olympic Games (Swift, 1999).

When one considers the money sponsors are willing to pay to advertise during major sporting events, it is clear that television network executives have spent their money well. For instance, a 30-second advertisement during the 1999 Super Bowl cost $1.6 million, up from $1.3 million the year before (Walters, 1999b; West, 1998). In fact, it was estimated that Fox sold $150 million worth of advertisement slots for the 1999 Super Bowl.

Sport coverage on radio is also prevalent. Most professional and major college sport teams have their own radio networks. Recently, sport talk radio has become very popular. The first 24-hour-a-day sport talk radio station, WFAN in New York, was introduced in 1987

(Haag, 1996; Mariscal, 1999). However, as a testament to the popularity of this programming format, there were an estimated 150 such stations only ten years later (Goldberg, 1998; Mariscal, 1999). Referred to by Goldberg (1998) as "the church of athletic self-opinion" (p. 213), sport talk radio allows fans to express their views, release their frustrations, and (theoretically) demonstrate their sport acumen. It allows for feedback and conversation—something noticeably missing with television viewing.

The Pervasiveness of Sport as Revealed through Sport-Related Movies and Videos

Yet another example of the pervasiveness of sport in today's society can be seen in the large number of sport-related movies and videos now available. Within the last few years, several popular movies with sport themes have appeared, including *Jerry McQuire*, *Tin Cup*, the *Major League* series, *The Fan*, *White Men Can't Jump*, *He Got Game*, *Hoop Dreams*, *Bull Durham*, *Necessary Roughness*, and *The Waterboy*, to name but a few. These and other movies, as well as highlight films from most sports, are readily available to fans in video format.

The Pervasiveness of Sport as Revealed through the Print Media

The pervasiveness of sport is also reflected in the print media (i.e., sport-related books, magazines, and newspaper coverage). With respect to sport-related books, simply venture into a bookstore and you will quickly see the importance of sport, as most bookstores have a special (and large) section for sport-related material. In fact, as of late 1998, the Amazon book company offered, online, approximately 6,000 books on baseball alone, as well as 4,000 books on football, 2,700 books on basketball, and 2,600 books on golf. Similar inventories are available from Barnes and Noble. There are also several sport-related magazines. In the late 1990s Amazon offered subscriptions to more than 100 different sport magazines.

Arguably, newspapers remain the print media with the strongest connection to sport. Every major and minor newspaper contains a sports section, and statistics show that news editors are expanding their coverage of sport relative to the rest of the paper (Lever & Wheeler, 1984). The "nation's newspaper," *USA Today*, includes a Sport section as one of its four major components, and it is often the largest of the four (how many of us have purchased a copy of *USA Today*, read the Sport section, and discarded the rest of the paper?). For example, in the Friday, November 14, 1997, issue of *USA Today*, the News section contained sixteen pages, the Money section twelve pages, the Life section fourteen pages, and the Sport section twenty-eight pages. In addition, this issue included a bonus basketball preview section containing fourteen pages. Thus, the editors allotted 50 percent of the newspaper's space to sport! Clearly, this amount of coverage indicates that the editors understand the place of sport in today's society and its importance to their target audience.

The Pervasiveness of Sport as Revealed through Sport-Related Internet Sites

The most recent evidence of the pervasiveness of sport in society is the Internet. Sport fandom has thrived on the World Wide Web. Need proof? Consider that in January 1999 the keyword "sport" resulted in approximately 20.5 million matches on Infoseek! The keyword "baseball" resulted in 3.3 million hits, while there were 4.1 million matches for football, 3.4 million for basketball, and 4.8 million for golf. The most popular Internet sites for sport include those by ESPN Sportszone, CBS Sportsline, CNN/SI, and *USA Today*. The number of individuals connecting to these sites is staggering. In fact, it has been estimated that these sites are called up over 100 million times per month (Alvarez, 1997; Grover, 1998). These impressive figures are not limited to the major websites. For instance, the Wimbledon site recorded approximately 40 million hits in one week during the 1997 tournament, while the Dallas Cowboys site averaged over 250,000 hits per night during the 1997 preseason (Alvarez, 1997). According to a recent article in *Sports Illustrated* (O'Brien & Hersch, 1997c), figure skater Tara Lipinski's personal site has received over 1 million hits, while professional race car driver Jeff Gordon's site has received more than 32 million hits. Truly, sport fandom has gone hi-tech.

Further evidence of the impact of sport on the Internet can be found in book and magazine articles that list and describe sport-related Internet sites. For example, Leebow (1999) recently published a book entitled *300 Incredible Things for Sports Fans on the Internet*, which, as the title implies, provides readers with the addresses to a number of fan-friendly sites. Several of the sites described in the book are directly related to sport fans and spectators. With respect to magazine coverage of sport on the Internet, *Sports Illustrated* recently began a weekly feature on sport in multimedia that contains "The Surfer" section, which describes several sport-specific Internet sites.

Summary of the Pervasiveness of Sport in Society

The statistics presented in this chapter paint a clear picture—sport has become a major component of modern life. The impact of the proliferation of sport is not limited to fans, but affects the lives of all members of society by taking up space in newspapers, commanding time on television (consider the reactions of nonfans when their favorite program is preempted by a sporting event), and serving as the focal point of conversation. Indeed, it is precisely this impact that provides validation and justification for the scientific study of sport fandom. Sport fandom touches the lives of most members of society by impacting entertainment choices, hero selection, emotionality and aggression, interpersonal relationships, psychological and societal well-being, and many other components of everyday living. The large impact of this phenomenon warrants our investigation.

It is important to note that, despite the prominent place of sport in society and its importance to so many people, social scientists have paid very little attention to sports fans (Melnick, 1989). In fact, one study found that less than 5 percent of the research in sport psychology and sport sociology has targeted the thoughts and behaviors of fans (Wann & Hamlet, 1995). Rather, the vast majority of sport-related research has investigated athletic participants (i.e., athletes, coaches, and officials). The lack of research on and about sport fans is unfortunate because, as the data provided here reveal, the consumption of sport is a major element of contemporary life.

OVERVIEW OF FOLLOWING CHAPTERS

Hopefully, the preceding pages have given the reader an overview of the pervasiveness of sport in today's society and made a strong case for the scientific study of sport fans. It should now be apparent that sport has a tremendous impact on society and its members (both fans and nonfans alike) and that social scientists should endeavor to further our understanding of sport fans and sport spectators. To this aim, this text focuses on two interrelated themes: the importance and impact of sport for fans and the importance and impact of fans for society. By integrating research and theory from both sport psychology and sport sociology, the analysis benefits from a multidisciplinary perspective. To fully understand sport fans within a societal context, one must consider both microlevel (i.e., sport psychological) and macrolevel (i.e., sport sociological) frameworks. Typically, the sport psychological viewpoint examines individual behaviors, traits, and characteristics. This perspective assists in our understanding of such fan-related phenomena as team identification, attendance decisions, personality traits associated with spectator violence, and hero worship, to name but a few. The sport sociological viewpoint tends to focus on the larger, macrolevel implications of sport fandom. This framework aids in our understanding of phenomena such as the structural context of sport, cultural values, collective behavior, and institutional functions.

This text has been divided into three sections. The first examines factors related to fan interest in and involvement with various sports, teams, and athletes. It includes three chapters. Chapter 2, "Becoming a Sport Fan," examines factors that influence an individual's decision to become a sport fan. It includes a discussion of the sport fan socialization process and the specific motives for sport fandom. Chapter 3, "Becoming a Sport Spectator," examines attendance at sporting events. It discusses the pressures applied to cities and other public agencies to build new sport facilities as well as the benefits for both fans (e.g., what fans get for their time and money) and society (e.g., what society receives for hosting a sporting franchise). Chapter 4, "Sport Fans and Their Heroes," focuses on the role and impact of sport heroes in society insofar as they shape the values and behaviors of their admirers. This chapter includes discussions of sport hero worship among youth, the relationship between personality variables and hero selection, and the impact of sport stars on their admirers.

The second section focuses on a darker side of sport fandom by examining spectator aggression. Chapter 5, "An Introduction to Spectator Aggression," provides a general overview of fan violence. It examines definitional issues, various forms of spectator violence, and the prevalence of fan violence throughout the world. Chapter 6, "Psychological and Sociological Causes of Spectator Aggression," examines the psychological (i.e., microlevel) and sociological (i.e., macrolevel) theory and research designed to account for spectator violence. It examines topics such as situational and environmental causes of fan violence (e.g., modeling, darkness, temperature, and crowding) as well as the larger societal factors that play a role in fan aggression (e.g., cultural, societal, and structural). This chapter also addresses the relationship between alcohol consumption and spectator aggression. Chapter 7, "Sport Spectator Riots"—the third and final chapter in this section—focuses on large-scale spectator aggression. It includes discussions about different forms of spectator riots, the personality characteristics of those who participate in riots and those who attempt to stop them, and soccer hooliganism.

The third section examines the advantages and disadvantages of sport fandom. Social scientists have debated the individual and societal costs and benefits of sport fandom and sport spectating for many years. While some have argued that sport fandom can have a positive impact on both the individual and society, others have contended that sport fandom has mainly negative effects. This section takes a critical look at both sides of the debate. Chapter 8, "The Psychological Consequences of Sport Fandom," focuses on the potential psychological costs and benefits of sport fandom. It begins with a critical examination of the argument that sport fandom has harmful effects on the individual fan. This argument is examined within a framework of existing theory and, where available, relevant research findings. The chapter also critiques the argument that fandom has positive effects on the individual fan, again referring to the research literature whenever possible. Chapter 9, "The Societal Consequences of Sport Fandom," examines the larger implications of sport fandom. The analysis includes "functional" (e.g., sport consumption contributes to societal integration) as well as "conflict" (e.g., sport fandom is a "cultural anesthesia") perspectives. The chapter also examines the feminist critique of spectator sport, which makes the case that sport contributes to masculine hegemony and reinforcement of the gender order.

PART I

The Desire to Follow Sport, Teams, and Athletes

| *Chapter Two* | **BECOMING A SPORT FAN** |

Throughout the pages of this text, we describe the behaviors, cognitions, and emotions of sport fans and the relationship between sport fandom and society. We concentrate on the "what" of sportfanship by examining such questions as "What factors impact fans' decisions to attend specific athletic contests?" (chapter 3); "What factors influence fans' decisions to choose athletes as heroes?" (chapter 4); "What factors contribute to fan violence?" (chapters 5, 6, and 7); and "What are the individual and societal costs and benefits of sport fandom?" (chapters 8 and 9). However, before answering these "what" questions, we must concern ourselves with the "why" of sport fandom. "Why do certain individuals become sport fans?" "Why have they chosen this recreational pastime over the plethora of other pastime options?" This focus on the "why" of sport fandom provides a unifying theme for the current chapter. We begin our investigation of the reasons underlying an individual's decision to become a sport fan by examining the sport fan socialization process. We then examine several factors associated with fan motivation.

SOCIALIZATION INTO THE ROLE OF SPORT FAN

Although survey data clearly indicate that most Americans consider themselves sport fans (D. Anderson & Stone, 1981; Lieberman, 1991; Thomas, 1986), it is equally evident that others have absolutely no interest in sport. Why do some members of society become passionate, lifelong fans while others never give sport a moment's notice?

The answer is best understood through an examination of the sport fan socialization process. Socialization is defined as the process of learning to live in and understand a culture or subculture by internalizing its values, beliefs, attitudes, and norms. With respect to sport fandom, we are specifically concerned with the process by which fans learn and accept the values, beliefs, attitudes, and norms of the sport fan culture (e.g., the notion of "never giving up," the jargon, terminology, rules of specific sports, players' statistics, and so forth). An understanding of the sport fan socialization process will not only further our comprehension of why certain individuals become fans, but will also assist us in explaining why certain groups (e.g., males, African Americans) are overrepresented among fans. Specifically, certain individuals or groups may be more likely than others to have been exposed to the sport fandom culture. Consequently, they are more likely to have learned and adopted the sport fan culture and the sport fan role.

Although a few authors have discussed the process of sport fan socialization (e.g., Kenyon & McPherson, 1973, 1974; McPherson, 1975), only a handful of empirical studies have been completed. The most extensive work in this area was done by McPherson (1976). He posits that four sources are mainly responsible for teaching the values, beliefs, attitudes, and norms of sport fandom. Referred to as socialization agents, they include the individual's family, peers, school, and community. To test the impact of these four socialization agents, McPherson asked Canadian adolescents to complete a questionnaire assessing the impact of each. He also included several items that measured the participants' degree of sport consumption. For instance, with respect to the impact of the family, the respondents were asked to report the number of family members who consumed sport, the frequency of their consumption, and the importance they attached to sport consumption. Sport consumption was viewed as a combination of three factors: (1) behavioral (e.g., attending games and buying tickets), (2) affective (e.g., loyalty to a team and mood changes while consuming the sport), and (3) cognitive (e.g., knowledge of the individuals, teams, and rules of the sport).

The data revealed that male and female participants reported different patterns of sport fan socialization. Males were most often influenced by their peers, followed by family and school. The community did not appear to be a significant agent in the sport fan socialization of males. As for female participants, family had the greatest influence, followed closely by peer groups. The community was also found to have a significant impact on the socialization of females, but to a lesser degree than family and peers. School did not appear to be a significant agent.

G. J. Smith, Patterson, Williams, and Hogg (1981) examined the socialization of sport fans by conducting extensive interviews with highly involved male sport fans. The participants were asked to identify the socialization agents who had the greatest influence on their becoming a fan. They were asked to choose no more than three from the following options: father, brother, friend, coach, mass media, no one. The respondents reported that their fathers had the greatest socializing influence, followed by friends. These results were similar to those obtained by McPherson (1976), who also found that family and peers were the two most important socialization agents for males.

A more recent examination of the impact of socialization agents on sport fandom was reported by Wakefield (1995). This researcher asked spectators attending a minor league baseball game to state their perceptions of family and peer acceptance of the activity (i.e., baseball spectating). Spectators were also asked for their perceptions of the quality of the event (e.g., they were asked to rate the stadium, food service, ticket value, etc.). Wakefield divided the participants into two groups: those who believed their family and friends viewed baseball spectating as unpopular and unfashionable (33 percent of participants), and those who said their family and friends viewed the activity as popular and fashionable (67 percent of participants). Those who believed their family and friends held negative attitudes reported more negative evaluations of the stadium and food services, lower perceptions of the value of the ticket, lower levels of involvement, and were less intent on attending a future game. Thus, the impact of the socialization agents was quite powerful, influencing the spectators' evaluations and enjoyment of the game, as well as their intentions to attend future contests.

Before concluding our discussion of sport fan socialization, two important points warrant mention. First, it is quite likely that the socialization process differs from one sport to another and among different ethnic groups (Kenyon & McPherson, 1973, 1974; McPherson, 1975). For instance, the values, beliefs, attitudes, and norms held by European soccer hooligans (a group of fans with a long history of violence) differ greatly from those held by North American golf fans. Further, different sport settings may give rise to different fan cultures. For instance, in his work on sport queues (i.e., ticket lines) Mann (1969, 1989) concluded that the queue is "a miniature social system . . . formulating its own set of informal rules" (p. 340). Other sport fan settings that may also develop their own miniature cultures include restrooms, "tailgating parties," sport memorabilia conventions, and Internet chat rooms.

The fact that the sport fan socialization process is related to culture, class, and ethnicity has three important implications for future research. First, researchers should conduct cross-cultural research to determine how the sport fan socialization process differs across various sociocultural contexts. Second, they need to document the components of the socialization process that are universal and those that are situationally specific. Third, researchers must be careful not to generalize their findings to groups that were not represented by their sample; for instance, research on U.S. fans may not reflect the socialization of fans in other countries.

A second important point to mention before concluding our examination of sport fan socialization is the fact that the findings reported by McPherson (1976) and G. J. Smith et al. (1981) are several years old. Consequently, the pattern of effects obtained by both researchers may not accurately reflect the sport fan socialization process today. This possibility is especially likely given the fact that gender differences in sport fandom change over time. For instance, consider the work of D. Anderson and Stone (1981). In 1960 these researchers asked several hundred Minneapolis residents to report on their sport fandom. Then, in 1975, they asked a second sample drawn from the same city to respond to the same items. Anderson and Stone found that the percentage of males who considered themselves sport fans rose from 64.2 percent in 1960 to 76.7 percent in 1975. However, female participants reported a much larger increase in self-described fandom. Although only 37.9 percent of the females in the 1960 sample claimed to be a fan, 60.2 percent did so in 1975.

Because of the strong possibility that the patterns of sport fan socialization have changed since the early 1980s, the authors conducted a study to examine current socialization patterns. Recall from chapter 1 that students from five universities were asked to complete a questionnaire assessing their sport involvement as fans. A portion of the inventory assessed the participants' perceptions of the impact of various socialization agents on their interest in sport fandom. First, the participants responded to a series of questions that assessed the importance of four different agents by rating the influence of their parents, friends and peers, schools, and community. These agents were specifically chosen to allow for a direct comparison to McPherson's (1976) findings. The participants were asked to rate the importance of each of the agents on a scale ranging from 1 (the agent had no influence) to 8 (the agent had a great deal of influence).

The results are presented in table 2.1. Multivariate analysis of variance revealed significant main effects for both the socialization agents and the participants' gender. Peers and friends were rated the most powerful agents, while community was the least influential agent. Male participants rated each of the agents as being more influential than did female participants. However, the two-way interaction was also significant. This finding suggests that while the gender difference in the influence of one's parents, schools, and community were minimal, males were much more likely to have been influenced by peers and friends. The finding that males were most strongly influenced by peers replicates McPherson's (1976) data, as does the finding that males were least likely to have been influenced by their community. Thus, for males, the pattern of sport fandom socialization was consistent from the 1970s to the late 1990s.

Such was not the case for the female participants, however. While McPherson (1976) found that school had the least amount of influence on female fans, the current female sample reported that it was the most powerful socialization agent. This change in the socialization process for female fans may reflect the impact of Title IX. Title IX, which was put into law in 1972, prohibits sexual discrimination in institutions receiving federal funding. This law has had a tremendous impact on high school and college athletics because it requires that schools provide equal opportunity to women athletes. Consequently, the number of women's sport teams at the high school and collegiate levels has increased dramatically in the last two decades (Greendorfer, 1993; Oglesby, 1989; M. A. Snyder, 1993). Perhaps the increase in participation has led to a greater prominence of female

TABLE 2.1

Estimates of Influence of Four Socialization Agents

SOCIALIZATION AGENT	ALL SUBJECTS	MALES ONLY	FEMALES ONLY
Parents	4.69	4.88	4.52
Peers and friends	5.47	6.02	4.99
Schools	5.14	5.25	5.04
Community	4.08	4.30	3.88

Note: Scores ranged from 1 (the agent had no influence) to 8 (the agent had a great deal of influence).

sports in school settings, thereby arousing greater interest in sport among the female student body. Certainly, these findings are consistent with this possibility, and they suggest that there may have been an added influence of Title IX, namely, the increased role of the school in socialization of female sport fans.

In addition to responding to the four items that directly assessed the impact of various socialization agents, the participants were asked to list the person (e.g., father, aunt, etc.) or entity (e.g., school, media, etc.) that had the greatest single influence on their becoming involved with sport as a fan. Responses to this open-ended item appear in table 2.2. Family exerted the greatest influence on socialization into sport fandom, as more than half of the male and female participants listed a family member (direct or extended) as the individual who provided the greatest influence. Within the family, fathers and siblings were most influential. The data also revealed that friends, peers, schools, and the media played prominent roles in the socialization process.

There were also several gender differences among the most influential socialization agents identified. Perhaps the most striking difference involved parents. Males were more likely than females to list their father; females were more likely to list their mother. The female respondents were also more likely to report being influenced by their spouse (i.e., husband), while male respondents were more likely to be influenced by their siblings (particularly their brothers). In addition to these gender differences, differences in nonfamily agents were also found. Males were more likely to report that the greatest influence came from the media or coaches, while females were more likely to list their boyfriend and school.

A final interesting result revealed by the data involved the gender of the socialization agents. The gender of the agent was mentioned in approximately 58 percent of the cases (e.g., father, sister, aunt, etc.). An examination of these agents reveals that they were far more likely to be male (51.1 percent) than female (6.9 percent). Thus, it is evident that both male and female sport fans are much more likely to be socialized into the sport follower role by males.

SPORT FAN MOTIVATION

Imagine a family comprised of a mother, father, son, and daughter. Let's assume that the parents are highly involved sport fans (e.g., they often discuss sport, frequently watch sport in person and on television, subscribe to several sport magazines, take family trips to

TABLE 2.2

Frequency of Socialization Agents Listed as the Single Greatest Influence

SOCIALIZATION AGENT	ALL SUBJECTS	MALES ONLY	FEMALES ONLY
Parents (both)*	1.3	0.0	2.4
Father*	34.7	38.7	31.3
Mother*	4.8	2.7	6.7
Stepfather	0.7	1.1	0.4
Stepmother	0.0	0.0	0.0
Parents total	41.5	42.5	40.8
Grandparents (both)	0.1	0.2	0.0
Grandfather	1.3	1.9	0.7
Grandmother	0.4	0.4	0.4
Grandparents total	1.8	2.5	1.1
Husband*	1.0	0.0	1.7
Wife	0.0	0.0	0.0
*Spouse total**	1.0	0.0	1.7
Son(s)	0.3	0.0	0.6
Daughter(s)	0.1	0.0	0.2
Children, gender not specified	0.1	0.0	0.2
Children total	0.5	0.0	1.0
Brother(s)*	7.7	10.7	5.0
Sister(s)	1.5	0.8	1.9
Siblings, gender not specified	0.1	0.0	0.2
*Siblings total**	9.3	11.5	7.1
Uncle(s)	1.7	1.9	1.5
Aunt(s)	0.1	0.0	0.2
Cousin, gender not specified	0.5	0.2	0.7
Entire family	0.4	0.0	0.7
Family total	56.8	58.6	54.8
Peers/Friends, gender not specified	8.5	10.1	7.1
Roommate	0.2	0.2	0.2
Boyfriend*	3.7	0.0	6.9
Girlfriend	0.0	0.0	0.0
Peers and friends total	12.4	10.3	14.2

continued on the next page

SOCIALIZATION AGENT	ALL SUBJECTS	MALES ONLY	FEMALES ONLY
School*	11.5	8.0	14.6
Teacher	0.1	0.0	0.2
School total*	11.6	8.0	14.8
Community	1.6	1.7	1.5
Played in band	0.2	0.2	0.2
Trainer	0.1	0.0	0.2
Military	0.1	0.2	0.0
Media*	5.4	6.9	4.1
Professional athletes	0.7	1.3	0.2
Myself	0.9	0.8	0.9
Playing sport	0.3	0.6	0.0
Coaches*	1.6	2.5	0.7
None/Cannot recall	2.0	2.5	1.5
Did not answer	6.5	6.1	6.9

Note: Numbers listed above are percentages. A * indicates a significant difference in the proportions of males and females listing the agent.

sporting events, and so on). Because of the parents' sport involvement, there is a good chance the children will become socialized into the sport fan role. However, this does not ensure that they will become sport fans. In fact, if you pause for a moment to consider your friends who are sport fans, you can probably recall situations in which one sibling was committed to the role of sport fan while another sibling displayed little or no interest in sport. Although the socialization processes were similar for both children, the results were not. This suggests that although early socialization influences are an important first step in the decision to become a sport fan, there are other important factors as well (Wann, 1997). One such factor is motivation. Some individuals who are socialized into the sport fan role may still reject the activity because they are not motivated by a specific factor. That is, although they are well aware of the values, beliefs, attitudes, and norms of the sport fan culture, they are not encouraged to engage in the activity by any perceived benefits. Similarly, some individuals who are only casually socialized into the sport fan role may become highly involved fans because they are strongly motivated by several specific factors.

The Most Common Sport Fan Motives

Although there are dozens of motives, researchers and theorists have identified the following as being the most common: group affiliation, family, aesthetic, self-esteem, economic, eustress, escape, and entertainment. You will find a brief description of these motives in table 2.3.

The Group Affiliation Motive In most instances, sport spectating is a social activity (Danielson, 1997). Whether it occurs at home, a restaurant, a bar, or the arena, sport tends to be consumed in a group

TABLE 2.3

Brief Descriptions of the Eight Most Common Sport Fan Motives

MOTIVE	DESCRIPTION
Group affiliation	Individual is motivated to participate in sport as a fan because it provides an opportunity to spend time with others.
Family	Individual is motivated to participate in sport as a fan because it provides an opportunity to spend time with family members.
Aesthetic	Individual is motivated to participate in sport as a fan because he or she enjoys the artistic beauty and grace of sport movements.
Self-esteem	Individual is motivated to participate in sport as a fan because it provides an opportunity to feel better about himself or herself.
Economic	Individual is motivated to participate in sport as a fan because he or she enjoys the potential economic gains afforded by sport gambling.
Eustress	Individual is motivated to participate in sport as a fan because he or she enjoys the excitement and arousal felt while watching sporting events.
Escape	Individual is motivated to participate in sport as a fan because it provides a diversion from the rest of his or her life.
Entertainment	Individual is motivated to participate in sport as a fan because it is perceived as an enjoyable pastime.

environment. For some individuals, it is precisely the social nature of sport spectating that attracts them to it. They are motivated by the group affiliation motive, that is, a desire to spend time with others (Gantz & Wenner, 1995; Guttmann, 1986; Melnick, 1993; Pan et al., 1997; Sloan, 1989; G. J. Smith et al., 1981).

Without question, humans are social beings, a fact reflected in a number of classical theories of human motivation (e.g., Alderfer, 1972; Fromm, 1941; Maslow, 1970). Sport fandom and sport spectating can help fulfill the human need for social interaction by providing a sense of belongingness. The fact that most spectators consume sport as a member of a social group suggests that fans do indeed use sport to satisfy social interaction needs (e.g., Mann, 1969). For instance, consider the work of Aveni (1977). This investigator examined the postgame celebration behavior of Ohio State football fans. He interviewed fans celebrating in the streets of Columbus, Ohio, after a Buckeye victory and found that 74 percent reported being with one or more friends. Similarly, Schurr and his colleagues (Schurr, Ruble, & Ellen, 1985; Schurr, Wittig, Ruble, & Ellen, 1988) found that greater than 95 percent of spectators attending college basketball games bought tickets that allowed them to sit with friends.

The Family Motive   The family motive is similar to the group affiliation motive. The family motive involves a desire to be a fan because it provides an opportunity to spend time with family members (Evaggelinou & Grekinis, 1998; Gantz & Wenner, 1995; Guttmann, 1986; Pan et al., 1997; Quirk, 1997; Weiller & Higgs, 1997). As one would expect, this motive is particularly common among sport fans who have children and/or are married (Wann, Lane, Duncan, & Goodson, 1998).

Family motivation and preferences for aggressive sports • Recently, researchers have begun to examine the relationship between tendencies toward family motivation and preferences for aggressive sports. Wann, Schrader, and Wilson (1999) hypothesized that individuals who use sport to bring their family together may prefer nonaggressive sports because they do not want to expose their children to violent behaviors. Past research by Wann (1995) had provided tentative support for this hypothesis. Specifically, Wann found that although level of family motivation was positively correlated with the enjoyment of watching nonviolent sports such as swimming and basketball, the enjoyment of viewing violent sports (e.g., professional wrestling and boxing) was negatively related to family motivation. Wann and his colleagues (1999) examined the relationship between family motivation and aggressive sport preferences by asking university students to report their favorite spectating sport (the participants were informed that this sport may or may not also be the sport that they most prefer to play) and degree of family motivation. The respondents' sport preferences were used to classify them into two groups: those with a preference for aggressive sports (e.g., boxing, football, and hockey) and those with a preference for nonaggressive sports (e.g., baseball, figure skating, and gymnastics). The results indicated that although respondents with a preference for nonaggressive sports did report higher levels of family motivation than those with a preference for aggressive sports, the difference was not statistically significant.

Wann, Schrader, et al. (1999) suggested that the failure to find a significant relationship between family motivation and preferences for particular sports may have been due to the homogeneity of the sample. Because the sample was comprised entirely of college students, there is a good chance that few married individuals were included (recall that these individuals report the highest levels of family motivation). Had the sample been more heterogeneous and contained a greater number of spouses and parents, perhaps family motivation differences between those preferring aggressive and nonaggressive sports would have reached statistical significance. To test this possibility, Wann, Lane, et al. (1998) replicated the previous research with a more diverse sample. They tested a random sample of spectators attending a college football game. The sample contained ninety-six individuals, forty-seven of whom (49 percent) were married and/or had children. However, the findings from this more heterogeneous sample again revealed that the two groups did not differ in their levels of family motivation.

A final study that examined the relationship between family motivation and preferences for aggressive sports was recently completed by Wann and Ensor (1999b). To improve on previous efforts, they first assessed college students' levels of family motivation and then asked each participant to list his or her five favorite spectator sports. Two formulae were used to classify participants into aggressive sport preference and nonaggressive sport preference groups. The first formula simply summed the number of aggressive sports listed. The second formula, labeled "the aggressive value index," took into consideration the ordering of the sports. Aggressive sports listed as the respondent's first favorite received a score of 5, aggressive sports listed as the second favorite received a score of 4, and so on. Nonaggressive sports received a score of 0 regardless of their place in the list. The relationship between family motivation and preference for aggressive sports was then tested by correlating the two aggressive sport preference scores with levels of family motivation. Consistent with the previous research (Wann, Lane, et al., 1998; Wann, Schrader, et al., 1999), the analyses failed to find significant relationships between family motivation and the number of aggressive favorite sports listed or between family motivation and the aggressive value index. Thus, it appears that one can safely conclude that persons motivated by family needs are equally likely to prefer aggressive and nonaggressive sports.

The Aesthetic Motive Another factor motivating an individual to become a sport fan is aesthetic motivation (Hemphill, 1995; Rinehart, 1996; Sloan, 1989; G. J. Smith, 1988; G. J. Smith et al., 1981; Wertz, 1985). The aesthetic motive involves an individual's desire to participate in sport as a fan because he or she enjoys the artistic beauty and grace of sport movements. Guttmann (1986, p. 177) provided an excellent description of the artistic nature of sport when he wrote: "If the runner's stride (and agonized grimace), the gymnast's vault (and forced smile), and the goalie's save (and muddled brow) are not forms of art, they certainly arouse in us emotions related to those we experience when we listen to one of Bach's cantatas or contemplate a still life by Chardin. Unquestionably, there are physical performances that live in the memory like the lines of a poem."

Mirroring Guttmann's sentiments, Heinegg (1985, p. 455) stated that "the literate fan may take an aesthetic tack: professional athletes perform with fabulous strength, speed, grace, and coordination. . . . Talented players, clearly, go about their work with as much precision and brio as ballet dancers or violinists." Heinegg notes that nonfans can also be inspired by the aesthetic value of sport performances, writing, "Even the anti-fan will sometimes stop in his tracks in front of the TV set and admire despite himself" (p. 455).

Certainly, artistic and stylistic sports such as figure skating, diving, and gymnastics are attractive to many fans because of their inherent beauty and the artistic expressions of the athletes. However, it is important to note that the aesthetic motive is not limited to fans of stylistic sports (Sargent, Zillmann, & Weaver, 1998). Rather, persons interested in other sports may also express a high level of aesthetic motivation. For instance, football fans who remember Lynn Swann (a wide receiver for the Pittsburgh Steelers) often describe the artistic nature of his leaping catches. Similarly, track and field fans often speak of the beauty and grace of such events as the discus, pole vault, and hurdles.

Aesthetic motivation and preferences for aggressive sports • Similar to the research on family motivation, investigators have become interested in the relationship between preferences for violent sports and aesthetic motivation. Wann, Schrader, et al. (1999) suggested that fans with a high level of aesthetic motivation probably prefer nonaggressive sports because the actions found in aggressive sports may "inhibit the graceful execution of sport movements" (p. 122). As an example of this possibility, Wann et al. noted the actions of hockey "goons" whose sole purpose is to disrupt the graceful flow of the other team's swifter and more athletic skaters.

Wann and Wilson (1999a) recently conducted a pair of studies designed to test the hypothesis that individuals with a tendency toward aesthetic motivation prefer nonaggressive sports. In the first study, college students were asked to complete a questionnaire assessing their level of aesthetic motivation and their enjoyment of watching seven aggressive sports (football, hockey, professional and amateur wrestling, martial arts, boxing, and rugby). The participants' enjoyment scores were combined to form a single index of enjoyment of violent sports. Wann and Wilson predicted that there would be a negative correlation between levels of aesthetic motivation and enjoyment of violent sports. However, contrary to expectations, the correlational analyses failed to reveal any significant relationships between the variables. In the second study college students were first asked to complete an inventory assessing their level of aesthetic motivation. They were then asked to watch five violent football plays and to rate their enjoyment of each. Once again, there was no significant relationship between aesthetic motivation and enjoyment of violent plays. Thus, it appears that sport fans who are motivated by the beauty and grace of sport movements are equally likely to enjoy violent and nonviolent sports.

Aesthetic or erotic? • In 1996 Guttmann published *The Erotic in Sports,* in which he examined the possibility that the aesthetic component of sport spectating possesses an erotic element (for additional work on sport eroticism, see Creedon, 1994; Duncan & Brummett, 1989; Hargreaves, 1993; S. Jones, 1993; McDonald, 1996). Guttmann argued that much of the aesthetic enjoyment derived from viewing sport contests lies in the erotic nature of sport movements. He states that it is "impossible to pretend . . . that aesthetic responses can be neatly separated from erotic ones" (p. 81). The fact is, the erotic nature of athletic competition was embraced and even celebrated by earlier societies (e.g., Greeks and Romans). However, by the seventeenth century, attempts were made to repress sport eroticism. Guttmann argues that these attempts continue today, despite numerous indications that sport has managed to maintain its erotic appeal. For instance, he notes that the costumes worn by female figure skaters are sexually suggestive and that the slow motion replays and close-ups found on televised sport enhance the erotic element of the athlete's performance. Further, he notes that the behaviors of athletes indicate their awareness of the erotic nature of their physical appearance and that they are willing to exploit their eroticism and attractiveness (e.g., the *Playboy* magazine pictorials of ice skaters Katarina Witt and Tonya Harding serve as strong examples of this point).

Guttmann's (1996) position is that the experience of erotic pleasure is a natural and acceptable response to viewing athletic performances (although he is careful to point out that not all athletic endeavors are erotic). Although he concedes that some individuals will disagree with him (e.g., certain religious groups and radical feminists), Guttmann makes a "plea for the acceptance of mutually admiring male and female gazes" (p. 163). He is also quick to point out that eroticism may have negative consequences as well. For instance, interest solely in an athlete's erotic appeal degrades the athlete. Further, on occasions, the erotic nature of sport performances may facilitate the sexually aggressive behavior of some spectators. For the most part, however, Guttmann does not place a value judgment on the erotic nature of sport. Rather, his main intention is to demonstrate the existence of the erotic nature of sport and to argue that it should be perfectly acceptable for athletes, coaches, fans, and social scientists to discuss sport eroticism. Guttmann concludes his text by observing, "The Greeks who gathered at Olympia for athletic festivals in honor of Zeus and Hera were candid about this pleasure [i.e., sport eroticism]. Perhaps, after two millennia of disapproval and denial, it is time for us to be as candid as they were" (p. 172).

The Self-Esteem Motive A fourth common sport fan motive is self-esteem enhancement (Gmelch & San Antonio, 1998; Pan et al., 1997; Sloan, 1989; Weiller & Higgs, 1997; Wenner & Gantz, 1989). This motive concerns an individual's desire to participate in sport as a fan because it provides an opportunity to feel better about himself or herself. That is, the individual uses sport fandom to help maintain a positive self-concept. For instance, when a team is victorious, fans often join the players in a celebration of their achievement and success. Indeed, fans often increase their association with teams subsequent to successful performances simply to bask in the team's accomplishments and boost their own self-esteem (Cialdini et al., 1976).

The Economic Motive Sport consumption and gambling go hand in hand. Perhaps the best evidence of this can be found in the many daily newspapers that publish the Las Vegas odds for sporting events in their sports sections. Some newspapers, including *USA Today*, also print winning lottery numbers in the sports section. The amount of money wagered on sporting events is staggering. One source estimated that legal and illegal sport betting exceeded $600 billion in 1998 alone (Crist, 1998).

For some individuals, it is the potential economic gain from sport gambling that attracts them to the role of sport fan. These persons are driven to consume sport by the economic motive (Chorbajian, 1978; Eastman & Land, 1997; Frey, 1992; Gantz & Wenner, 1995; Guttmann, 1986). Although one can find sport gamblers in all demographic categories, college students appear to be disproportionately likely to be motivated by sport gambling opportunities (Layden, 1995).

It was noted earlier that some sport fans may not have been socialized into the role of sport consumer. Rather, they become sport consumers because of specific motives. It is likely that this is the case for many sport gamblers. It seems reasonable to assume that many fans with high levels of economic motivation may not have been socialized into the values, beliefs, attitudes, and norms associated with sport fandom. In fact, they may not even be sport fans at all (see Guttmann, 1986, for a similar argument). Instead, they simply see sport fandom as an opportunity to acquire financial gains (not unlike someone who purchases stock in a company he or she knows little or nothing about). Wann (1995) has provided strong empirical support for this argument (see also Trail, James, & Madrigal, 1998). He found no relationship between the level of economic motivation and self-proclaimed fandom. Although other motives were positively related to the degree that one's mother and father were sport fans, there was no relationship between the level of economic motivation and perceptions of one's fandom. Levels of economic motivation also showed small and insignificant relationships with the degree that the individual's friends were fans and the individual's level of team identification. Thus, individuals who were motivated to become sport fans due to economic reasons did not perceive themselves as sport fans, did not view their parents or friends as fans, and did not have particularly high levels of team identification. Therefore, many economically motivated fans are, by definition, not fans at all. Instead, they participate in the pastime simply for the potential monetary rewards that accrue through sport wagering.

The Eustress Motive A number of theorists have suggested that many individuals fail to receive a sufficient amount of stimulation in their everyday lives (e.g., Elias & Dunning, 1970; Howard, 1912; Klapp, 1972; Klausner, 1968; McNeil, 1968; M. Zuckerman, 1984). Consequently, they explore other opportunities to gain stimulation and excitement. One such opportunity can be sport fandom and spectating. For example, Brill (1929) stated, "The life of man in America or in any of the industrialized countries today, laboring on the farm, in the factory, in the office, is not the natural life of man. He is still an animal formed for battle and conquest, for blows and strokes and swiftness, for triumph and applause. But let him join the crowd around the diamond, the gridiron, the tennis court or the ring. . . . Let him identify himself with his favorite fighter, player or team. . . . He will achieve exaltation, vicarious but real" (p. 434). Brill's statement suggests that even though life often fails to meet our need for excitement and stimulation, these desires can be fulfilled through sport spectatorship.

Persons who participate in sport fandom to gain excitement and stimulation are motivated by eustress (Gantz, 1981; Gantz & Wenner, 1995; Sloan, 1989; G. J. Smith, 1988). Eustress refers to positive forms of arousal and stimulation. Thus, sport fans with high levels of eustress motivation become involved with the pastime because they enjoy the excitement and arousal they experience watching sport. It is important to note that although fans usually view the suspense of sport spectating as pleasurable (Bryant, Rockwell, & Owens, 1994; Eastman & Riggs, 1994), these stressful reactions are not always positive. Some fans (i.e., those with low levels of eustress motivation) do not enjoy the anxiety associated with sport spectating and go to great lengths to avoid this anxious state. Thus, for these fans, the stress they experience watching their favorite team compete should be referred to as distress (i.e., negative stress). However, one of the advantages of sport fandom is that it is a voluntary activity. Consequently, fans who become uncomfortably aroused and excited watching a favorite team compete can simply remove themselves from the situation (i.e., leave their seat at the arena, turn off the television set, etc.; see Eastman & Riggs, 1994).

The Escape Motive The escape motive is another popular reason individuals become sport fans (Gantz & Wenner, 1995; Krohn, Clarke, Preston, McDonald, & Preston, 1998; Sloan, 1989; G. J. Smith, 1988; G. J. Smith et al., 1981). The fan participates in the activity because it provides a diversion. Individuals who are disgruntled by their home life, work, college experience, and so on are able to temporarily forget their troubles through sport fandom. Wann (1997) suggests that the use of the escape motive may be particularly prevalent during personally difficult and/or stressful times. He notes that historically, many individuals have used sport spectating as a diversion during wartime. For instance, President Roosevelt's decision to allow professional baseball to continue during World War II was designed to provide an escape for North Americans. In explaining his decision, Roosevelt stated that Americans "ought to have a chance for recreation and for taking their minds off their work" (see McGuire, 1994, p. 66).

Escaping from overstimulation and understimulation • Although it is clear that sport fans often use the pastime as a diversion, what is less known is from what they are attempting to escape. For instance, Sloan (1989) argued that sport could provide "an escape from work and the other tediums of life" (p. 183). G. J. Smith (1988) concurred, writing that "the search for excitement represents one of the most familiar means of escape" (p. 58). These statements suggest that individuals use sport fandom to escape from their understimulating (i.e., tedious and boring) lives. However, Heinegg (1985) argued that sport serves as "a flight from the pain of existence" and "worldly cares and crises" (p. 457). This perspective implies that sport fans use the pastime as an escape from their overstimulating lives. Zillmann, Bryant, and Sapolsky (1989) recognized both possibilities by stating that "spectatorship relieves from boredom" and "relaxes tensions" (p. 250). Similarly, Krohn et al. (1998) stated, "People use athletic events to escape for many reasons" including "to take a break from the monotony of a repetitive job" or to escape the "difficulties they face with their own work" (p. 282).

Thus, sport fans may use sport as an escape from both overstimulation and understimulation. For instance, consider two avid sport fans who meet at their favorite bar every Monday night to watch Monday Night Football. Both individuals view the game as an opportunity to escape their daily routines. One individual is a police officer who considers her life very stressful. She views the game as an escape from overstimulation. The other individual works on an assembly line and finds her life extremely boring. She perceives the game as an opportunity to escape from understimulation.

Recently, Wann and Rochelle (1999) empirically examined the use of sport as an escape from overstimulation and understimulation. They attempted to determine if sport fans use sport spectating for both forms of escape and if one form was more common than the other. They asked college students to state the extent to which they believed their life was stressful or boring. The researchers also assessed the participants' levels of escape motivation. Correlational analyses revealed positive relationships between the respondents' level of escape motivation and their perceptions of life as boring and stressful. Those who felt their life was stressful and those who believed their life was boring both reported using sport fandom as an escape. A second questionnaire asked participants to select which of the following two statements was most accurate: "I feel that my life is overstimulating and, consequently, use sport spectating as an escape from this excitement," and "I feel that my life is understimulating and, consequently, use sport spectating as an escape from this boredom." The results indicated that 64 percent of the respondents used sport as an escape from overstimulation, while 36 percent used sport as an escape from understimulation. Those respondents with high levels of stress were particularly likely to use sport as an escape from overstimulation. These results suggest that fans use sport as an escape from both overstimulation and understimulation and that utilizing sport as an escape from overstimulation is more common.

The Entertainment Motive Many individuals become involved in sport fandom for entertainment motives (Gantz, 1981; Gantz & Wenner, 1995; Krohn et al., 1998; Sloan, 1989; G. J. Smith, 1988). Here, sport spectating is viewed as being similar to other recreational pursuits, such as going to the theater, watching television, listening to music, or reading.

A number of researchers have attempted to document the characteristics of sporting events that spectators and fans find most enjoyable and entertaining. As one might expect, this body of research suggests that watching one's favorite teams succeed is extremely enjoyable and entertaining (Su-Lin, Tuggle, Mitrook, Coussement, & Zillmann, 1997; Wann & Schrader, 1997). However, Zillmann and his colleagues suggest that the entertainment and enjoyment derived from sport viewing is more complex than the simple successes and failures of one's favorite team (Bryant, 1989; Izod, 1996; Sapolsky, 1980; Zillmann et al., 1989, Zillmann & Paulas, 1993). They argue that to fully understand the entertainment and enjoyment value of sport spectating, one must not only consider the favored team's performance, but also the opponents. Specifically, their disposition theory of sport spectatorship argues that a spectator's enjoyment of watching a sporting event is a function of his or her alliance with the team, the team's performance, and his or her dislike of the team's opponent (i.e., the spectator's "disposition"). The enjoyment of watching a team succeed is expected to increase with positive sentiments and decrease with negative ones. The enjoyment derived from watching a team lose is expected to increase with negative sentiments and decrease with positive sentiments toward the team. Therefore, spectators are predicted to be happiest (and most entertained) when their favorite teams succeed and when their least favorite teams fail (see R. H. Smith et al., 1996). They are hypothesized to be least happy when their favorite team fails and when their least favorite team succeeds. Although Zillmann and his associates provide strong empirical support for the basic tenets of disposition theory, an investigation by Mahony and Howard (1998) indicates that spectators enjoy games featuring a disliked team only to the extent that the team is viewed as a threat to the favorite team.

Research has also examined the extent to which sport fans are entertained by the violent content found in sports. A persistent theme in media circles has been that "violence sells" and that in producing violent programming media moguls are merely giving the public what it desires. Some research suggests that the impressions of media executives are correct—sport fans do enjoy violence. This appears to be particularly true for male fans and for fans with a propensity toward violent behavior (Bryant, 1989; Bryant, Comisky, & Zillmann, 1981; Bryant & Zillmann, 1983; Kaelin, 1968). Similarly, when the commentary of the announcers describes the opponents as "hated foes" rather than "good friends," spectators report greater levels of enjoyment watching the contest (Bryant, Brown, Comisky, & Zillmann, 1982).

However, some investigations have failed to find a relationship between sport violence and entertainment. In one such investigation (Russell, Di Lullo, & Di Lullo, 1989) men were shown a film clip of fast-paced hockey action that included several on-ice brawls. Other men viewed the same clip with the violence edited out. In contrast to the research cited above, the participants rated the two versions as equally entertaining. In this instance, the violent content added little or nothing to the entertainment value of the contest. Other studies make a similar point with respect to televised action dramas (Diener & DeFour, 1978; see Cantor, 1998, for a review). Thus, the jury is out on fans' enjoyment of sport violence.

A final investigation of the sport factors viewers perceive as entertaining was recently completed by Wann and Wilson (1999b). These authors examined the entertaining features of spectator sports by asking individuals attending one of two college men's basketball games to list the reasons they enjoyed the game. The research was conducted at two different arenas: an older arena in use for over four decades and a brand new, state-of-the-art arena. They found that the most frequently listed correlates of enjoyment were the game itself and the competition. The social nature of the event, exciting plays, the entertainment and recreational value of the event, and the players themselves rounded out the top five most commonly cited reasons for enjoyment. Surprisingly, spectators attending at the new arena were not especially likely to mention the arena or atmosphere as an enjoyment factor.

Current Issues in Sport Fan Motivation

In this section, we examine several important issues related to the eight sport fan motives just described. Specifically, we review the accurate measurement of the motives, compare the prominence of different motives, identify demographic differences in sport fan motivation, and discuss the classification of the motives as either intrinsic or extrinsic.

Measuring Sport Fan Motivation In 1986 Guttmann commented that one of the greatest problems in the study of fan motivation was that most of the work was subjective in nature. Although a number of social scientists had offered elaborate descriptions of various fan motives, their writings were based on subjective observation rather than objective data. Wann (1995) addressed this problem by developing a questionnaire to assess sport fan motivation. The questionnaire, labeled the Sport Fan Motivation Scale (SFMS), contains twenty-three items divided into eight subscales (each subscale represents one of the aforementioned motives). The group affiliation, aesthetic, self-esteem, economic, eustress, escape, and entertainment subscales contain three items each, while the family subscale is comprised of two items. A copy of the SFMS appears in table 2.4. You are encouraged to complete the items in the table to determine your own motivational pattern. Simply answer each item and then sum your responses for each of the subscales (subscale designations follow each item in table 2.4).

Initial research by Wann and his colleagues indicated that the SFMS scale is reliable and valid whether administered through either pencil and paper or telephone interview formats (Wann, 1995; Wann & Ensor, 1999a; Wann, Lane, et al., 1998; Wann & Rochelle, 1999; Wann, Schrader, et al., 1999). However, Trail et al. (1998) suggested that the instrument is not without problems. They note that, as is often the case with the initial edition of a psychometric instrument,

TABLE 2.4

The Sport Fan Motivation Scale

Instructions: Answer each of the following questions about sport spectating using the 1 to 8 scale below. In the space next to each item, simply indicate (by writing a number) how well each item describes you. There are no right or wrong answers, simply be completely honest in your responses. Remember, these questions are about sport spectating, not sport participation.

THIS IS NOT AT ALL DESCRIPTIVE OF ME	1	2	3	4	5	6	7	8	THIS IS VERY DESCRIPTIVE OF ME

_____1. One of the main reasons that I watch, read, and/or discuss sports is that doing so gives me the opportunity to temporarily escape life's problems. (escape subscale)

_____2. One of the main reasons that I watch, read, and/or discuss sports is so I can bet on the sporting events. (economic subscale)

_____3. One of the main reasons that I watch, read, and/or discuss sports is that I get pumped up when I am watching my favorite teams. (eustress subscale)

_____4. One of the main reasons that I watch, read, and/or discuss sports is for their artistic value. (aesthetic subscale)

_____5. One of the main reasons that I watch, read, and/or discuss sports is that I enjoy the beauty and grace of sports. (aesthetic subscale)

_____6. One of the main reasons that I watch, read, and/or discuss sports is that I enjoy being physiologically aroused by the competition. (eustress subscale)

_____7. Sports are enjoyable only if you can bet on the outcome. (economic subscale)

_____8. One of the main reasons that I watch, read, and/or discuss sports is that doing so makes me feel good when my team wins. (self-esteem subscale)

_____9. One of the main reasons that I watch, read, and/or discuss sports is that doing so allows me to forget about my problems. (escape subscale)

_____10. Making wagers is the most enjoyable aspect of being a sports fan. (economic subscale)

continued on the next page

_____11. One of the main reasons that I watch, read, and/or discuss sports is because most of my friends are sports fans. (group affiliation subscale)

_____12. I enjoy watching sporting events because to me sports are a form of art. (aesthetic subscale)

_____13. To me, watching, reading, and/or discussing sports is like day-dreaming because it takes me away from life's hassles. (escape subscale)

_____14. One of the main reasons that I watch, read, and/or discuss sports is I am the kind of person who likes to be with other people. (group affiliation subscale)

_____15. I enjoy sports because of their entertainment value. (entertainment subscale)

_____16. I enjoy watching sports more when I am with a large group of people. (group affiliation subscale)

_____17. I enjoy watching sports because it increases my self-esteem. (self-esteem subscale)

_____18. I like the stimulation I get from watching sports. (eustress subscale)

_____19. I enjoy watching, reading, and/or discussing sports simply because it is a good time. (entertainment subscale)

_____20. To me, sports spectating is simply a form of recreation. (entertainment subscale)

_____21. To me, my favorite team's successes are my successes and their losses are my losses. (self-esteem subscale)

_____22. I like to watch, read, and/or discuss sports because doing so gives me an opportunity to be with my spouse. (family subscale)

_____23. I like to watch, read, and/or discuss sports because doing so gives me an opportunity to be with my family. (family subscale)

Note: Subscale designations are in parentheses following each item. To determine your SFMS subscale scores, simply sum the items for each subscale (group affiliation subscale includes items 11, 14, and 16; family includes 22 and 23; aesthetic includes 4, 5, and 12; self-esteem includes 8, 17, and 21; economic includes 2, 7, and 10; eustress includes 3, 6, and 18; escape includes 1, 9, and 13; entertainment includes 15, 19, and 20).

the first version may need to be fine-tuned. For instance, Trail and his colleagues present data suggesting additional items may be needed for the family motivation subscale and that the various subscales (i.e., motives) have excessive overlap (i.e., questionable discriminant validity). The work by Trail et al. highlights the importance of test refinement and suggests that better and more accurate versions of the SFMS may be forthcoming.

Comparisons of the Prominence of the Fan Motives Four studies have compared participants' scores on the eight SFMS subscales to determine the most common and least common motives (Wann, 1995, Study 1; Wann, Schrader, et al., 1999, Studies 1, 2, and 3). In each of the four studies, the highest scores were found on the entertainment subscale, while the lowest scores were found on the economic subscale. Other researchers recently confirmed this pattern (Wann, Bilyeu, Brennan, Osborn, & Gambouras, 1999). Table 2.5 presents the mean SFMS subscale scores collapsed across the four studies. In addition to the entertainment motive, the eustress and group affiliation motives were also prominent. The family and escape motives, along with the economic motive, appear to be the least common motives. By comparing your SFMS subscale scores (see table 2.4) with the

TABLE 2.5

Mean **Sport Fan Motivation Scale** *Subscale Scores Reported in Wann (1995) Study 1 and Wann et al. (1999) Studies 1, 2, and 3*

SUBSCALE	MEAN	RANK
Group Affiliation	13.30	3
Family	5.92	7
Aesthetic	11.04	5
Self-esteem	12.54	4
Economic	5.36	8
Eustress	15.28	2
Escape	10.40	6
Entertainment	17.49	1

Note: N totaled 569 for the four studies combined.

average scores reported in table 2.5, you can determine how your motivational pattern compares with that of others.

Demographic Differences in Sport Fan Motivation Researchers have also used the SFMS to examine demographic differences in fan motivation, specifically, age, gender, and race.

Age and sport fan motivation • Two research projects involving five separate studies have examined the relationship between age and the eight fan motives (Wann, 1995; Wann, Schrader, et al., 1999). The results failed to reveal consistent, significant relationships between age and sport fan motivation. Thus, it can be concluded that age has very little, if anything, to do with sport fan motivation.

Gender and sport fan motivation • The same five studies also examined gender differences in fan motivation (Wann, 1995; Wann, Schrader, et al., 1999). In four of the five studies, females reported significantly higher levels of family motivation than did males. Further, each of the studies revealed that males had higher levels of eustress and self-esteem motivation; data from four of the five samples also revealed that males had higher levels of aesthetic motivation. There were no consistent gender differences for the other motives. Thus, one can conclude that: (1) female fans are more likely than male fans to be motivated by the opportunity to spend time with family, and (2) male fans are more likely than female fans to seek out excitement and arousal, experience feelings of self-worth, and enjoy the artistic nature of sport performances.

Because males are more likely than females to be motivated by eustress, one would expect males to report greater enjoyment of close and exciting contests. Su-Lin et al. (1997) asked college students to view one of eight live television broadcasts of an NCAA men's basketball tournament game. The investigators classified the contests into one of four suspense categories: minimal suspense (final score difference of 15 or more points), moderate suspense (10–14 points), substantial suspense (5–9 points), or extreme suspense (1–4 points). At the conclusion of the contests, the respondents rated their enjoyment of the game. Participants reported the greatest levels of enjoyment for the most suspenseful contests. However, the data also revealed an interaction between suspense and gender. Male respondents reported linear increases in enjoyment as the contest became more suspenseful (i.e., their enjoyment steadily grew with increases in suspense). Female participants reported a different pattern of effects. Although these participants also reported increases in enjoyment from minimal to moderate suspense and from moderate to substantial suspense, they reported a dramatic decline in their enjoyment of the game in the extreme suspense condition. Thus, not only are female fans less likely to be motivated by the excitement of the contest and become fans because of the excitement of spectator sports, they are also less likely to enjoy the game if it becomes too suspenseful.

You may have been surprised to learn that males consistently report higher levels of aesthetic motivation than females. Stereotypically and anecdotally, female sport fans are believed to gravitate toward artistic and graceful sports (e.g., figure skating and gymnastics), while male fans tend to prefer combative sports (e.g., boxing, football, and hockey). Indeed, research conducted by Sargent et al. (1998) documented these gender differences in sport preferences (see also Pan & Baker, 1999; Roloff & Solomon, 1989). These investigators assessed the television viewing preferences of college students. Compared to female respondents, male participants reported greater preferences for violent and aggressive (i.e., combative) sports; females reported greater preferences for elegant and stylistic sports.

Thus, females appear to prefer stylistic sports, sports that are often aesthetically or artistically expressive. Males, meanwhile, prefer more combative sports. However, this finding appears to contradict Wann (Wann, 1995; Wann, Schrader, et al., 1999), who found that males reported greater levels of aesthetic motivation. This apparent contradiction may be resolved by considering the difference between aesthetic sport movements (e.g., the spinning, twirling dismount of a gymnast, the graceful swing of a home-run hitter, the behind-the-back dribble of a point guard, etc.) and aesthetic sports (i.e., stylistic sports). While female fans clearly prefer aesthetic sports, male fans may be more likely to view the movements and skills of combative sport participants as being aesthetically pleasing and artistically expressive. Perhaps that is why females are less likely than males to regard sport as aesthetically pleasing. Male fans are more likely to enjoy the artistic nature of all sports, while female fans tend to merely enjoy "artistic" sports. Preliminary support for this proposition was provided by Sargent et al. (1998), who found that although males and females were equally likely to view each of the stylistic sports as "elegant," males were more likely to view several other sport types in this manner (see also Roloff & Solomon, 1989).

Race and sport fan motivation • To date, only one study has examined race differences in sport fan motivation (Wann, Bilyeu, et al., 1999). In this exploratory investigation, Caucasian and African-

American college students were asked to complete the SFMS. The results revealed that the Caucasian participants reported higher levels of fan motivation than the African-American participants on four subscales: eustress, self-esteem, escape, and family. There were no significant racial differences on the remaining subscales. At first glance, this finding appears to suggest that African Americans are less interested in sport fandom than Caucasians are. However, as noted in chapter 1, research shows that many African Americans exhibit a high interest in sport fandom, maybe higher than Caucasians (Schurr et al., 1985; Schurr et al., 1988).

Thus, we are left with a contradiction. Wann, Bilyeau, et al. (1999) considered the possibility that there may be sport fan motives that are particularly relevant to minority groups such as African Americans that are not assessed by the SFMS. That is, African Americans and Caucasians may favor particular kinds of fan motives. This notion is consistent with research indicating that the self-schemas of both groups differ (Oyserman, Gant, & Ager, 1995) and with research showing that African Americans and Caucasians report different rates of interest for various sports (Papazian, 1998; Wenner & Gantz, 1989). Wann et al. note that the SFMS was constructed on the basis of current theory and research in sport psychology and sport sociology. Because this research was carried out by Caucasian researchers and tested on Caucasian participants, other motives more applicable to minority groups may have been overlooked. Thus, additional research on the motivational patterns of minority sport fans is needed to better understand the underlying reasons for their sport fandom.

The Intrinsic and Extrinsic Motivation of Sport Fans Social scientists have often found it useful to differentiate between intrinsic and extrinsic motivation (Deci, 1971; Deci & Ryan, 1985; Harackiewicz, 1979; M. Ross, 1975). Intrinsic motives lie within an individual and reflect interest in and enjoyment of a task. Extrinsic motives lie outside an individual and involve the rewards and benefits received for performing a task. Recently, researchers have used the SFMS to assess sport fans' intrinsic and extrinsic motivation. According to Fortier, Vallerand, Briere, and Provencher (1995), intrinsic motivation includes aesthetic pleasures, stimulation, and enjoyment of the activity itself. These desires are reflected in three of the SFMS subscales: aesthetic, eustress, and entertainment. With respect to extrinsic motivation, Fortier et al. (1995) state that this form of motivation involves "a wide variety of behaviors where the goals of the action extend beyond those inherent in the activity itself" (p. 25). The remaining five SFMS subscales (self-esteem, escape, economic, group affiliation, and family) all reflect extrinsic desires because all involve using fandom as a means of acquiring a goal (i.e., fandom is used to acquire self-esteem, an escape, economic gains, and time with friends or family).

Comparison between motivational patterns of athletes and fans • Wann, Schrader, et al. (1999) predicted that individuals who were intrinsically motivated as athletes would also be intrinsically motivated as fans. Those with a tendency toward extrinsic player motivation were expected to adopt an extrinsic motivational pattern as a fan. To test this hypothesis, the researchers asked college students to complete the SFMS and the Sport Motivation Scale, a valid and reliable measure of an athlete's intrinsic and extrinsic motivation (Fortier et al., 1995). Consistent with their hypothesis, Wann and his associates found consistency between sport fan and athlete motivational patterns. Those who were involved in sport as a fan for intrinsic reasons also were intrinsically motivated as athletes, while those with extrinsic fan motivation were extrinsically motivated as athletes.

The relationship between intrinsic/extrinsic fan motivation and team identification • Wann, Brewer, and Royalty (1999) examined the relationship between intrinsic and extrinsic fan motivation and level of team identification. These investigators hypothesized that highly identified fans should be more likely than lowly identified fans to adopt an extrinsic motivational perspective. They hypothesized that a team's performance has a strong impact on the self-concept of highly identified fans (see chapter 1 for an elaboration on this point). Because these fans place a great deal of importance on the team's success, they were expected to exhibit an extrinsic motivational pattern. To test their predictions, the authors asked college students to complete the Sport Spectator Identification Scale (Wann & Branscombe, 1993) and the SFMS. The results indicated that, contrary to predictions, both highly and lowly identified fans favored intrinsic motives. The authors concluded that although team performance is clearly important to highly identified persons, their main reasons for being a sport fan are based on the activity itself.

SOME FINAL THOUGHTS

If nothing else, the sections in this chapter highlight the multifaceted nature of sport fan socialization and motivation. However, as with so many topics relevant to sport fandom, there is still much we do not know about the socialization process and the specific motives underlying individuals' decisions to participate in this pastime. Because of the void in our understanding of these processes, there are several directions future research should take. Three such paths that may be most especially fruitful in furthering our understanding of how and why individuals become sport fans are described below.

First, recent empirical data on the sport fan socialization process and the relative importance of various socialization agents are almost nonexistent. In fact, an examination of the works cited in this chapter reveals that all but one was completed before 1981. Clearly, additional research is needed before we have a clear understanding of the socialization process.

Second, future work should explore the possibility of group-level differences in sport fan socialization and motivation. Recall that Wann, Bilveu, et al. (1999) found preliminary evidence of racial differences in sport fan motivation. Because members of various racial, ethnic, and class groups often experience different socialization processes, it stands to reason that they may also differ in motivation patterns. Further, because certain motives may only be relevant for specific groups, an understanding of fan motivation across several groups has the added benefit of discovering fan motives not previously identified.

And third, the majority of recent empirical work on the motives of sport fans has used the Sport Fan Motivation Scale (Wann, 1995; Wann, Schrader, et al., 1999). As noted, although preliminary work has substantiated the reliability of validity of the scale, there is room for improvement (see Trail et al., 1998). Further, relying so heavily on a single instrument can lead to a somewhat distorted and biased picture (i.e., the SFMS only measures the eight motives included in the instrument). Hopefully, researchers will continue to refine this instrument and/or develop additional tools for assessing sport fan motivation. Such an endeavor is critical to the advancement of knowledge on this topic because, as Wann (1997) noted, "Data collected by sport researchers is only as good as the tests and questionnaires used to acquire the data" (p. 32).

Chapter Three | BECOMING A SPORT SPECTATOR

As noted in chapter 1, throughout the world millions of people invest time, energy, and financial resources for the opportunity to consume sport. For some, the opportunity to spectate a sporting event requires little effort, such as those who need only to make a short drive across town to attend a local professional, college, high school, or club team contest or those who choose instead to watch a sporting event on television. Others have to travel great distances and spend considerable income on transport, food, lodging, tickets, and parking to indulge their passion for spectator sports. This chapter examines spectator behavior by identifying the psychological factors that promote and maintain sport spectatorship, with particular attention focused on the direct consumption of sport through attendance at sporting events. Thus, the chapter addresses the underlying factors involved in one's decision to attend a sporting event. It is important to note the distinction between the information presented in this chapter and our discussion of fan motivation in the previous chapter. Although the two topics are certainly related, they are not identical. That is, the factors underlying one's decision to become a sport fan and the factors responsible for his or her attendance decisions need not be the same. For instance, although an individual may be motivated to participate in fandom because it provides an escape from his or her life, the same individual may consume sport for entirely different reasons. Thus, once again it seems appropriate to separate our examination of sport fandom and sport spectating.

In his book *Sports Spectators* Guttmann (1986) observed that there had been little research interest in the factors related to sport spectating despite its popularity as an entertainment choice. However, since the publication of his book, we have evidence of an increasing interest in the sport consumer. In fact, investigators from several different perspectives and theoretical backgrounds (e.g., psychology, philosophy, sociology, marketing) have greatly expanded our understanding of the social, psychological, and economic issues related to sport spectatorship behavior.

THEORETICAL APPROACHES TO SPORT SPECTATING

Several theoretical perspectives have been employed to explain the motives underlying the attendance decisions of sport spectators. The majority of these theories can be classified into one of five somewhat independent categories: salubrious effect theories, stress and stimulation seeking theories, catharsis and aggression theories, entertainment theories, and achievement seeking theories (Schwartz, 1973; Sloan, 1989; Zillmann & Paulas, 1993). Each of these theories is briefly described below. As you will note, several of these theories share commonalties with the sport fandom motives discussed in chapter 2.

Salubrious effect theories (also referred to as recreation theory and diversion theory) reflect the belief that spectators are attracted to a game for its pleasure and the physical and mental well-being derived therefrom. Similar to the escape motive of sport fandom discussed in chapter 2, salubrious effect theories also suggest that attending a sporting event can serve as an escape (Lever & Wheeler, 1984; McPherson, 1975; Sloan, 1989). Similar to the notion of eustress presented in the previous chapter, stress and stimulation seeking theories focus on the positive or negative stresses that can result from direct or indirect sport consumption. Here, spectators are attracted to a game because of their need for arousing and stimulating experiences (Branscombe & Wann, 1994; Gantz & Wenner, 1995; Sloan, 1989).

Catharsis and aggression theories reflect the belief that spectators are attracted to a game for its aggressive and violent content (Iso-Ahola & Hatfield, 1986; Sloan, 1989). There is little question that many spectators are attracted to and enjoy the violent nature of some sports (Bryant, 1989; Bryant & Zillmann, 1983). However, catharsis and aggression theories go beyond merely suggesting that individuals are attracted to sport spectating because they like aggressive content. Rather, proponents argue that when spectators view an aggressive sporting event, their own aggressive tendencies are released, resulting in a more calm and less aggressive psychophysical state. However, as we shall see in an upcoming chapter, this notion of catharsis has been strongly challenged by researchers. Rather than becoming less aggressive subsequent to the consumption of violent sports, spectators tend to display an increased level of aggression.

Entertainment theories suggest that spectators are attracted to a game because one or more specific components of the contest will provide them with pleasure (Duncan, 1983; Gantz, 1981; Sloan, 1989; Zillmann et al., 1989). This theory includes the notion of aesthetics discussed in the previous chapter. Achievement seeking theories of sport spectating are consistent with the self-esteem motive presented in chapter 2. This viewpoint suggests that individuals are attracted to sport spectating because of their identification with the achievement of others (Anderson, 1979; Branscombe & Wann, 1991; Murrell & Dietz, 1992; Zhang, Pease, Hui, & Michaud, 1995).

THE THEORY OF PERSONAL INVESTMENT

Although each of the theories described here has, at least to some extent, stimulated research and/or aided our understanding of sport spectating, there are three critical concerns one must bear in mind when evaluating the value of these approaches. First, and perhaps most basic, some of the aforementioned approaches lack empirical support (e.g., the notion of catharsis).

Second, in addition to being fairly unidimensional in nature, these theoretical perspectives overlap with the sport fandom motives discussed in chapter 2. Some overlap is not only inevitable, but desirable. Because the constructs "sport fandom" and "sport spectating" share much in common, it is perfectly understandable that the theories used to account for both will have common ground. However, as noted earlier in this text, it is equally apparent that the two activities are distinct. Consequently, one cannot fully account for both activities with the same theory, hence the necessity for a separate theoretical approach to sport spectating.

Third, these theoretical approaches tend to focus on a specific component of the spectating process. Limited acknowledgment is given to the interrelationships among the variables that might impact attendance and consumption decisions. As Guttmann (1986) correctly observed, sport spectating is multidimensional and highly complex, that is, a number of factors help determine an individual's attendance decisions. To be valid, a theory of sport spectating must reflect the multidimensionality of the activity. Indeed, in an effort to address this problem, Zhang and his colleagues developed the Scale for Attendance Decision (SAD) (Zhang et al., 1995, 1997). The SAD is a psychometrically sound, twenty-seven-item index specifically designed to assess the multiple psychological factors affecting spectator attendance. This scale contains five factors (i.e., subscales): game attributes (e.g., aggressive play, speed of game), game convenience (e.g., day of week, weather), home team (e.g., quality, history), economic consideration (e.g., ticket prices, advertising), and opposing team (e.g., quality, star player). A similarly valid and reliable instrument for assessing sport consumer behavior was developed by Madrigal (1999). This instrument, the FANDIM scale, contains twenty-four items that assess eight different dimensions related to sport consumer behavior: aesthetics (e.g., admiring the beauty of sport), camaraderie (e.g., socializing with friends), evaluation (e.g., analyzing performances), fantasy (e.g., imaging oneself as an athlete), flow (getting "lost" in the action), personalities (e.g., following famous athletes), physical attraction (e.g., admiring the athletes' bodies), and vicarious achievement (e.g., the "thrill of victory").

To address the concerns just described, a more general theory of motivation was needed for organizing, identifying, and interpreting the important psychological factors influencing spectator attendance decisions. Specifically, we sought a general theoretical framework that had empirical support, was consistent with the notion that sport fandom and sport spectating are not identical, and was multidimensional in nature. The theory of personal investment seemed most appropriate (Maehr & Braskamp, 1986). This theory identifies three dimensions that are critical in determining motivation: (1) perceived options, (2) sense of self, and (3) personal incentives (see figure 3.1).

FIGURE 3.1

The theory of personal investment as applied to sport spectating decisions

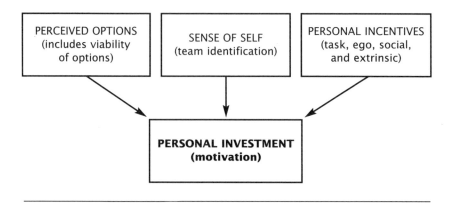

The value of the theory lies in its generality—it represents an integration of several motivational factors (e.g., achievement and affiliation). Further, it focuses on the choices and decisions made by individuals and the meanings they assign to them. This theoretical approach allows us to critically examine the factors underlying an individual's decision to invest time, energy, and personal resources to attend sporting events (or observe through the media). It should be noted that the tenets of personal investment theory have been used previously to understand sport behavior. Specifically, Duda and her colleagues (Duda, 1989; Duda, Smart, & Tappe, 1989) used this approach to account for decisions made by sport participants and nonparticipants and to study predictors of exercise adherence.

Perceived Options

Within personal investment theory, perceived options refer to one's understanding of the behavioral alternatives available in a specific situation. An attendance decision requires weighing the costs and benefits of several different entertainment options. On any given weekend, a potential consumer has a number of recreational options. For instance, he or she could, in addition to attending a sporting event, go to a movie, play a round of golf or a set of tennis, dine out, see a nightclub show, and so on. If one chooses the sporting event option, he or she is still faced with an important decision, namely, having to choose among the various sporting venues, ranging from amateur sports (e.g., little league, junior and senior high school sports) to collegiate and professional events. Of course, the number of options available is directly related to the geographical area in which one resides. For example, in Houston, Texas, on one weekend (i.e., from Friday night to Sunday night) over thirty-seven sporting events (based on a *Houston Chronicle* newspaper listing) were identified. This figure does not include little league competitions and other formal or informal recreational sporting events. Nor does it include indirect consumption options. As noted in chapter 1, there are dozens of indirect sport consumption options available, particularly to cable or satellite television subscribers. In smaller communities, however, the direct consumer may be limited to one or two weekend sporting events (e.g., a Friday night football game at the local high school). However, this person may still have access to many indirect options.

Research suggests that the direct (i.e., personal attendance) and indirect (i.e., television, radio) consumption options are sometimes at odds with one another. There is evidence that the number of televised sport options is negatively related to direct spectator attendance (Demmert, 1973; Noll, 1974; Zhang & Smith, 1997). To counter this, home games are often "blacked out" unless all stadium or arena tickets are sold. However, when questioning spectators who attended a minor league hockey game, Zhang, Pease, and Smith (1998) found a positive correlation between attendance and degree of watching home and away games on television. These researchers suggested that there may be a reciprocal relationship at play. Specifically, they argued that by providing information and generating interest about sport through media coverage, sport management is able to increase fan identification. Consequently, increased team identification leads to increases in direct sport consumption (Wann & Branscombe, 1993).

The Viability of Identified Options Once a consumer has identified his or her options, the next task is to determine the viability of each (Maehr & Braskamp, 1986). The direct consumer must determine if the value of attending the event is greater than the costs associated with attending. For example, although one may want to attend the Super Bowl, ticket availability and cost, travel requirements, and time away from one's family or job may make it an unrealistic option. The indirect sport consumer must decide whether or not time spent watching a televised event will prove sufficiently satisfying to warrant the time invested. Thus, we have a formula for estimating the viability of a sporting event option: $V = B - C$. In this formula, B refers to the benefits gained from attending the event, C refers to the costs associated with attending the event (financial, time, etc.), and V refers to the viability of the option. If the benefits of attendance outweigh the costs, the individual will most likely view the option as viable. If, on the other hand, the costs outweigh the benefits, the option will probably be perceived as nonviable.

A number of factors impact perceptions of the viability of an option, including availability and financial cost. Below, we examine how these factors impact sport spectatorship decisions.

The future availability of an option • Maehr and Braskamp (1986) note that to understand the viability of an option, one must consider its future availability. In the case of sport spectators, this refers to the availability of an event (or similar events) in the near or distant future. Event availability can have both positive and negative influences on attendance decisions. For example, attending an Olympic event may be a once in a lifetime happening (i.e., low future availability), thereby increasing the attractiveness of attending. For other options, such as with little league baseball games, the opportunities for future attendance are much greater. Consequently, the spectator may choose not to attend now, knowing that he or she will be able to attend in the future with little difficulty.

For some events the lack of future options may actually decrease the likelihood of attendance. A clear example of this occurred when the Houston Oilers of the NFL announced a year in advance that they were moving the franchise to Nashville, Tennessee. During their last year in Houston, attendance at Oilers' games dropped by approximately 50 percent. Those who chose not to attend may have reasoned that, because future attendance was not a viable option (i.e., it would take a great deal of time and expense to see the team play in Nashville), it made little sense to continue rooting for the team, and the decision was made to not attend. In addition, the Nashville stadium was still under construction during the following season. Consequently, the team was forced to play its home games in Memphis, Tennessee, a three-hour drive from Nashville. As was the case with attendance in Houston the previous season, attendance in Memphis was well under expectations. Many may have thought that, because the team would not be competing in Memphis the next year, why support the team by purchasing tickets?

The financial requirements of an option • Another important factor determining the viability of an option involves its financial cost (e.g., Eitzen, 1996; Hansen & Gauthier, 1989; Schofield, 1983; Zhang et al., 1995). Costs can range from no financial outlay (e.g., attending children's little league competitions) to the prohibitive costs of attending professional sporting events. Research generally shows a negative relationship between ticket prices and frequency of attendance (e.g., Baade & Tiehen, 1990; Bird, 1982; Hansen & Gauthier; 1989, Zhang et al., 1995). Additional expenses that must be considered when assessing the viability of an event include food, beverages, parking, memorabilia, and travel costs. A fan cost index (FCI) produced by Team Marketing underscores the importance of the financial issue (McGraw, 1998). The FCI is based on the cost of four average-priced tickets, two small beers, four sodas, four hot dogs, parking for one car, two game programs, and two twill caps. In 1999 it cost a family of four an average of $266.61 to attend an NBA game, $258.50 for an NFL game, $254.48 for an NHL game, and $121.36 for an MLB game ("Hoop tickets," 1999). The cost of attending an NBA, NFL, or NHL game is approximately 30 percent of the average household's weekly earnings; it's 16 percent for MLB games. Unfortunately, a weekly trip to the ballpark or arena for a professional sporting event may no longer be a viable option for many fans.

Although the majority of research on the financial factor has involved attendance at professional sporting events, cost factors also appear to be an issue at the collegiate level. Pan et al. (1997) surveyed basketball season ticket holders at an NCAA Division I-A university in the United States. They reported that economic factors accounted for 24 percent of the variance in the season ticket holders' decision-making process; it was a better predictor than team schedule and various social factors. As expected, respondents with lower reported income assigned greater importance to economic concerns than did those with higher incomes. Seventy-two percent of the season ticket holders reported relatively high incomes ($60,000 or more). This finding suggests that, as one might expect, higher levels of disposable income are directly related to the purchase of season tickets. Interestingly though, even for those with considerable disposable income the economic issue was still the most important factor affecting their attendance decisions.

Other factors influencing the viability of an option • In addition to future availability and cost, the viability of an option is impacted by several other factors. Factors such as driving distance to the event (Schurr et al., 1988), stadium/arena access and parking (Hay & Rao, 1982), day and time of the event (Hill, Madura, & Zuber, 1982; Zhang et al., 1995), quality of the event (J. C. Jones, 1984; Noll, 1974; Whitney, 1988), and weather (Noll, 1974; Pan et al., 1997) also help determine the viability of an option. For example, although an individual may consider the cost of a sporting event acceptable, he or she may not choose this option because the walk from the parking lot to the stadium is simply too long. Similarly, another potential spectator may choose not to attend because he or she had to attend work or school at the time of the event.

Sense of Self

A second major component of the theory of personal investment involves the sense of self. According to Maehr and Braskamp (1986), sense-of-self factors are a "more or less organized collection of perceptions, beliefs, and feelings about who one is" (p. 59). The aspect of the self that is most relevant to sport spectating is identity (there are other components of self with minimal relevance to sport spectating). Identity is defined as the way an "individual perceives himself or herself as associated with certain groups and holds selected others to be significant" (Maehr & Braskamp, 1986, p. 59). With respect to sport spectatorship, we refer here to team identification (or player identification) as outlined in chapter 1.

Team Identification and Sport Spectating Team and/or individual athlete identification may be the most important psychological factor impacting attendance. A number of researchers have found that degree of team identification and level of team commitment are positively related to game attendance (e.g., Murrell & Dietz, 1992; Wakefield, 1995; Wann & Branscombe, 1993; Wann, Roberts, & Tindall, 1999). For instance, consider a study recently conducted by Pease and Zhang (1996). These researchers investigated several factors related to attendance at six Houston Rockets NBA games and found that team identification was the best predictor. Included in the general identification factor were items related to an individual's knowledge about the team, confirming previous research (D. F. Anderson, 1979; Murrell & Dietz, 1992). The analysis of demographic variables related to team identification showed significant differences for age and ethnicity. Older spectators tended to have lower team identification than younger ones. Older and younger spectators appeared to have different needs (e.g., social, political). With respect to ethnicity, Hispanics reported higher levels of team identification than did African Americans, Caucasians, or Asians. Pease and Zhang suggest that, because there are very few Hispanic NBA players, for some Hispanics, higher levels of identification are related to increased self-esteem and decreased alienation; that is, team identification provides them with a sense of belonging and attachment to a larger social structure (Branscombe & Wann, 1991; for more on this topic, see chapters 8 and 9).

Loyalty, free agency, and attendance decisions • The concept of team loyalty is closely related to team identification. Consequently, one would expect that loyal (i.e., "die-hard") fans are more likely to attend games than are disloyal (i.e., "fair-weather") fans (Wann & Branscombe, 1990a). Within the last few decades, there has been some concern over the impact of player free agency on fans' team loyalty and game attendance. In free agency, introduced to professional sports in the 1970s, athletes are not bound to one team and can negotiate with other teams for higher salaries. The result has been a dramatic increase in player movement and roster turnover. Has increased player movement eroded fans' loyalty to their favorite teams? Isn't it difficult for a fan to maintain his or her loyalty to a team when its composition is dramatically different from year to year? If free agency has resulted in lower fan loyalty, it may be reflected in lower attendance. Kahane and Shmanske (1997) examined the possible impact of free agency by investigating the relationship between roster turnover and attendance in MLB. Using the period from 1990 to 1992, they found that teams experienced an annual turnover rate of

27 percent. For each percentage point of player loss (i.e., turnover) yearly attendance was reduced by between six thousand and twelve thousand fans. Although this study did not attempt to account for factors such as player quality, the results do suggest that player turnover and the potential reduction in fan loyalty have a detrimental affect on attendance.

Disposition theory and attendance decisions • So far we have discovered that highly identified, loyal fans are more likely to attend their team's games than are less identified fans. This finding is consistent with marketing research showing that positive consumer attitudes are directly related to product purchase; consumers are less likely to purchase a product for which they hold a negative attitude (e.g., Fazio, Powell, & Williams, 1989). However, in the case of sport consumption, the disposition theory of sport spectating suggests a contrary finding. Recall from chapter 2 that disposition theory states that not only do spectators enjoy watching their favorite team play well, but they also gain great satisfaction observing a despised team being humiliated, particularly if the team is viewed as a threat (Mahony & Howard, 1998; Sapolsky, 1980; Zillmann et al., 1989). Consequently, sport fans consume sport not only when they hold a favorable attitude toward the product (i.e., their favorite team is playing), but, in some instances, when they hold negative attitudes (i.e., when a despised team is playing). For example, consider a die-hard Dallas Cowboys fan. Obviously, this person is going to enjoy attending a Cowboys' game. However, this fan would also enjoy attending a Washington Redskins' game if this heated rival of the Cowboys was soundly defeated. This is quite contrary to marketing research for consumer products. For instance, it makes no sense for someone who likes toothpaste brand A but despises toothpaste brand B to use the latter.

Personal Incentives

Maehr and Braskamp (1986) define personal incentives as those environmental components perceived to be attractive or unattractive. Personal incentives reflect the goals or reasons for becoming a spectator or continuing to spectate. There are four different types of personal incentives, each of which is influential in sport spectating decisions. Two of the personal incentives are intrinsic in nature: task incentives and ego incentives. Task incentives involve the activity itself, that is, the individual engages in the activity simply because of the enjoyment derived. With respect to sport spectating, task incentives refer to an individual's desire to attend a specific sporting event because he or she enjoys one or more components of that sport. Ego incentives involve competition with others and demonstrating one's superiority at a task. Thus, with respect to sport spectators, ego incentives refer to the desire to watch a favorite team perform well and succeed.

The two other personal incentives are social incentives and extrinsic rewards, both extrinsic in nature. Social incentives refer to the interpersonal relationships resulting from participation in an activity. This incentive is related to the pleasure received from spending time with, or gaining the approval of, others. Social incentives are highly relevant to sport spectatorship behaviors as many individuals engage in the activity in the company of intimate others. Extrinsic rewards involve direct benefits gained from participating in an activity. In sport settings, promotions such as "giveaway days" are clear examples of extrinsic rewards.

Task Incentives: The Importance of the Game and Attendance
Rather than consume all sports equally, spectators typically express strong preferences for certain sports. For instance, a college basketball fan can have as much loathing for auto racing as she has love for basketball. This points out the importance of task incentives in sport spectating decisions. There are certain aspects about particular sports that attract fans to those sports. For instance, some spectators may be primarily attracted to fast-paced action, graceful sport movements, or "extreme" sports.

One component that researchers have been especially interested in is a sport's violent content. In one study, the number of hockey spectators who attended home games following their team's most violent contests was compared with attendance figures following nonviolent games. The results indicated no differences in attendance as a function of game violence. What was related to increased attendance was winning streaks by the home team (Russell, 1986).

Conversely, another investigation found a positive relationship between on-ice violence and attendance (J. C. Jones, Ferguson, & Stewart, 1993). Using a somewhat different design, the investigators discovered that total penalty minutes predicted attendance in NHL cities in both the United States and Canada. However, when the most extreme forms of violence were considered (e.g., major penalties and misconducts), a positive relationship was found only for American cities. The researchers suggest that during the league's expansion into the United States, the sport was marketed specifically on its violent content. Consequently, American spectators grew to enjoy a more violent form of the game.

Regardless of the mixed results, violence does sell in some sports. In a sport such as boxing, spectators would neither attend nor watch on television if the fighters were not allowed to hit each other. Even with the fanciest of footwork, ratings would plummet and arenas would be empty. Certainly, there is an audience for violent entertainment. However, research shows that it is an audience largely comprised of people who are themselves aggressive. As noted elsewhere, "aggressive individuals seek out and attend entertainment featuring aggressive themes" (Arms, Russell, Dwyer, & Josuttes, 1999).

Ego Incentives: Team (and Player) Success and Attendance As discussed earlier in this text, fans often view their favorite teams as an extension of themselves. Fans experience the "thrill of victory" when their team wins and the "agony of defeat" when their team loses. Thus, for many fans an important ego incentive is associated with spectating sporting events, namely, the positive affect they experience watching their team perform well. Accordingly, it should not be surprising that several studies have documented a positive relationship between team success and attendance (e.g., Baade & Tiehen, 1990; Brooks, 1994; Fullerton & Merz, 1982; Hay & Rao, 1982; J. C. Jones, 1969; Noll, 1974; Zhang et al., 1995). In fact, some researchers have suggested that team performance is the most important factor in attendance decisions (Guttmann, 1986; Zhang et al., 1995).

Attributions of team success and attendance • Although fans are more likely to attend games when a team is playing well, the relationship between team performance and attendance is more complex than that. To truly understand this relationship, one must consider not only the team's performance, but also the spectators' attributions about that performance. Attributions are estimates of the causes of a behavior. With respect to sport fans, attributions refer to the causes of their team's performance. Statements such as "my team won because of their talent," "they lost because of poor officiating," and "that athlete only succeeded because he is on steroids" are all examples of attributions. Although researchers have identified a number of different attributional dimensions (see chapter 7), the one most relevant for attendance decisions is locus of causality. This dimension concerns the extent to which an individual believes that the cause of a behavior was internal or external (e.g., Heider, 1958; Kelley, 1967; Weiner, 1989). Internal attributions reflect the belief that a behavior was caused by the individual. For example, beliefs that a team was victorious because of their hustle or skill are examples of internal attributions. External attributions reflect the belief that a behavior was caused by the environment or setting. For instance, beliefs that a player performed poorly because of the weather or bad luck are examples of external attributions.

Iso-Ahola (1980) was the first researcher to examine the interrelationships between locus of control, team performance, and attendance decisions (see also Wann, Roberts, et al., 1999). He presented subjects with descriptions of upcoming contests and had them indicate their attendance decision. The descriptions contained four variables: past performance of the home team (i.e., successful or unsuccessful), reasons for the home team's past performance (i.e., internal or external), past performance of the visiting team, and reasons for the visiting team's past performance. The findings revealed that individuals were less likely to attend a game when the home team had been unsuccessful, the cause of their poor performance was internal (e.g., low ability), and the visiting team had been successful because of internal factors. Apparently, fans see little opportunity for their team to win such games and, as a result, are less likely to attend. The participants reported they were most likely to attend a contest in which both teams were successful and the cause of their performance was internal. Fans may be attracted to these games because they figure them to be exciting, well-played contests in which the favored team has a reasonable chance of success.

Team performance, team identification, and attendance • It warrants mention that although successful team performance is an important criterion for determining spectator attendance, fans do attend games played by teams with less than stellar records. In fact, in some cases, teams with long histories of poor performances still attract millions of spectators each year. An obvious example would be the Chicago Cubs MLB franchise. Although the Cubs have not won a major-league pennant since 1945, they still draw large numbers of spectators to their games, sellouts being quite common. This seems to contradict earlier findings that showed a positive relationship between team performance and attendance. Wann and Branscombe (1990a) suggest that to account for the contradiction, we have to consider the spectator's level of team identification. These researchers have found that highly identified fans are much less likely to "jump ship" when their team begins to perform poorly. Consequently, these fans will continue to support the team and attend their games even during trying times (e.g., the Chicago Cubs Die-Hard Fan Club).

Of course, not all fans attending contests played by poor teams identify highly with one or both of the teams. Rather, it is more likely that some feel only a moderate or a low sense of connection to the team. For these individuals, neither team identification nor ego incentives (i.e., the team is playing poorly) account for their attendance. Consequently, there must be one or more additional incentives operating to affect their behavior. Several of these additional incentives are discussed below.

Social Incentives: Group Affiliation and Attendance For many fans, the primary incentive for attending spectator sports lies in the social nature of the event. The specific social incentives vary from spectator to spectator. For instance, for some the opportunity to spend time with family members serves as sufficient incentive for attending a sporting event. For others, the social setting may be used for business purposes or to gain social status by being seen in public.

A number of authors have commented on the social atmosphere as an underlying reason for attendance at sporting events (e.g., Pan & Baker, 1999; Pan et al., 1997; Wakefield, 1995; Zhang et al., 1995). In fact, some have suggested that social outcomes may be more important than the competition itself (Branscombe & Wann, 1991; G. J. Smith, 1988). Melnick (1993) observes that sport spectatorship enhances people's lives by "helping them experience the pure sociability, quasi-intimate relationships, and sense of belonging that are so indigenous to the stands" (p. 46). In supporting of Melnick's observations, Spreitzer and Snyder (1975) found that 84 percent of men and 75 percent of women viewed sport as a good means of socializing with other people.

Extrinsic Rewards: Promotions, New Stadia, and Attendance For many spectators, the opportunity to observe highly skilled athletes perform in a social environment provides ample incentive to attend sporting events. However, there is evidence suggesting that some individuals require additional incentives before they attend a game. Two of the most common extrinsic rewards observed in sport today are promotions and a new sport stadium/arena.

Promotions and giveaways • To attract fans, team marketing strategists dole out many extrinsic rewards in the form of giveaways (e.g., autographed balls, hats, posters, etc.), free entertainment (e.g., fireworks shows, the San Diego Chicken), and opportunities to interact with the players (e.g., autograph and photo opportunity days). A recent, highly successful giveaway at professional games has tapped into the Beanie Baby craze (Beanie Babies are small stuffed animals). MLB teams in New York and Houston increased their attendance by over ten thousand spectators per game on Beanie Baby giveaway days. A Beanie Baby promotion at an NBA game in Philadelphia increased attendance by more than 50 percent. Although one-day promotions provide an incentive for attending a particular game, they appear to have little influence on a spectator's continuing attendance (Stotler, 1989). Thus, the impact of extrinsic rewards appears to be short-lived—personal and social incentives most likely have longer-lasting effects.

Many extrinsic reward incentives are convenience factors (Zhang, Smith, Pease, & Lam, 1998), such as accessibility of parking, security, stadium aesthetics, concessions, ticket services, and schedule convenience. Research involving minor-league hockey spectators found "satisfaction with ticket service" (e.g., ordering services, ticket office personnel, and convenience of ticket sale location) and "satisfaction with event amenities" (e.g., pregame activities and souvenirs) to be highly predictive of game attendance (Zhang, Smith, et al., 1998). Similarly, satisfaction with amenities (e.g., half-time shows and dance team performances), satisfaction with accessibility (e.g., arena access and parking), and satisfaction with audiovisuals (e.g., scoreboards) were significantly associated with attendance at professional basketball games. In both samples, satisfaction with amenities was the strongest predictor of attendance. Clearly, this suggests that extrinsic rewards do enhance a game's entertainment value and increase spectator attendance.

The building of new sport arenas and stadia • Many professional and college teams have built new stadia and arenas in recent years in the hope that they will attract greater numbers of fans (as well as fans willing to pay higher ticket prices). The chance to attend a sporting event in a flashy new stadium is another example of an extrinsic reward. From the days of the "exploding scoreboard" introduced by White Sox owner Bill Veeck at Chicago's Comiskey Park in 1960, facility enhancements have undergone major changes. In planning new stadia and arenas for the twenty-first century, Murphy (1997) suggests that instead of building facilities in which all spectators have the same experience, new venues must provide for a variety of spectating options. He argues that to be most "fan friendly," different amenities need to be located in different tiers of the stadium. He calls this approach to stadium structure "microclassification." For example, consider the recently built Turner Field, home field of the Atlanta Braves of MLB. This ballpark has aptly been described as a cross between a baseball park and Disney World.

Roberts (1997) discussed the problems involved in constructing sport arenas (which she calls the "American Pyramids") that serve not only as venues for watching a game but also as extrinsic rewards in and of themselves. She argues that sport franchises need more corporate suites and executive dining facilities and must provide better spectator amenities in order to keep the "machine oiled and running at top speed" (p. 34). The sport stadium is becoming a "signature piece" for a city. Michael Hallmark of NBBJ Sports and Entertainment states that "just as the movie industry reinvented itself with new multiplex theaters, we will have to make our new venues so exciting, equal to most spectacular theme parks, that families, kids, moms and dads, everyone will be drawn to our unique destinations of fun, civic pride and comfort" (cited in Roberts, 1997, p. 36). Roberts describes the stadia of the future as having "smart seats" with individual video units providing miniature scoreboards and replays, food and beverage service ordering, e-mail hookups, and other computer driven technology (remember when it was considered a luxury to have a seat with a cupholder?!).

In addition to influencing the spectating option, the location and accessibility of new stadia and arenas are also important components of the extrinsic reward package (Hansen & Gauthier, 1989; Mulrooney & Farmer, 1996; Schofield, 1983). In the past, sporting facilities were often located in suburban areas. Land was readily available and there was good accessibility to major highways. It was also believed that the safer environments of suburban locations provided an additional incentive for potential spectators. Today, however, new stadia and arenas are being constructed in or close to the central areas of a city (e.g., Atlanta, Cleveland, Baltimore, Houston, Denver, and Toronto). Politicians and economists justify the location as a way of rejuvenating a decaying downtown area and enhancing a city's image. It is believed that the inner-city location will enhance ticket value. This incentive was suggested by Williams (1998) in his description of the location of a baseball stadium in downtown Houston: "you will park your car downtown, walk past a restaurant or bar and maybe stop. As you get closer to the stadium, the buzz around it will get louder. Inside, the buzz will be even louder. You will see downtown. People are having fun just because they are there" (p. A37).

SOME FINAL THOUGHTS

This chapter has focused on several psychological factors related to spectator attendance using personal investment theory as a conceptual framework (Maehr & Braskamp, 1986). Based on the relevant literature, it seems appropriate and useful to analyze sport spectatorship from this perspective. Research indicates that the via-

bility of entertainment options, one's sense of self (i.e., team identification), and incentives all impact the decision to attend sporting
events. However, in closing, a few additional comments are in order.
First, although we have presented the three motivational components of personal investment theory separately (i.e., options, sense
of self, and incentives), this was not meant to suggest that they are
independent entities. Rather, Maehr and Braskamp observe that they
are interactive constructs and that one must understand their interrelationships to fully comprehend how the motivational variables
direct human behavior. With respect to sport spectatorship, this
means that spectators' perceptions of the viability of their options,
their level of team identification, and the attractiveness of incentives
all interact in complex ways to impact decision making. For
instance, an individual with high team identification may believe
that paying $1,000 for a ticket to see her team play in a champi-
onship game is quite reasonable. Conversely, a lowly identified fan
of the same team may view this attendance option as very unattractive (Wann & Branscombe, 1993).

Second, it is important to note that the theory of personal investment says that although the underlying motives for sport fandom and
sport spectating may be similar, they are far from identical, hence the
need for separate approaches to understanding both. For instance,
some individuals are motivated to become fans because of group affiliation motives; consequently, they choose to spectate because of
social incentives. However, other individuals may be motivated to
attend a sporting event simply because the stadium is new, the parking is readily accessible, and there will be a fireworks display after the
contest. It seems doubtful that these individuals are motivated to participate in sport fandom for the same reasons.

Third, although research involving spectator behavior has
expanded over the past decade, there is still much we do not know.
For instance, most of the research has focused on the direct sport consumer with little research focused on the indirect consumer.
Similarly, we know little about the sport fan who is a nonspectator
yet follows a favorite team through the print media, radio talk shows,
and the Internet. Also, most of the research has involved professional
or collegiate sports, sports with high levels of media coverage and
strong fan allegiances. Unfortunately, there is little empirical work
on factors affecting attendance at high school, club, or children's
sporting events.

In closing, the data presented here and in chapter 1 suggest that
interest in spectator sports continues to be very high. However, some

reports indicate that it is actually declining. For example, Roper Starch Worldwide reported a 13 percent decline in public interest in spectator sports since 1992. This decline may be attributed to Generation X (defined as people born between 1965 and 1976). Simmons Market Research Bureau reports that for the Generation X population sport consumption decreased between 1984 and 1991 (Turco, 1996). Attendance at professional basketball declined 3.3 percent, while professional football declined 10.2 percent. Similar declines in sport television viewing have been reported. It appears that this age group, for whatever reasons, is not as involved with sport spectatorship as were previous generations.

| **SPORT FANS AND THEIR HEROES**

There is no shortage of candidates for the designation of sport hero. Indeed, virtually every sport can muster an array of outstanding athletes either from an earlier era or from among those who are still active. Perhaps the importance of heroes in contemporary society is most evident in our interest in Halls of Fame. Many heroes have been enshrined in Halls of Fame, keeping alive memories of their past achievements for future generations to admire. As a predominantly North American phenomenon, Halls of Fame have become a growth industry, their numbers increasing at an astonishing rate during the latter half of the twentieth century (G. Lewis & Redmond, 1974). Virtually every city and region in North America boasts some version of a Hall of Fame to honor a sport and/or its heroes. Not only do they serve as repositories for archival materials and a focal point for collective and individual nostalgia (E. E. Snyder, 1991), but Halls of Fame also frequently provide a boost to local tourism.

Thus, many fans engage in hero worship, placing their favorite athletes on rather lofty pedestals. Consequently, to truly understand the behaviors of sport fans, we would be remiss not to include a discussion of the importance of heroes in the lives of sport fans. The current chapter is designed to provide such an analysis by highlighting the role and impact of sport heroes in society insofar as they shape the values and behaviors of their admirers (in this text, "heroes" will be used as a non-gender-specific term referring to both male and female athletes). Our analysis focuses on several important topics, including the extent to which the sportsworld serves as a major category from which individuals draw heroes, the impact of sport heroes on individuals and society, the relationship between personality and exemplar choices, and people's perceptions of former heroes who have fallen from grace. Before investigating these issues, we must first develop a basic understanding of the hero worship phenomenon as it relates to sport fans.

AN INTRODUCTION TO HERO SELECTION

In this section, we introduce hero worship by briefly examining several basic, but important, components of the phenomenon. Specifically, we examine the notion of "true" heroes, the functions of heroes, and the impact of media on the creation of heroes.

"True Heroes" versus Those "Less Deserving": Setting Standards for the Status of Hero

Sportswriters are in general agreement that sport heroes are blessed with exceptional physical ability. After that, opinions differ as to the patterns of attributes indicative of a true hero. Some make a distinction between short-term heroes, or "celebrities" (Barney, 1985), and heroes who persist through the years (long-term heroes). Others see consistency in clutch, high-pressure situations and the ability to capture the public's imagination as important heroic qualities (Cramer, Walker, &, Rado, 1980).

Although outstanding athletes are plentiful and can potentially serve as role models for aspiring youngsters, the personal qualifications of many are suspect. In recent years we have seen too many would-be heroes disappoint their followers. With disturbing regularity we learn of star athletes' involvement with illegal drugs, gambling, tax fraud, domestic violence, and an assortment of other criminal activities. What is sorely needed is a set of standards for distinguishing between true heroes and those who lack the requisite qualities. One such set of standards, offered by Barney (1985), is presented briefly below. It might be useful to keep these criteria in mind as this chapter unfolds. Of course, these standards represent an ideal that most candidates for hero status only approach. Still, they provide a reference for parents and others in selecting desirable role models for themselves and their children.

Most of what we know about our heroes is based on information that is filtered, often sanitized, by media sources. The bulk of that information speaks to Barney's (1985) first criterion, performance excellence (i.e., physical excellence). Relatively little attention is paid by the media to the other criteria because it represents less newsworthy aspects of a hero's life. Secondly, the hero must also display moral excellence in all aspects of his or her life, acting with honesty, humility, generosity, sportsmanship, and self-control. An additional requirement is that candidates give unselfishly of their energies and talents to assist those less fortunate than themselves. Barney's fourth criterion requires the individual to have demonstrated theoretical and practical wisdom. For instance, heroes should act responsibly in dealing with personal decisions regarding money, drugs, gambling, and the like. Finally, true hero status should not be accorded an athlete in his or her lifetime. Too often, unsavory bits of information come to light long after an outstanding athlete has been established as a role model for aspiring youngsters. The sheer passage of time is assumed to bring a more objective and balanced perspective of a candidate's qualifications.

The Functions of Heroes

Heroes are not all of the same stripe, nor do they perform the same functions. Various researchers have speculated about the important societal functions that heroes serve. Some of these speculations are plausible, while others are a bit far-fetched. Moreover, the suggested functions are largely untested. In fact, some are stated in such vague form that it is not even possible to evaluate their merit. Here, we examine a number of these hypothesized functions.

Leadership Function One of the most often cited functions of heroes is they serve in some form of leadership capacity. Indeed, if heroes are capable of influencing at least some of their admirers, then we should view them as leaders, albeit of a special type. On occasion, a single outstanding performance will catapult an athlete into the media's spotlight. Overnight she becomes a recognized expert on her sport with others looking to her for advice and inspiration. As such, her role in the sport is now that of a leader exercising what Gibb (1969) called "unsought leadership." Bear in mind that she has been accorded leadership status solely on the basis of athletic excellence.

There are several implications associated with this type of leadership. In most cases, one can assume that less gifted and less famous cocompetitors are equally if not more knowledgeable regarding the intricacies of their sport. As elsewhere, the selection of effective sport leaders is far from a lighthearted exercise. If the overnight expert is subsequently called upon to serve her sport in a leadership capacity, the chances are slim that she will possess the requisite attributes for effective leadership. Yet such "leaders" are often called upon to head up various political, commercial, and charitable campaigns. The question of their effectiveness will be touched upon in a later section in connection with Magic Johnson's stint as a spokesperson for a national AIDS campaign.

Idealized Social Order In the view of some scholars, the presence of a hero can prompt admirers to strive toward an idealized social order. This can vary from maintaining the status quo to extending current behavioral norms to creating entirely new modes of behavior (J. C. Harris, 1986; Klapp, 1969). Those who epitomize the existing social order by affirming current standards represent "reinforcing heroes" (Klapp, 1969). Their values and goals are those that society has traditionally approved. However, there is also what Klapp termed the "seductive hero," whose actions tempt us to violate traditional norms of conduct. Olympic gold medalist snowboarder Ross Rebagliati's involvement with a marijuana subculture illustrates one such seductive direction. Finally, there are "transcending heroes" who separate themselves from traditional societal orthodoxy and propose entirely new approaches to social order. Utopians and a hodgepodge of gurus would be included in this category.

Compensatory Function Another category of heroes includes those whose exploits rekindle the traits and values associated with a bygone era. Such values may seem all but lost in today's world, with some wishing for a return to the "glory" days. For example, the epic solo voyage of Sir Francis Chichester, who circled the globe in his 54-foot *Gypsy Moth IV*, brought forth a flood of nostalgic memories to Britons eager to relive the glorious days of the empire. British adventurer Richard Branson's recent attempts to circle the globe in a hot air balloon may, too, have stirred such sentiments in his fellow countrymen.

Interpersonal Involvement Sport heroes are, for the most part, in the public domain. As mentioned, there are precious few opportunities for fans to engage in significant personal interactions with them. Most interactions, such as those that occur at book signings, fan appreciation days, and the like, are quite impersonal. Nevertheless, social relationships may be forged among fans who share in their admiration of a particular sport figure. Friendships can develop among members of fan clubs just as they often do among those who collect and trade sports cards. On a much grander scale, Goodhart and Chataway (1968) see entire nations drawing closer together as they share in their admiration of a common hero.

Fitness Motivation   Another potential function of sport heroes involves the ability of top-flight athletes to prompt their fans to participate in sport and exercise activities (certainly, an obese and unfit North American population could benefit from such an influence). Indeed, current evidence suggests that this notion may have merit. For instance, in-depth interviews with committed male fans revealed that many were motivated to emulate their sport hero's activity in just this way (G. J. Smith et al., 1981). It is interesting to note that sport and exercise psychologists are continually seeking innovative and effective strategies for improving adherence to exercise programs. Perhaps one such novel approach could include using individuals from the sportsworld to serve as positive role models. Indeed, some fitness magazines appear to be doing just this by having famous athletes author "Question and Answer" columns.

Economic Function   Franchise owners have long recognized the value of having a celebrity or star player on their rosters. For example, during the Victorian era British cricketer Dr. W. G. Grace consistently drew enormous crowds to matches. Sandiford (1982) has described him as "perhaps the most dynamic sports hero in British history" (p. 9). Interestingly, some clubs doubled the admission prices to matches in which he was scheduled to play. High admission prices were an irritant then as they are now. Player salaries are generally cited as the reason for the high cost of tickets. How do tomorrow's fans feel about player salaries? Bibby (1995) reports that among a national sample of young Canadians, 86 percent expressed the view that the salaries of professional athletes are excessive.

Heroes as Media Creations

The media plays a major role in creating heroes, a theme that will surface a number of times in this chapter. For example, it occasionally happens that an athlete achieves celebrity status because of public interest in his or her controversial, sport-irrelevant activities. Deford (1969) has coined the term *impact champions* to describe those athletes who are able to "establish a notoriety and an impact that can be turned into box office" (p. 33). The off-court antics of basketball player Dennis Rodman or, from an earlier era, those of professional wrestler Gorgeous George spring to mind as prime examples.

An interesting example of the gatekeeping function of the mass media can be seen in a report by Wachs and Dworkin (1997). They describe the case of two extremely talented athletes, basketball player Magic Johnson and diver Greg Louganis, who had recently tested positive for the AIDS virus. However, stories in the mainstream press following their announcements of their condition were framed in strikingly different ways. Self-described as "too heterosexual," Johnson was "framed as a hero for living with a stigmatized illness" (p. 332). The reasons the media cast him as a hero were twofold: his attempt to increase public awareness of AIDS and his openness and grace in dealing with the illness. By contrast, Louganis was "framed as a carrier who was morally responsible for alerting the heterosexual community to this risk" (p. 332). The "risk" involved an incident in which Louganis hit his head on the diving board and subsequently bled in the swimming pool. Certainly, this is an extremely negligible risk, if a risk at all. Thus, we see two outstanding athletes, both stricken with AIDS, yet the media offered entirely different treatments of the two stories. Wachs and Dworkin note that "Louganis is a hero only to smaller, fragmented interest groups . . . as a hero to gay men." Johnson "is unequivocally labeled a courageous hero to everyone" (p. 339).

SPORT HEROES IN CONTEMPORARY SOCIETY: PREVALENCE, SELECTION, AND INFLUENCE

With the basic understanding of hero worship provided in the preceding section, we begin a discussion of sport heroes. It seems that the most appropriate topic to open such a discussion centers on the size of the sport category as a source of heroes. Next, we discuss the process of selecting a sport hero and the influence of such heroes on individuals and society.

The Sportsworld as a Source of Heroes: The Prevalence of Sport Heroes in Contemporary Society

Our focus here involves the extent to which sport is a common category from which large numbers of people choose their exemplars. Estimates of the size of the sport exemplar category vary widely. Further, research suggests that the prevalence of hero worship differs across the life span. Interviews with a large sample of adults revealed that although exemplars were common among younger respondents, older respondents reported having fewer heroes (M. D. Smith, 1976). However, the negative, linear pattern of effects implied by these data is overly simplistic. A more accurate model would characterize the relationship between age and number of personal heroes as curvilinear, specifically, the inverted-U curve depicted in figure 4.1. A review of the literature led J. C. Harris (1986) to propose just such a relationship. She noted that very young children do not have heroes as

FIGURE 4.1

Hypothesized relationship between age and the number of sport heroes

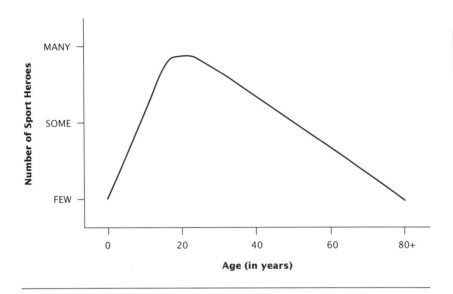

we commonly think of them. Only later do youngsters come to acquire heroes, the number of heroes rising to a peak in the late teens and early twenties, then slowly declining thereafter.

The Sportsworld as a Source of Heroes for Children Averill (1950) replicated one of the earliest investigations of children's hero choices (Darrah, 1898). While a sport category was nonexistent among 12- to 14-year-old Americans prior to the 1900s, by mid-century it had emerged as an important category, accounting for 23 percent of choices. More recent data confirm the finding that sport figures serve as a relatively common exemplar category for children. For instance, in the 1970s a sample of over two thousand U.S. 7- to 11-year olds was asked for "the name of a famous person you want to be like." Restricting the child's choices to famous people resulted in athletes being nominated by 13 percent of the sample (Foundation for Child Development, 1977). Even more recently, among school children in North Carolina, 28 percent chose athletes in response to a question that restricted choices to famous heroes (J. C. Harris, 1994). Similarly, data collected by Wallis (1999) confirmed that athletes remain a visible category for youngsters. In this research, interviews with over one thousand children ages 6 to 14 were conducted in twenty-five U.S. cities.

The children were asked, "Of all the people you know or know about, who are the top three you look up to most?" The preeminence of relatives was seen in their answers, as parents (79 percent) and grandparents (19 percent) received top billing. Athletes (13 percent) were also frequently mentioned on the lists. However, some researchers have contradicted these findings. For instance, when California youngsters were asked to specifically name their favorite sport figure, the item was left blank by 37 percent of the boys and 57 percent of the girls (Bredemeier, Weiss, Shields, & Cooper, 1986).

A Canadian study of schoolchildren provides evidence suggesting that sport is just as visible a category for Canadian youngsters as it is for American youth (Russell & McClusky, 1985). Tenth-grade students in the Medicine Hat, Alberta, public school system completed a survey that tapped various dimensions of the exemplar question. Their nominations were elicited in response to an open-ended, nondirective item that asked the children to "indicate the person, past or present, from any walk of life, that you admire the most." Their selections fell into four major identifiable categories as shown in figure 4.2. Clearly, sport was a significant, although minor, source of exemplars for boys. Equally clearly, girls drew their role models largely from other sources.

Recent evidence also suggests that there may be cultural differences in the extent to which athletes are chosen for exemplar status. Each of the studies cited above involved North American school children. Contradictory findings have been reported in Africa, where athletes are seldom chosen as personal role models. For example, children in Brazzaville, Congo, were asked, "Who would you like to resemble the most?" Athletes and entertainers made up what was described as a very small category (Didillon & Vandewiele, 1985).

The Sportsworld as a Source of Heroes for Adults   Adults are very unlikely to look to the sportsworld for their personal heroes. Since 1947 Americans have been asked annually by Gallup pollsters to name a living man and woman from any part of the world whom they most admire. While the wording has varied slightly from year to year and nominations have been restricted to people "they had heard or read about," sport has remained a negligible category accounting for less than 1 percent of the choices (T. W. Smith, 1986).

A Methodological Note   Note should be taken of an important methodological point. Researchers and pollsters have frequently sought to identify personal heroes by the use of questions that exclude vast numbers of individuals who might otherwise be considered. Questions are often framed such that choices are restricted to living individuals, famous people, or sport figures. As a result, valid comparisons across studies are problematic. Moreover, people who are deceased, unheralded, or not involved in sport may in fact be the principal exemplars in the lives of their admirers. That is to say, restrictive wording does not allow Uncle Harold or Grandma Ethel to be recognized as a major source of inspiration in a child's life. Taking into account the restrictive wording of questions put to respondents in numerous studies, an overview indicates that sport is an exemplar category of limited importance for males and a very minor category for females.

Selecting a Sport Hero: The Importance of Similarity

Research in social psychology has established the fact that individuals tend to be attracted to others who share similar traits, characteristics, backgrounds, and so on (e.g., Byrne, 1971; Byrne, Clore, & Smeaton, 1986). Consequently, it should not be surprising that a number of studies have found that sport fans tend to resemble their exemplars and that some dimensions of the resemblance likely form the basis of hero selection. For instance, the schoolchildren in

FIGURE 4.2

Relative size of exemplar categories

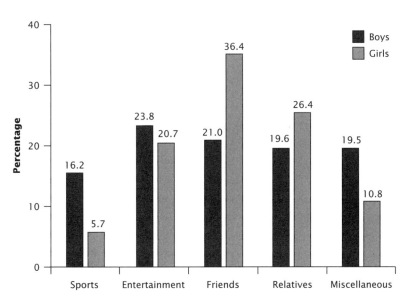

Medicine Hat were asked to indicate the extent to which they resembled their exemplar choices (the basis of resemblance was unspecified). The youngsters stated they least resembled sport figures, followed by entertainers, friends, and relatives. However, a closer examination of the data revealed a gender difference in perceptions of resemblance. Boys believed they bore a closer resemblance to their sport and entertainment choices than did girls. On the other hand, girls felt a greater resemblance to their friends. The researchers also sought to determine the extent to which individuals make an effort to be like their nominee. Efforts to emulate were weakest for the sport category, followed by entertainment, friends, and, finally, relatives. However, the analysis again yielded an interaction. Consistent with the previous pattern, boys reported making a greater effort to emulate exemplars from the sport and relatives categories, whereas girls strove to emulate friends.

With respect to specific traits, research suggests that fans tend to resemble their heroes on both sport-related and unrelated dimensions. For instance, researchers have found that among children who identified an athlete as their hero, 59 percent chose a sport figure who excelled at the youngster's favorite sport (Cooper, Livingood, & Kurz, 1981). Further evidence of a common bond between hero and admirer is seen in two other studies. Russell (1979) found that junior hockey players tended to nominate stars in the professional ranks who played the same position as themselves. Equally compelling is a study by Castine and Roberts (1974), who found that 56 percent of the black college athletes in their sample chose sport idols who played the same position as they were currently playing.

Research on sport-unrelated traits has focused on race and gender. Two-thirds of black college students and three-quarters of white students chose athletic heroes whose race matched their own (Vander Velden, 1986). A different study found that black athletes did not nominate a single white sport figure as an exemplar (Castine & Roberts, 1974). With respect to gender, one study found that male heroes were chosen by 100 percent of the boys and the majority of girls (83 percent) (J. C. Harris, 1994; see also Balswick & Ingoldsby, 1982). Similarly, 83 percent of boys in the Medicine Hat study chose male exemplars, in contrast to only 54 percent of the girls (Russell & McClusky, 1985).

Ties to a hero based on gender and race may be quite resilient. College students were asked to judge the guilt or innocence of heavyweight boxer Mike Tyson following his rape conviction. Eighty students still thought him innocent while twenty believed he was guilty.

After being shown a film titled *Mike Tyson: The Movie,* which depicted his delinquent past and his problems with women, twenty-five white women changed their verdict from innocent to guilty. However, all male participants and all black participants stuck to their earlier verdict of innocent (Eisenman, 1994).

It is important to note that there are other important resemblance factors in addition to sport type, playing position, race, and gender. Because youngsters assign different levels of importance to the various components of the self (Harter, 1993), they may desire sport heroes who resemble themselves on a variety of different traits and characteristics. One might speculate, for example, that left-handers tend to select other lefties while disabled persons disproportionately select physically challenged athletes as their personal heroes.

The Influence of Sport Heroes: For Better or for Worse

Yet another important topic in the understanding of sport heroes concerns the extent to which sport heroes have the ability to influence their admirers. It is important to note that virtually all sport fans are distanced from those they admire. They may have seen their heroes perform from their seat in the stands, watched them on television, or read of their exploits, but they are unlikely to have interacted with them on an interpersonal level for any length of time. Consequently, the influence process spans an enormous gulf. Information about the sport hero is subjected to media filters and can be altered by the impression management strategies of the athletes themselves. Thus, to best understand the process by which admirers are influenced by those they hold in high esteem, we need a theoretical framework that reflects the fact that heroes can exert influence from afar. Such a theoretical perspective can be found in observational learning.

Observational Learning and Sport Hero Worship Observational learning involves the vicarious learning of behaviors and attitudes through imitation and modeling (Bandura, 1973, 1986). According to this perspective, sport heroes can exert considerable influence on their admirers without the requirement of meaningful interaction. Rather, simply watching a sport hero's behavior and the consequences of that behavior can influence a fan's decision to adopt or reject the hero as an exemplar choice. Consider the case of the aggressive behaviors displayed by some sport personalities. According to obervational learning, aggressive behaviors are often acquired through the observation of the aggression of others. Youngsters attending to the aggression displayed by their sport hero take particular note of whether the aggression "paid off," that is, whether the hero was successful or unsuccessful in attaining his or her goal. Note is also taken of whether the aggression meets with the approval or disapproval of others. In short, the fan carefully monitors the positive and negative consequences of his or her hero's actions. Under conditions where the model's aggression is rewarded and draws approval from others, the acquisition of aggressive behaviors by an attentive admirer will be maximized. The individual is less likely to imitate the model's behavior when it results in punishments and disapproval. Thus, young fans can be influenced simply by observing their sport heroes, learning a number of positive (e.g., diligence, teamwork, sportspersonship, etc.) and negative behaviors (cheating, poor sportspersonship, etc.).

It is important to note that even when the hero's behavior is punished, it may still be learned. The newly acquired behaviors may simply not be displayed in the presence of the disapproving agent. In the absence of the agent, the previously learned behaviors may be freely exhibited. This has important implications for the influence of sport heroes. Specifically, the influence may be more powerful than it first appears. Although the youngster is inhibited from displaying antisocial behaviors in the presence of disapproving agents such as parents and coaches, the youngster may imitate the hero's negative actions when these persons are absent.

Assessing the Influence of Sport Heroes: Sport Heroes as Agents of Social Change It seems logical that the status and prestige given to sport heroes make them ideal role models for those who admire them. We might also assume that they are in a position to have considerable influence on their followers. Community leaders across North America have acted on this assumption and established innumerable programs in which outstanding athletes are called upon to exert a positive influence on their admirers. Popular athletes talk to would-be dropouts about the importance of staying in school, give motivational speeches, lend their name and energies to fund raising drives, urge people to avoid drugs and practice safe sex, and so on. Other more commercially minded athletes promote a range of products from breakfast cereals to jockey shorts to feminine hygiene products.

The logic of these programs draws a measure of support from attitude change experiments. Research suggests that, in the short run at least, high-status or prestigious communicators are generally effective in changing the attitudes of an audience in the desired direction (Petty & Cacioppo, 1985, 1986). However, it is important to note that a change in attitude does not necessarily result in a corresponding change in behavior. This point is relevant because, after all, it is usually a change in behavior that is the goal of the enterprise. Even assuming that heroes are able to change the attitudes of their admirers, do the latter actually stay in school, donate money, practice safe sex, and buy jockey shorts? It is this question that lies at the heart of what is called program evaluation research. Parenthetically, we are obliged to say that evaluation research is rarely conducted and that many seemingly worthwhile social programs continue to be funded (often at enormous cost) without any concrete evidence of their effectiveness.

Anecdotally, it might seem obvious that athletes are highly influential, serving as effective role models for a majority of our youth. When they speak, people listen and follow the advice. However, there is good reason to be skeptical. It may be that the superstars of sport are no better than other spokespersons in shaping public attitudes and behaviors. There are three lines of evidence that substantiate our skepticism.

First, as noted earlier, almost a century of intermittent research on people's heroes, exemplars, and role models indicates that sport figures represent a minor choice category, especially for females. Despite indications that most Americans describe themselves as sport fans (see chapter 1) and millions participate in sport or exercise programs (Thomas, 1986), it appears that they do not draw their personal heroes from the sportsworld, at least not in large numbers. Our heroes appear, instead, to be drawn from among our friends and relatives, certainly not the people who make the headlines, appear on the evening news, or are invited to address the student body.

Second, data gathered in the Medicine Hat investigation also shed doubt on the influence of sport heroes (Russell & McClusky, 1985). The researchers found that with respect to admiration, the youngsters' ratings did not differ across the four exemplar categories of "entertainment," "sports," "friends," and "relatives." However, when we turn to the critical question of influence, there were major differences across the categories. Overall, influence ratings were lowest in the entertainment category, slightly higher in sport, followed by friends and relatives, the most influential. Thus, sport figures were not only a minor category, but they also had less influence than exemplars from other walks of life. The point regarding influence was aptly made by Rosenberg (1973) when he observed that "not all significant others are equally significant" (p. 830).

The third reason for questioning the ability of star athletes to act as influential role models arises from studies evaluating the impact of the previously discussed incident in which Magic Johnson announced his HIV infection. On November 7, 1991, Johnson announced to the world that he had tested positive for the AIDS virus. The media coverage of his press conference and his national campaign to educate the public were touted as having made people more aware of the personal risks they face with unprotected sex and generated a greater understanding of the disease itself. Underlying all of this was the hope that people would adopt more responsible sexual practices.

The effectiveness of the Johnson campaign was examined by Sumser (1992). In the summer of 1991, this researcher administered a questionnaire asking college students about the sources of AIDS infection (e.g., blood donations, the dentist's office, etc.) and the likelihood that they would get infected. Three weeks after Johnson's press conference, the questionnaire was again administered to the same students. Somewhat surprisingly, there was no change in their ratings of personal risk, nor were they any better informed on the topic. Probably no event in recent history has been given such widespread and intense media attention and involved such a charming and likeable spokesperson. Indeed, it is hard to imagine a more persuasive individual. Yet, the students held firmly to their beliefs. As a footnote, what Sumser did find to be effective in changing attitudes and behaviors regarding AIDS is knowing someone personally who is infected. That seems to strike home!

On a more positive note, other assessments of the impact of Johnson's announcement have shown a more positive influence on people's attitudes and on some behaviors. Interviews with male Chicagoans revealed an increased concern that an "acquaintance" will get AIDS. However, that concern remained unchanged for them personally, as did their perceived risk of contracting the disease (Kalichman & Hunter, 1992). The subjects were more likely to seek out additional information on AIDS and more likely to discuss the topic with friends in the future. Interestingly, among blacks in the sample, concern about the subject of AIDS did rise following Magic's disclosure. Perhaps this finding again shows the impact of one's similarity to the sport hero.

It might be hoped that Johnson's announcement had a stronger impact on youngsters. In the case of black junior high school students in Cleveland, the results were in some ways puzzling (Zimet et al., 1993). While they wanted to know more about the disease following the announcement, other findings were contrary to those predicted by the researchers. For example, students saw themselves as *less* likely to become infected with the AIDS virus and *more* anxious about interacting with an AIDS victim after the announcement. Similar findings were reported among New England adolescents (Brown, Baranowski, Kulig, Stephenson, & Perry, 1996). Because worries about the disease have been linked to less risky sexual behavior, the fact that students worried less following the announcement is disheartening. After all, the ultimate goal of celebrity speakers is to change some aspect of their audience's behavior, in this case, their sexual practices.

There was only slightly better news at the University of Florida (Penner & Fritzsche, 1993). Students were asked to imagine that a graduate student who had contracted the AIDS virus through a blood transfusion was in desperate need of help with a class project (stuffing envelopes and making phone calls as part of a survey he was conducting). Were he to fail the course, he would be forced to drop out of school. The response to his appeal was enthusiastic. Fully 83 percent of the male participants volunteered to assist one week after the announcement, a stark contrast to the results found just prior to Johnson's disclosure when none of the male participants volunteered. Among women, 63 percent were already volunteering their help prior to the announcement. In this instance, Johnson may have been preaching to the choir. However, when asked the amount of time they would volunteer, the female participants reported an increase from before to after the announcement. Of course, the increase in helping will not continue indefinitely, several months at best. Still, we should be thankful for any gains realized on this and other health issues, however short-lived they may be.

While Johnson's motives were noble, the results of his efforts would appear to have been something less than what he and others had hoped for. Why the dismal results? Marketing research suggests that Johnson may not have been perceived as a credible spokesperson for the AIDS cause (Ohanian, 1991). Beyond having contracted the AIDS virus, he was not likely to have been viewed as an expert on the topic. While he most likely appeared trustworthy and physically attractive (two components of credibility), he lacked the third and often most critical component, expert knowledge of the topic. Often, it is the communicator's perceived expertise on the topic that best predicts changes in buying behavior or, in this case, sexual practices.

Quality of the Sport Hero The superstars of the sportsworld, regardless of whether we judge them to be superior or inferior role models, signify "success" to legions of their followers. The fact that heroes are adored by the media, lavishly rewarded by society, and highly skilled at whatever it is they do speaks to their potential to influence others. Consequently, one of the most important topics surrounding the influence of sport heroes has to do with their quality. In light of the fact that admirers do make an effort to emulate their heroes, we should be concerned with the quality of heroes in contemporary society. As Butt (1987) aptly put it, "The athlete contributes more to the audience than an enactment of competence and competition. He also contributes his way of life. Whatever the admired athlete does, the crowd, particularly the young, tend to emulate" (p. 257).

One of the difficulties in understanding the impact of a hero's quality is the elusiveness of the concept. Depending upon which aspects of a model's behavior an observer attends to, one admirer may see the hero as approaching sainthood while another may see him or her in a much less flattering light. For example, consider tennis star John McEnroe. Some of his fans would describe him as skilled, sincere, and intelligent, while others might instead describe him as immature, loud-mouthed, and petulant—two perspectives resulting in qualitatively different evaluations of the same sport figure.

THE IMPACT OF PERSONALITY ON THE ADMIRATION OF SPORT HEROES

In this section we examine the role played by personality in sport hero worship. Unfortunately, our understanding of this relationship is rather limited. However, a start toward such an understanding was made in the Medicine Hat study (Russell & McClusky, 1985). The youngsters were asked to complete scales assessing aggression and self-esteem and a measure tapping the strength of their belief in fate. The fate scale assessed the participants' levels of external and internal locus of control. Those with an external locus of control possess a fatalistic view of the world, believing that the events in their lives occur as a result of chance and are predetermined. Conversely, people who have a more internal orientation believe that they can personally influence the events in their lives, that they control their own destiny.

The results of the correlational analyses are summarized in table 4.1. With respect to aggression, the data revealed positive relationships, but only for girls. That is, girls scoring high on the measure of aggression generally expressed a greater admiration for their exemplar. Positive correlations were also found between aggression and the degree to which girls were influenced by their exemplars and their efforts to emulate that person. The more aggressive girls also believed that they in some way(s) resemble their choices.

TABLE 4.1

Relationships between Gender, Personality Variables, and Aspects of Exemplar Choice

	PERSONALITY VARIABLE	
Aggression	**Self-esteem**	**Fate**
BOYS		
No correlation	**Positively** related to:	**No correlation**
	(1) admiration of exemplar	
	(2) influence by exemplar	
	(3) resemblance to exemplar	
	(4) efforts to emulate exemplar	
	(5) quality of exemplar	
GIRLS		
Positively related to:	**Positively** related to:	**Negatively** related to:
(1) admiration of exemplar	(1) admiration of exemplar	(1) admiration of exemplars
(2) influence by exemplar	(2) number of exemplars	(2) influence by exemplar
(3) resemblance to exemplar		(3) quality of exemplar
(4) efforts to emulate exemplar		

Positive correlations were also found for scores on the self-esteem inventory. Boys with high self-esteem provided higher ratings of admiration, influence, resemblance, and made greater efforts to emulate their choice. And, perhaps most importantly, they chose exemplars of superior quality. A positive relationship between self-esteem and the strength of admiration for the exemplar was also found for girls. Note too, girls with high self-esteem also identified a greater number of exemplars in their lives.

Finally, scores on a measure of internal-external locus of control (i.e., the fate scale) were related to ratings of admiration and influence, but only for girls. The relationships were negative, indicating that girls with a belief in fate were less likely to admire and less likely to be influenced by their exemplar than schoolmates with an internal locus of control. Their exemplar choices were also of inferior quality. Thus, the Medicine Hat research established that personality is significantly related to sport hero worship in a number of important ways.

The findings presented here only touch on three aspects of personality; they barely scratch the surface of the relationship between exemplar attributes and individual differences among admirers.

Clearly, much remains to be learned about the interplay between personality traits and hero selection. Other traits such as level of moral reasoning (Bredemeier et al., 1986), authoritarianism, and sensation seeking spring to mind as likely predictors of exemplar choice. For example, it seems reasonable to predict that individuals with a high degree of sensation seeking would be more likely to nominate the likes of race car driver Jacques Villeneuve or daredevil Evil Knievel as their sport heroes.

A ROGUES' GALLERY

Most sports have been rocked by scandal at some point in their history. Promoters, managers, officials, and athletes alike have all stained the image of their sport at one time or another. Antisocial behaviors by high-profile athletes in particular seem to inflict the greatest damage on the reputation of a sport. Regardless of whether their notoriety stems from social excesses, criminal conduct, or behaviors that violate traditional norms, the media are generally quick to condemn them. Unfortunately, the athlete's sport often suffers collateral damage.

The decade of the nineties has seen the emergence of a research literature addressing public perceptions, attitudes, and beliefs about athletes who have somehow discredited themselves in the public eye. The public has been witness to steroid use, tax fraud, barbaric actions in the ring, rapes, family violence, and horrific murders by elite athletes who were previously held in high esteem by their fans. These crimes are committed by more than just an inconsequential minority of athletes. Consider the situation with respect to the NFL. An archival investigation by Benedict and Yaeger (1998) revealed that 21 percent of players on NFL rosters had been charged with serious criminal offenses ranging from resisting arrest and armed robbery to kidnapping and homicide. Bear in mind that many of these players had multiple charges. Certainly, many of these men enjoyed celebrity status and were admired by legions of football fans. Even those warming the bench were at the very least admired by fans from their hometown.

The Influence of Villainous Heroes

Interestingly, the likes of Hitler, Al Capone, Charles Manson, and other infamous persons occasionally appear in general surveys intended to identify youngsters' most admired person. The question of influence is equally (if not more) important in the case of these villainous persons as it is with exemplars who project a positive image. Fortuitously, a means of assessing the influence of villains (as well as positive idols) has been developed by McEvoy and Erickson (1981). The degree of negative influence that a villain has on an individual is described at one of five levels. Level I involves little more than simple disdain for the villain. At Level II, in addition to disliking the villain, the individual engages in minimal role playing, taking pleasure when the villain stumbles, becoming disheartened when he enjoys success. Influence at Level III takes the form of the individual using the villain as a point of comparison. By contrasting his own merits and achievements with those of the villain, the individual is able to validate his or her own worth. The individual at Level IV acts in ways decidedly different from those of the villain. At this level the individual consciously rejects behaviors he attributes to the villain (e.g., clothing styles, political views, and religious practices). Influence at Level V is stronger and more overt than that at the previous levels. Here, the individual publicly opposes the intensely disliked villain. For example, the individual may mount a letter-writing campaign attempting to block the induction of an athlete with a criminal record into a Hall of Fame.

Recently, Melnick and Jackson (1998) extended the work of McEvoy and Erickson (1981) by exploring the influence of villainous characters in the lives of youngsters. Sixty-nine percent of a sample of New Zealand teenagers indicated they knew of at least one person from the public domain whom they regarded as a villain, that is, the youngsters judged to be "bad." Politicians (42 percent) and criminals (18 percent) topped the list of single, most disliked villains followed by a significant number of athletes (11 percent). In breaking the athlete category down by gender, only 4 percent of the girls identified athletes as personal villains in contrast to 28 percent of the boys. This gender difference seems reasonable in light of the previously mentioned finding that boys are more likely than girls to have sport figures as heroes.

Melnick and Jackson (1998) also assessed the degree of the villains' negative influence across the five levels. The results were encouraging. At all levels of influence a clear majority of the sample responded contrary to the direction represented or suggested by their villains. Still, it should be noted that a small percentage of the sample at Levels I (4 percent) and II (9 percent) disagreed with statements assigning negative influences to their choices, leaving open the possibility of their having positive influences (i.e., adopting the values, beliefs, and attitudes of their villain).

Melnick and Jackson (1998) have opened up an important line of inquiry. Future research might consider the impact of villains on the small core of individuals who admire them, examining the manner in which their values, beliefs, and behaviors are shaped by those whom society regards as reprobates and evildoers. Equally important, future research should also concentrate on the traits and characteristics of individuals who adopt villains as personal heroes.

The Fall from Grace

Fans' cognitions play a critical role in their attempt to explain why an athlete "falls from grace." A drug scandal that occurred at the 1988 Seoul Olympics will serve to illustrate how ardent admirers interpret events surrounding a disgraced athlete. Canadian sprinter Ben Johnson tested positive for anabolic steroid use and was immediately stripped of his gold medal; his world record 100-meter time was also disallowed. A shocked Canadian public sought answers to the cause of Johnson's disgrace.

Ungar and Sev'er (1989) approached these questions from an attributional perspective, attempting first to determine if Canadians believed Johnson's downfall resulted from internal or external causes. Under normal conditions the answer would be clear. The "fundamental attribution error" tells us that people tend to attribute internal causes to an actor and place less emphasis on external causes (L. Ross, 1977; M. L. Snyder & Jones, 1974). However, this was not a normal situation. Rather, it was a rare occurrence involving a national hero with whom Canadians had formed a close "unit relationship" (Heider, 1958); that is, Canadians had developed a strong sense of identification with Johnson. As a result of this intense identification, the threat posed to Johnson's future was also threatening to his countrymen. Under these special circumstances, Ungar and Sev'er predicted that attributions for Ben's plight would reflect a defensive interpretation of events, one emphasizing external explanations (see chapter 8 for further discussion of defensive attributions).

To test their prediction, they asked University of Toronto students to complete a series of attributional questions during the week following the Seoul announcement. As expected, the students judged external factors to have been more important than internal factors in bringing about Johnson's downfall. Indeed, he was seen as the victim of sabotage as often as he was thought to have knowingly taken steroids. In yet another defensive interpretation of events, responsibility for Johnson's steroid use was attributed to his handlers—few participants thought he was personally responsible.

Tall Poppies Feather has pursued an interesting line of inquiry by examining the public's reactions to people who have achieved fame in their chosen field (e.g., politicians, entertainers, sport figures) and then subsequently fallen from grace. Feather calls these persons "tall poppies." J. R. Grove and Paccagnella (1995) describe a corresponding "tall poppy syndrome" by which people show "a tendency to closely scrutinize high-profile individuals, search for reasons to 'cut them down to size,' and experience satisfaction if they suffer a reversal of status" (p. 88). We are most likely to cut down persons whose outstanding achievements are seen to be the result of external assistance rather than attained through their own efforts and ability. In the words of Feather, Volkmer, and McKee (1991) the tall poppies most likely to be lopped off are those seen to be "self-centered, quick-tempered, and uncaring in their attitudes, and whose integrity and concern for others is suspect" (p. 91).

The results of several studies will serve to highlight the gist of the tall poppy syndrome. Feather et al. (1991) examined the responses of university students to prominent public figures in Australian society (i.e., politicians, entertainers, and sport people). Although there were only three figures in each domain, the most favorable attitudes were directed toward sport figures. Their success was also more often attributed to their personal efforts and ability and less to their having received external assistance. In contrast to politicians and entertainers, students saw the sport figures as more deserving of their success. Finally, the students were less pleased about a hypothetical fall on the part of an athlete.

Grove and Paccagnella (1995) looked further at tall poppies using prominent athletes, some of whom may have disappointed their fans by their actions. Two groups were compared. Group A contained athletes who attracted media publicity for being gay, being HIV positive, or for using steroids. Athletes in Group B participated in the same sports with no publicized links to the foregoing. A sample of university students expressed more favorable social attitudes toward those in Group B by liking them, wanting to be like them, and wanting to mix with them socially. The athletcs in Group A paid a further price for their associations with controversial issues. The students saw them as less worthy, judged them to be rule-oriented, and felt they lacked self-control. Their integrity was also called into question as they were thought to be less honest and trustworthy than those in Group B.

Feather (1991) narrowed the focus of his investigation to consider the role of attitudes and self-esteem in people's reactions both to tall poppies in general and after their fall. The tall poppy in question was sprinter Ben Johnson. Feather's results showed that those who felt that tall poppies should be rewarded were themselves highly competent at what they do. These same individuals were also characterized by high self-esteem. On the other hand, those who were negatively disposed toward tall poppies and wanted to see them toppled scored lower on measures of personal competence and self-esteem.

Interestingly, these relationships are reversed after the fall of a tall poppy (Feather, 1991). For example, Johnson drew support from those respondents who were low on competence and especially from those who were low in self-esteem. By way of explanation, Feather offers the view that "the winner is more likely to identify with and to favor other winners and the loser tends to identify with and to support other losers" (Feather, 1991, p. 124). Thus, our reactions to highly successful and less than successful others is likely influenced by our own level of competence and self-worth.

SOME FINAL THOUGHTS

People generally acknowledge having a personal hero or heroine they admire and from whom they draw direction. The sources of their heroes are varied, with perhaps the greatest numbers drawn from among friends and relatives. However, sport is also a visible category providing significant numbers of exemplars for youngsters, especially in the case of males.

The critical issues emerging from matters of hero selection center on the quality of exemplars and the lessons they teach their admirers. Some heroes display attributes that can serve their admirers and society well (e.g., honesty, humility, and good sportspersonship). However, others who are accorded hero status impart values that can seriously erode the moral fabric of society. We are all too quick to enshrine individuals in sport Halls of Fame, often with an eye only on their performance record while turning a blind eye to the unsavory aspects of their lives. Consequently, a chary look at seemingly worthy candidates is warranted (cf., Barney, 1985).

PART II

Spectator Aggression

Chapter Five | AN INTRODUCTION TO SPECTATOR AGGRESSION

Spectator aggression has been an ongoing concern for sport and civil authorities, as well as the general public, since the dawn of sport. In fact, spectator violence may be the most well researched aspect of sport fandom. Psychologists and sociologists alike have spent countless hours developing theories and conducting investigations with the goal of understanding the violence among those who watch sport. We take a critical look at much of this theory and research in the next three chapters. In the first chapter, we introduce sport spectator aggression. This chapter includes discussions of basic topics such as operational definitions of aggression, forms of spectator aggression, the prevalence of these acts, and those groups with a vested interest in the curtailment of fan violence. Chapter 6 centers around two different yet overlapping perspectives on spectator aggression: psychological (microlevel) and sociological or social-psychological (macrolevel). Psychological approaches to spectator aggression tend to focus on the role played by specific aspects of a spectator's personality and unique physical environmental factors. Conversely, sociological and social-psychological viewpoints tend to rely on larger social phenomena such as culture, social structure, and the social environment. Chapter 7 examines large-scale riots. It includes a discussion of the various forms of spectator riots, characteristics of those participating in sport melees (as well as those serving in peacemaker roles), and an examination of hooliganism.

DEFINITIONS AND DISTINCTIONS

Seldom is there a consensus of opinion among social scientists on matters of definition, and the concept of aggression is no exception. Several examples will suffice to illustrate the diversity of theoretical viewpoints. For instance, aggression has been defined as:

- "behavior that results in personal injury and in destruction of property" (Bandura, 1973, p. 5)
- "any form of behavior that is intended to injure someone physically or psychologically" (Berkowitz, 1993, p. 3)
- "any form of behavior directed toward the goal of harming or injuring another living being who is motivated to avoid such treatment" (Baron & Richardson, 1994, p. 7)
- "behavior that intends to destroy property or injure another person, or is grounded in a total disregard for the well-being of self and others" (Coakley, 1998, p. 180)

It quickly becomes apparent that the task of crafting a definition of the concept acceptable to all is fraught with complexities (see Baron & Richardson, 1994; Tedeschi & Felson, 1994, for an extended discussion of this issue). In this text, we have chosen to utilize Coakley's (1998) definition (see above) because it seems to best capture the violent acts of sport fans. That is, acts of fan aggression include: taunting opposing players, coaches, and fans; harassing officials; using profanity; throwing things on the field of play; spilling a beverage on another fan; refusing to move out of someone's line of sight; obscene gestures; and pushing, shoving, or striking another person. Each of these acts fits nicely into Coakley's conceptualization of aggression. Finally, it warrants mention that Coakley views violence as a subset of aggression; it refers specifically to physical acts, that is, the physical assault of another.

Hostile versus Instrumental Aggression

Before proceeding, we note an important conceptual refinement formulated by Buss (1961) that involves a distinction between hostile and instrumental aggression. "Hostile aggression" refers to actions intended to harm another person who has annoyed or otherwise provoked an individual. With this form of aggression, the goal is simply the pain and suffering of the victim. By contrast, "instrumental aggression" refers to interpersonal aggression that serves as a means to achieving some goal other than the victim's suffering. The violence is simply a means to an end. To illustrate these distinct forms of aggression, consider a group of basketball spectators heaping scorn on a rival player. Clearly, the abusive and obscene shouts would be categorized as verbal aggression. If the spectators were responding to a player's poor sportspersonship and they wanted to inflict psychological pain on her, they would be displaying hostile aggression. However, if the rival player was standing at the free throw line and the spectators' intent was to impair her performance, their behavior would be considered an act of instrumental aggression.

Studies conducted with spectators at several sporting events reveal several interesting differences in the use of hostile and instrumental aggression (see Wann, Carlson, & Schrader, 1999; Wann, Schrader, & Carlson, in press). For example, hostile aggression is more common than instrumental aggression among hockey and basketball spectators. Furthermore, officials are more likely to be the targets of hostile aggression than of instrumental aggression, perhaps because the spectators realize that officials are trained to be impartial and, consequently, are somewhat immune to the influence of instrumental aggression. Aggression directed toward opposing players is equally divided between the two forms. Research also suggests that it is those fans who most strongly identify with a team who display the greatest amount of both hostile and instrumental aggression.

THE VARIOUS FORMS OF SPECTATOR AGGRESSION

As suggested above, Coakley's (1998) definition of aggression allows for the inclusion of a great number of aggressive acts. Certainly, this seems reasonable in light of the many forms spectator aggression may take. As an excellent example of this, consider the following "letters to the editor" written by some sport spectators in the last few years, as well as the cartoon found in figure 5.1. This is a letter from a football fan who attended a Buffalo Bills–New York Jets game in Buffalo with his wife and another couple:

> Trying to avoid getting wet from the rain while entering the stadium was a snap compared to the challenge of avoiding the beer being thrown on the people from under-age drinkers in the upper deck. . . . Although my wife and myself are not prudes, the language that was exchanged between some intellectual in my section with some gentleman below us was nothing any child should have to hear. . . . The four of us decided that one half of pro football was enough loyalty for any team. As we were walking out to our van some thoughtless idiot

couldn't wait in line to the men's room and urinated across from a concession stand. . . . A suggestion: Instead of putting a dome on the stadium, use the money to cage in five sections of the stands. Make anyone who wants to drink, fight or vomit sit in these sections. This would allow the person who wants to go to a football game with his family to enjoy the action on the field and not in the stands. I know four loyal fans who will be watching Bills' football from our living rooms from now on.

Another football fan had the following to report to his local newspaper after attending a Cleveland Browns–Buffalo Bills game with his family in Cleveland.

The fans made up cheers that used the Big F every other word. The language was worse than a bar fight. The smell would knock you over with drinks all over the place. In the men's room, it was wall to wall people urinating on the floor! My 9-year-old son was in tears, begging to go home after the first quarter. Not only was the drinking out of control, the lady in front of us smoked so much dope, along with the booze, her friends had to carry her out. I felt very sad that day . . . that professional sports has deteriorated to such a mess. . . . Sports and the beer companies are not the problem; just part of a total moral breakdown in society. . . . Needless to say, I won't be back to Cleveland.

And, from an indoor lacrosse fan who attended a Rochester, New York, Knighthawks game with his family, we read the following:

I was embarrassed and appalled by the poor sportsmanship and behavior of the Knighthawks fans and management. Picture this: As every member of the opposing team was introduced, the fans yelled the word "sucks," and to make matters worse, the word was flashed on the announcement screen . . . If this continues, I will give up my season tickets. I can't control the fans, but management can clean up its act.

If, as Coakley (1998) suggests, aggression involves "behavior that intends to destroy property or injure another person, or is grounded in a total disregard for the well-being of self and others," then our three letter writers certainly have something to complain about. Clearly, sloppy beer drinkers, obscene language, public urination, rancid odors, marijuana smoke, poor sportspersonship, and offensive

FIGURE 5.1

Much to the dismay of many sport spectators (including the family depicted in this cartoon), attending sporting events to "become a part of the action" has taken on a new and violent meaning in recent years

scoreboard messages should all be considered as aggressive acts because they involve destruction of property, injury, or disregard for others. Thus, these statements stand as testaments to the wide array of spectator behaviors that should be classified as aggressive.

To aid in the classification of such acts, J. M. Lewis (1980) developed the following typology for categorizing violent fan behavior: verbal assaults, disrupting play, throwing missiles, fighting, and vandalism.

Verbal Assaults

Verbal assaults refer to the use of obscenities, vulgarities, and threatening words directed by sport spectators at the targets of their derision (e.g., other spectators, players, coaches, and officials). Common sense tells us that profanity and vulgarity have no place at the ballpark. Spectators are obligated to exercise self-control and when such is not the case, event managers should impose strong, negative sanctions upon those who are unwilling or cannot control their mouths. Even so, research suggests that verbal assaults are quite common at sporting events (a fact that is all too obvious to many of us). For instance, a *USA Today* call-in survey of over five hundred fans found that approximately three-quarters of the sample had shouted insults at players, coaches, or officials ("Fan Insults," 1991). Fifty-six percent said there should be some limits on heckling, but a surprising 41 percent said that fans should be able to say whatever they want. Twenty-seven percent of the respondents believed that verbal abuse was offensive, but 18 percent found it funny. The remaining 55 percent said it should be ignored.

Not to be outdone by American sport fans, soccer spectators at Worker's Stadium in Beijing, China, have become so profane at soccer matches that the press and stadium officials refer to their behavior as the "Beijing Curse." Among their favorite chants is "Shobi! Shobi!," a crude reference to a part of the female anatomy (Mravic & Kennedy, 1998).

Throwing Missiles

Consider the following list of items: a softball, a shot glass, a Walkman, a golf ball, plastic bottles, beer cans, a sanitary napkin dispenser, and a fortune in small change. Although this may read like the typical items found at a garbage dump, in actuality it is a list of objects New York Yankee fans hurled at the Seattle Mariners during the first two games of the American League Division Series in 1995. It seems as though garbage time has taken on a new meaning in spectating sports. Often used to refer to the final minutes of a basketball blowout when players seek to pad their scoring averages, garbage time has also come to mean the unseemly practice of basketball, baseball, and ice hockey spectators throwing anything and everything at players, coaches, officials, and each other (see figure 5.2). The danger of throwing missiles goes without saying. It has prompted the commissioner of MLB to issue a directive to all teams prohibiting the giveaway of items before games that can be easily thrown on the field, such as baseballs and Frisbees. Parenthetically, the last MLB forfeit occurred on August 10, 1995, when Los Angeles Dodger fans ended a game by lobbing baseballs on the field.

Ice hockey fans are perhaps the most creative missile throwers. At Hamilton College in Clinton, New York, for example, a game was delayed for several minutes because a traditional ritual had gotten out of hand. It is the custom at this school for fans to throw things at the opposing goalie after the home team's first goal of the season. But consider the articles attendants gathered up before play could resume: tennis balls, oranges, apples, melons, two live mice, a dead squid, and a life-sized, anatomically correct, inflatable doll. The school president didn't find anything funny about the incident and

FIGURE 5.2

Unfortunately, throwing missiles has become a sport in and of itself

Copyright 1991, USA TODAY. Reprinted with permission.

banned all spectators, except players' family members, from the next home game, stating, "Extreme antisocial acts warrant censure" (Wolff & O'Brien, 1994, p. 19).

Disrupting Play

Although not a frequently observed fan behavior, occasionally fans will decide to become "a part of the action" and run onto the field, thereby disrupting play. Usually without malevolence, they attempt to shake hands with a favorite player, request an autograph, or demonstrate a sport skill (e.g., sliding into second base). We see less and less of this behavior because it is now network policy to refrain from showing those responsible for the disruption. When such disruptions occur, viewers are simply told that someone has run onto the field and security is trying to apprehend them. The bursts of applause viewers hear signifies that the individual has been caught and escorted out of the stadium. Needless to say, drunkenness and disrupting play go hand in hand.

Judges treat this behavior very seriously. In Detroit, where baseball fans are notorious for running onto the field and stopping play, a man was charged with disorderly conduct and received a ten-day jail sentence. Said the judge, "The unruly fan could have injured himself, ballplayers and police officers when he ran onto the field and stopped the game" ("Rowdy Detroit Fans," 1995).

Fighting

Although not a common occurrence at most sporting events, spectator fighting is an ugly, dangerous affair when it does occur. Not only do the combatants risk serious injury, but oftentimes, innocent spectators are injured as well. At the very least, these incidents are frightening and likely to ruin the game and day for those involved as well as those unfortunate enough to have witnessed it. It is not surprising that when these incidents are sorted out, drunkenness is often found to be a contributing factor. The surliness, belligerence, and bravado that oftentimes accompany excessive drinking can easily turn into fisticuffs following an unintentional push or shove. Frustration over a heartbreaking loss or a perceived mistake by an official can also cause opposing fans seated in close quarters to begin fighting.

Vandalism

The willful or malicious destruction of public or private property is, on occasion, observed at sporting events. Disgruntled fans are obviously more likely than contented ones to take out their frustrations on wall displays, concession stands, elevators, urinals, and flower beds. A few years ago, the president of the Boston Bruins of the NHL and the Boston Garden made an interesting comment when he observed that winning teams save money in vandalism costs. He was referring to the fact that the cost of vandalism after a Bruins win amounts to about $500, while the cost to the building after a Bruins loss amounts to about $5,000. Observed the CEO, "When the Bruins or Celtics lose a game in which there are high expectations the other way, the building bears the brunt of fan dissatisfaction" ("Ah, Those Sunday Victories," 1983).

ASSESSING THE MAGNITUDE OF SPECTATOR AGGRESSION

In this section, we examine the magnitude of spectator aggression. Specifically, we will investigate the prevalence and severity of these acts.

The Prevalence of Spectator Aggression

The methodological difficulties faced when attempting to empirically assess the prevalence of spectator aggression need to be fully appreciated. Researchers are presented with several daunting problems. First, more likely than not, researchers are forced to rely on secondary data sources. Use of archival data (e.g., encyclopedias, yearbooks, police reports, daily newspapers, popular magazines, sport news telecasts, etc.) raises questions about data availability, comprehensiveness, and media distortion. Second, investigators must select the appropriate time period for their research. For instance, they must decide if data should be gathered over the course of several weeks, months, or years. Similarly, researchers face a third dilemma, deciding on which sport or sports to include in their work. Should they monitor all popular sports, just those that are combative in nature, or a single sport? A further difficulty lies in the selection of a geographical area. The researcher could choose to focus on all of North America or limit the work to the United States, a specific region, a few states, or even a single state or town. In previous efforts, researchers have focused on a single sport in a single city (Dewar, 1979), two sports in the rural West (Bryan & Horton, 1976), all sports in the eastern and midwestern United States (J. M. Lewis, 1982), all sports in the province of Ontario, Canada (G. J. Smith, 1978), and all sports in the world (Mann, 1979). These divergent geographical areas reveal the magnitude of choices open to researchers. Finally, researchers must choose their operational definition of fan violence. For example, they must determine the number of spectators that must be involved for an incident to qualify as a "riot" as well as the behaviors considered to be "violent."

Despite these formidable problems, a small number of researchers have attempted to assess the frequency of spectator violence. Based on his analysis of seven U.S. newspapers and the *New York Times*, J. M. Lewis (1982) found an average of 14.2 serious spectator disorders per year over a twelve-year period. Similarly, G. J. Smith (1978) calculated an average of 13.5 major disorders per year in the Province of Ontario over a ten-year period, based on a content analysis of the *Toronto Globe and Mail*. Smith acknowledged that such estimates are obviously very crude, not especially reliable, and undoubtedly underestimate the frequency of the problem.

The figures presented by J. M. Lewis (1982) and G. J. Smith (1978) suggest that the prevalence of spectator violence in North America is quite low. Indeed, when one considers the thousands of sporting events that take place each year at the high school, college, and professional levels, "the record of behavior among sports fans is surprisingly nonviolent" (Coakley, 1998, p. 203). While anecdotal data and the mass media sometimes suggest otherwise, the conclusion that fan violence at North American sports events is relatively infrequent appears to be justified (M. D. Smith, 1983).

Increases in Spectator Aggression   The absence of quantitative data spanning several years makes it difficult to determine if spectator aggression is on the rise. M. D. Smith (1983) was of the opinion that in absolute numbers, incidents of spectator aggression, serious or otherwise, have probably increased in frequency since 1960. However, he also pointed out that the number of sporting events has also risen, raising the question of whether there has been a relative increase in fan violence. Smith also observed that the mass media have a tendency to exaggerate fan violence with eye-catching, sensationalized headlines. As a result, "false evidence" is produced, leading to "false consciousness." The net effect of this process is to distort the public's perception of the problem (Melnick, 1986). While the frequency, magnitude, and pattern of spectator aggression in North America is still to be determined, people's perceptions of what they believe is real are important because, as Thomas observed six decades ago, "If men define situations as real, they are real in their consequences" (quoted in Merton, 1967, p. 19).

The Severity of Spectator Aggression

The decade of the nineties bore witness to several sport-related, spectator tragedies. Consider the following newspaper headlines:

- "Forty Killed in S. African Soccer Melee" (January 14, 1991)
- "Ten Die in Melee After Soccer Game in Santiago, Chili" (June 7, 1991)
- "Fourteen Killed, 378 Hurt in Colombian Soccer Celebrations" (September 7, 1993)
- "Soccer Tragedy Stuns: 84 Deaths in Guatemala Tied to Fake Tickets, Rowdy Crowd" (October 18, 1996)
- "Spectators Stampede at Soccer Match in Lusaka, Zambia: 9 Dead, 78 Injured" (June 18, 1996)
- "Soccer Violence Leaves Two Dead, 40 Injured at Soccer Game in Bangladesh" (September 28, 1998)

Upon reading these headlines, a few observations come immediately to mind. First, soccer may well be the most popular sport in the world, but it is also the deadliest! Second, serious sport crowd violence is not restricted to a single country or continent; rather, it is global in nature. Third, the magnitude of spectator disorder at North American sporting events pales in comparison to that in the rest of the world. Of course, this isn't to say that tragedies never occur. For example, in New York City in 1991 eight people died and dozens were injured in a rush to get inside a gymnasium where a charity basketball game was played. The legal capacity of the facility was 2,730 but an additional 2,000 people were sold tickets. When they pushed through the front doors to get inside, the situation turned tragic ("Overcrowding Causes Deaths," 1991). Further, a 19-year-old man was stabbed to death in Niagara Falls, New York, when a YMCA basketball game turned into a melee involving fifty players and fans fighting each other with mops, brooms, crowbars, pipes, and anything else they could find ("Player Charged with Murder," 1992).

Setting aside the more serious forms of spectator violence for a moment, we do have indirect evidence that spectator disturbances have become more severe. More than four decades ago, Calisch (1954) surveyed high school principals, physical education teachers, and game officials for their opinions about the incidence, prevalence, and cause of spectator behavior problems. The most often chosen problem was "excessive booing." Our guess is that many principals today would gladly trade their most serious spectator behavior problems for "excessive booing."

PERCEPTIONS OF SPECTATOR AGGRESSION AMONG INTERESTED PARTIES

Listed and briefly discussed below are the perceptions of several interested parties who have strong opinions about fan violence. Because of their relationship to spectator sports, these groups tend to have a vested interest in both the understanding of fan violence and in methods for reducing its prevalence.

The American Public

It's unfortunate that there are no recent, national data on American attitudes about fan violence. The best available is found in the *Sports Illustrated Sports Poll '91*, a national survey of America's participation, attitudes about, and involvement in sport. To the question, "How concerned are you about violence or disturbances in the stands?" 76 percent said they were "very concerned," 12 percent said they were "fairly concerned." Only 12 percent reported that they were "not concerned." These data clearly suggest that the general public is interested in the control of violence in the stands.

Professional Journals

As is to be expected, there has been considerable editorial comment on the seriousness of fan violence in the United States. Typical was a column written by Ryan, editor of the *Physician and Sportsmedicine Journal*. He wrote, "We must take specific steps if we are to protect spectators (from themselves as well as from others) and prevent public entertainment from becoming a source of death and personal injury" (1984, p. 43).

Daily Newspapers

Newspaper editors and editorial boards have also been quick to condemn fan misbehavior at sporting events. To quote from *USA Today* ("Rowdies Spoil Fun," 1988), roughnecks are: "spoiling sporting events across the USA—professional and amateur—with booze, abusive language and fighting. They're taking the fun out of sports and driving families away from many sporting events. . . . We have to get the roughnecks and rowdies out of the stands—and the fun back in the game" (p. 12A). Similarly, a cover story appeared in the June 16, 1992, issue of *USA Today* headlined "Violence and High School Sports." The conclusion drawn in this article was that although violence at high school sporting events has always existed, it appears to be increasing at an alarming rate (Gregg, 1992).

Stadium General Managers

A further indication that fan violence at sporting events should be taken seriously is reflected in the efforts of stadium general managers to ensure a safe, secure, and fan-friendly environment for their patrons. For example, the New England Patriots of the NFL instituted a policy in which they revoke season tickets for inappropriate behavior. A total of seventy Patriot fans lost their season tickets in 1995 for the following offenses: drunkenness, throwing objects on the field, fighting, abusive and/or foul language, and disorderly behavior (Weisman, 1995).

City Law Enforcement Officials

Most certainly, law enforcement officials are keenly interested in curbing sport spectator aggression. For instance, consider the novel approach adopted by the Philadelphia Eagles management in an attempt to reduce the violence occurring at Eagles' NFL home games.

The city of Philadelphia, in cooperation with the Eagles management, arranged for a court to be set up in the basement of the stadium to "mete out instant justice to the drunk, the disorderly and the vulgar" (McCallum & Hersch, 1997). In its very first Sunday of operation, seventeen defendants pleaded guilty to a variety of summary offenses (less than a misdemeanor) and were fined an average of $300 each.

Sport Officials

Maybe the most appropriate group to consult about fan violence is sport referees and officials. Although they maintain no formal statistics, the sixteen-thousand-member National Association of Sport Officials (NASO) believes that spectator violence is increasing. When fans scream "Kill the umpire," some really mean it. Referee legislation has been adopted in eleven states and is being considered in at least five more (Littlefield, 1997). One New Jersey attorney estimates that he works on as many as twenty cases each year involving assaults on sport officials.

Apart from the anecdotal, there are a number of research studies that have investigated the stress experienced by baseball and softball umpires (Rainey, 1994), basketball referees (Rainey & Winterich, 1995), and volleyball officials (Stewart & Ellery, 1996). The general methodology is to ask the official, "How much stress do you experience while umpiring (refereeing, officiating) games?" Perhaps unanticipated was the relatively low levels of stress reported across the three studies, the average score falling between "very little" and "a moderate amount." On average, only 3.6 percent of the officials surveyed reported high rates ("quite a bit" and "a great deal") of stress.

In a recently published study by Rainey and Duggan (1998), several hundred certified basketball referees in the state of Ohio were asked, "Have you ever been physically assaulted while refereeing (including before or after the game)?" Approximately 14 percent of the sample ($n = 98$) reported at least one assault. The most common assailants were players (41 percent), followed by parents (20 percent), coaches (19 percent), and spectators (15 percent). Rainey and Duggan found that spectators committed a disproportionately high percentage of assaults (28 percent) at the high school level.

SOME FINAL THOUGHTS

The sections in this chapter reveal that although the overwhelming majority of sport spectators are well-behaved and simply wish to observe an entertaining, well-played contest, a very small minority have a different agenda. It is this latter group that draws our attention lest they turn a day at the ballpark into "an afternoon of hell." Indeed, it is the actions of this far-from-silent minority that mandates our concern and investigation of sport spectator aggression. Most certainly, the mass media do not miss a chance to remind us that all is not well in the stands. For instance, baseball writers now have a new "score card" to share. In addition to the standard one that informs us about at bats, hits, runs scored, RBIs, and errors, readers are now provided with scores of the violence in the stands. For instance, consider the report of a San Francisco Giants–Los Angeles Dodgers game played at Candlestick Park ("Brawl Games," 1988). This game's "score card" showed twelve citations, seventy-five ejections, and eighteen arrests. Although anecdotal data such as this fall short of the mark in making a case that fan violence is systemic throughout sport, at the very least, they command those formally (sport researchers) and informally (sport fans) interested in sport to pay greater attention.

Chapter Six | # PSYCHOLOGICAL AND SOCIOLOGICAL CAUSES OF SPECTATOR AGGRESSION

A number of social scientists from a variety of disciplines have made important contributions to our understanding of sport spectator violence. In the current chapter we take a critical look at much of the theory and research generated by these investigators. The chapter centers around two distinct yet overlapping perspectives on spectator aggression: psychological (microlevel) and sociological or social-psychological (macrolevel). Psychological approaches to spectator aggression tend to focus on the impact of specific aspects of a spectator's personality and unique physical factors found within spectating environments. Conversely, sociological and social-psychological viewpoints tend to rely on the impact of larger social phenomena such as culture, social structure, and social environments. It is extremely important to remember that these viewpoints frequently overlap. While some theories and topics relevant to spectator aggression are specific to a single viewpoint, others involve both micro- and macrolevel considerations. We conclude this chapter with a discussion of the impact of alcohol on fan aggression.

PSYCHOLOGICAL APPROACHES TO UNDERSTANDING SPECTATOR AGGRESSION

In this section, we examine spectator violence from a psychological viewpoint. We begin by touching on several theoretical frameworks from psychology that provide insight into spectator aggression. Thereafter we examine specific situational and environmental causes. A concluding section focuses on the impact of the observation of sport violence on the aggressive tendencies of the viewers.

Psychological Theories of Spectator Aggression

Here we briefly review several theoretical viewpoints that have been used to advance our understanding of episodes of spectator violence. We begin with classic approaches to aggression and their application to spectator violence. We then examine two newer theoretical approaches to the problem.

The Frustration-Aggression Hypothesis   Given virtually any outburst of violence, be it among athletes on the field of play or spectators in the stands, commentators will typically seize upon some disheartening aspect of the situation as the cause. For example, a crowd disturbance is likely to be attributed to the frustration experienced by local fans witnessing their team's poor performance. Ever mindful of the daily annoyances and setbacks in their own lives, people have little difficulty accepting the commentators' analysis as an insightful explanation for the violence.

Originally formulated in 1939 by a group of Yale psychologists, the frustration-aggression hypothesis proposed that when people are blocked or in some way thwarted in their efforts to attain a goal, aggression will inevitably result. Similarly, when we observe an act of aggression, the theory assumes the existence of a prior state of frustration (Dollard, Doob, Miller, Mowrer, & Sears, 1939). However, this sweeping view of frustration as the cause of aggression was not without its shortcomings. For instance, consider the hockey enforcer who obeys the orders of his coach to attack an opposing player. There is no clear sense in which the goon's act of instrumental aggression originated with his being frustrated. Critics also had observed that people don't always respond with aggression when they are frustrated. For example, some increase their efforts to attain their goals, others pursue alternate goals, and still others regress to behaviors that are typical of an earlier stage of their development (e.g., sulking and pouting).

N. E. Miller (1941) subsequently proposed a more general formulation of the frustration-aggression hypothesis. It allowed that "frustration produces instigations to a number of different types of response, one of which is an instigation to some form of aggression" (p. 338). This revised position accommodated many of the criticisms by providing for a number of nonaggressive responses to frustration. However, the dominant and most likely response to frustration remained aggression.

Factors affecting the relationship between frustration and aggression • Our everyday lives are chock-full of frustrations, a few major, most minor. However, we do not as a rule see violent confrontations erupting all around us. Whether or not we act aggressively when frustrated is governed by several considerations. Two prominent considerations involve the severity of the frustration and the presence of aggressive cues. With respect to the degree of one's frustration, consider the reactions of spectators waiting in a queue (i.e., line) to purchase tickets to an important game. When a "sold out" announcement is made, one would expect fans near the front of the line to be highly frustrated and more likely to react in a violent manner than fans near the back of the line. Alternatively, hockey fans learning of the suspension of their star player at a crucial point in the playoffs would predictably be likely to respond with some manner of aggression, verbal or otherwise. Just such an incident preceded the Montreal hockey riot of 1955 when the commissioner of the NHL suspended Maurice "The Rocket" Richard for the balance of the season in what most Canadians saw as an unfair, draconian ruling (Lang & Lang, 1961).

A second important consideration determining whether or not one responds to frustration with aggression is the presence of aggressive cues, that is, people, events, objects, and so forth that have long-standing associations with aggression. Aggressive cue theory proposes that frustration simply produces a readiness to aggress and that actual aggression is more likely to occur in the presence of aggressive cues (Berkowitz, 1989, 1993). In his reformulation of the frustration-aggression hypothesis, Berkowitz developed a cognitive neoassociation model wherein frustration and other aversive stimuli create negative affects. If the individual interprets the resulting unpleasant state as one of anger, then the likelihood of aggression is increased. However, note that if the frustration is not interpreted as an unpleasant event, aggression need not result. Note also that under these conditions aggressive cues need not be present for aggression to occur. Rather, they serve to intensify one's aggressive response to being blocked in his or her efforts to attain a goal.

Social Learning Theory   Social learning theory, developed by Bandura (1973, 1986), provides a theoretical framework within which much of human aggression can be understood. Social learning theory has enjoyed widespread applications to a range of questions surrounding human aggression. For the present purposes, the model provides a valid explanatory framework for understanding the effects of watching violent sports either as a direct or an indirect sport consumer.

According to the social learning perspective, aggression is similar to numerous other social behaviors in its acquisition and maintenance. While biological factors (e.g., hormones) are recognized as having an influence, albeit limited, in the acquisition of aggressive behaviors, it is direct experience and observation that are most critical. Simply put, a major tenet of social learning theory is that individuals often learn to act aggressively by watching the violent actions of others (recall that observational learning was discussed in the previous chapter in regard to the influence of exemplars on their admirers).

A second focus of the theory is on the factors that instigate aggression. Such factors as incentives, direct orders, and aversive conditions can produce aggressive behaviors on the part of an individual. More germane to spectatorship is the role of models in instigating aggression among those observing their actions.

Finally, social learning theory considers the means by which aggression is regulated. Certainly, externally administered rewards and punishments influence one's aggressive behavior, as do self-regulatory mechanisms such as guilt. Equally important is the influence of vicarious reinforcements or punishments. The attentive observer takes note of whether a model is rewarded in some fashion for their aggression, such as with praise and wealth, or if the model is punished, for instance, with social disapproval. What does this mean for students of sport fan violence? It means that when a football fan sees his favorite player deliver an especially vicious hit on an opposing player and receive praise from his teammates for doing so, the spectator might be inclined, given sufficient provocation, to model the same behavior on the obnoxious opposing team's fan seated a few feet away.

Recent Psychological Theories of Spectator Aggression: Self-Esteem Maintenance and the Need for Excitement More recent models of spectator aggression in sport have been proposed by Wann (1993) and Apter (1992). These recent advances qualify as "psychological" because each focuses in large part on psychological needs (i.e., the need for self-esteem and the need for excitement).

The self-esteem maintenance model • The central concept in Wann's self-esteem maintenance model is the extent to which individuals have developed strong allegiances with a sport team. Those with strong team identification are predicted to respond differently to team losses than those with only weak ties. Wins by a favorite team tend to enhance one's social identity and self-esteem both in the case of spectators who strongly identify with the team and ones with weaker ties.

However, team losses lead to quite different behaviors. Spectators low in identification engage in "cutting off reflected failure," or "CORFing." CORFing involves decreasing one's association with an unsuccessful team to protect one's psychological well-being (C. R. Snyder, Lassegard, & Ford, 1986). Thus, sport fans can sometimes distance themselves from a losing team, thereby preserving a positive self-image and maintaining self-esteem. Research suggests that CORFing is not available to highly identified fans and, consequently, their self-esteem falls with the poor performance of their team. Rather, they engage in a process of "blasting," or derogation, as a means of restoring damage to their positive identity and lowered self-esteem (Branscombe & Wann, 1992b, 1994). The hostility of highly identified individuals then is likely to be directed at players on the opposing team and its fans. Accordingly, there is a heightened potential for spectator aggression when highly identified individuals witness their favorite team's defeats. It should also be noted that, because their aggression is designed to assist them in regaining a positive self-image, the self-esteem maintenance model involves instrumental spectator aggression.

The need for excitement • The general public is frequently outraged and mystified by the seemingly mindless acts of violence that have occurred in and around sport sites. The wanton destruction of property and unprovoked assaults on persons seem to defy explanation. What is equally difficult to appreciate is that for some troublemakers these activities are pleasurable and satisfy a basic need for excitement. Such a theory has been proposed by Apter (1992) to account for the motivations of violence-prone individuals attracted to sporting events.

Apter (1992) notes that the opportunities for people to take risks have been shrinking in recent decades, leading some to search for excitement in activities that carry a degree of personal risk. The model allows that individuals seeking excitement do so in a "protective frame" within which they judge themselves to be safe. Should they miscalculate their margin of safety, they are in peril of slipping over the "dangerous edge" into a trauma zone where harm can result. Thus, for example, a contingent of football fans may invade the pitch en masse. Individually, they may feel relatively safe. However, some will have miscalculated their margin of safety and suffer injury or find themselves in police custody. Mindless acts of spectator violence then are anything but mindless and in some instances may be initiated solely by a need for excitement.

The Contribution of Specific Environmental Influences to Spectator Aggression

It is a sweltering hot afternoon at the ballpark as you take your seat sandwiched between two other spectators. The roar of a capacity crowd is ringing in your ears. Further, and most unfortunately, you find yourself downwind from the sweaty man on your left who is desperately in need of a shower. You reflect on the striking contrast in vantage points as you look across the diamond at the executive suites, where a privileged few enjoy the game from their spacious, air-conditioned surroundings.

Viewing conditions such as those endured by the spectator in our example (e.g., oppressive heat, noise, crowding, and foul odors) are not uncommon in the experience of many who attend sporting events. Is it more than idle speculation to suggest that when these aversive conditions occur individually or in combinations, the quality of interpersonal relationships deteriorates? On the following pages we explore several environmental factors capable of playing a key role in facilitating interpersonal aggression: noise, temperature, atmospheric ionization, and crowding. Before embarking on this exploration, however, it warrants mention that our coverage of environmental influences is far from exhaustive. Rather, scientists working in the area of environmental psychology have identified additional factors that can increase aggressive behaviors, including foul odors (Rotton, Frey, Barry, Milligan, & Fitzpatrick, 1979), darkness (Page & Moss, 1976), and secondhand smoke (Zillmann, Baron, & Tamborini, 1981).

Noise An integral part of the spectator experience at many sporting events is extreme noise levels. Capacity crowds in domed stadia, arena sound systems, or the roar of engines at racing events create conditions that would be intolerable in most other nonsport contexts. Researchers have clearly demonstrated that noise can contribute to aggressive behaviors (e.g., Geen & McCown, 1984) because it leads to heightened physiological arousal, a state shown to facilitate aggression (Baron & Richardson, 1994). However, several considerations come into play in determining the strength of this factor. Noise occurring at irregular intervals and noise over which the individual has no control produce the strongest effects. Further, the effects of aversive noise levels are also more pronounced when the individual is already angered. For example, spectators in the midst of a noisy environment and enraged by an official's controversial call would be especially likely to give violent expression to their feelings.

A simple study by Knipmeyer and Prestheldt (cited in O'Neal & McDonald, 1976) nicely illustrates how noise can influence aggression. Small groups of all-female and all-male participants threw foam rubber balls at a same-sex confederate during a 3-minute period. Background noise accompanied the activity: either 88 dB noise of a boxing crowd, the same intensity of white noise, or silence. More balls were thrown at the confederate under the two experimental noise conditions than when there was silence.

Temperature   Heat is another physiologically arousing environmental condition that can stimulate aggression. For instance, researchers found that soaring temperatures in Texas are accompanied by an increasing incidence of rape and homicide (C. A. Anderson & DeNeve, 1992). Texas also provided the setting for a sport-related test of a heat-aggression hypothesis. The records of MLB provided figures on the number of batters hit by errant pitches over three seasons of play. As the temperatures recorded at game time rose, so too did the number of batters hit by pitchers (Reifman, Larrick, & Fein, 1991). Skeptical of "hit batters'" as a measure of aggression? In point of fact, it appears to be a valid reflection of a pitcher's aggression. The researchers went to considerable lengths to rule out rival explanations, such as fatigue or sweaty palms.

Regarding those in the stands, there is every reason to assume that thay also become increasingly hostile as temperatures rise to 100˚+ levels. A wealth of archival and experimental evidence points to a positive (causal) relationship between temperature and interpersonal aggression (e.g., Baron & Richardson, 1994). Indeed, Dewar (1979) noted in his investigation of spectator behavior at baseball games that violent outbursts were most likely to erupt during warmer weather.

Ions   Although not as frequently studied as noise and temperature, the balance of ionization in the atmosphere is another environmental factor that can affect aggression. The atmosphere varies in the extent to which air molecules carry a preponderance of positive or negative electrical charges. Negative ions have long been thought to be beneficial, whereas positive ions were generally believed to have adverse effects. Positive ions are the product of automobile emissions, machinery, winds, air conditioners, and crowds. Consequently, spectators at most sporting events find themselves in a situation that has an excess of positive ions. Recently, investigators have begun to examine the implications of atmospheric ionization for interpersonal relations among audience members and the hypothesized positive effect of negative ions.

One of the first such investigations examined the influence of negative ions on mood and physical aggression (Baron, Russell, & Arms,

1985). Participants in this experiment were classified as either Type A or Type B personalities. The profile of the Type A personality identifies such individuals as hard driving, impatient, and somewhat hostile. Atmospheric ionization theory suggests that Type As would exhibit less aggression in the "beneficial" atmosphere of a negative environment. However, this was not the case. Rather, there were no changes in the aggression of the more easygoing, affable Type B participants; there was, however, an increase in overt aggression by Type A individuals.

Equally interesting implications for the behavior of spectators are seen in a follow-up investigation. A major effect of negative ions appears to be that of intensifying one's existing feelings toward a stranger (Baron, 1987). Participants who found they had attitudes in common with a stranger and, consequently, were likely to have a positive impression of him, liked him even more in a negative-ion environment. On the other hand, when they had few attitudes in common and consequently disliked the stranger, negative ions intensified their dislike. We might cautiously extend these findings to suggest that viewing an event in a hostile and positive-ion environment will result in an intensification of existing interpersonal tensions and a greater potential for violence. This might be particularly true for spectators with Type A personalities. Of course, if an atmosphere of interpersonal goodwill prevails, negative ions could further enhance the quality of interactions among spectators.

Crowding   Crowding is yet another environmental factor found to facilitate aggression. Crowding is a subjective feeling of discomfort arising from a perception that too many people are present in a given situation. Early investigations (e.g., Freedman, Levy, Buchanan, & Price, 1972) showed that in crowded circumstances males became distrustful and hostile toward one another whereas females viewed crowding as a rich social occasion. However, when working on a common task over an extended period of time (one and a half hours), males seemingly develop a team spirit and an increased liking for each other (Marshall & Heslin, 1975). In the context of a sporting event, one might speculate that men's initial hostility toward one another gradually gives way to liking when they have opportunities to interact and share a common focus for several hours.

The Observation of Violence

North American media are awash with images of violence. Movies, television, and even evening news stories prioritized by a "if it bleeds, it leads" criterion provide the public with a steady diet of mayhem.

Largely overlooked in the debate on media violence is the aggression found in many of our more popular sports (e.g., boxing, pro wrestling, football, soccer, and hockey). Thanks to satellite technology, sporting events staged in any part of the world can now be viewed live and made available to millions of spectators. Here, we examine the impact of the observation of sport violence on the individual viewer (see also Zillmann & Paulas, 1993). We examine the effects of observing televised sport violence as well as the impact of witnessing violence in person in sport arenas and stadia. As we shall see, it matters not whether sport spectators view violence on television or from their seats in the stadium or arena. In either case, increases in player hostility seemingly cause spectators to become more aggressive themselves.

Before beginning our discussion, two important points deserve mention. First, research suggests that before a combatant sporting event takes place or appears on television, the media have often unwittingly set the stage for interpersonal conflict. Pregame hyperbole intended to stimulate viewer interest in an event may activate stored memories or negative schema, what cognitive psychologists call priming effects. References to "upcoming battles," "revenge," "taking no prisoners," even aggressive sport names (Wann & Branscombe, 1990b) can activate negative schema in some viewers. These, in turn, cause them to judge others unfavorably and see them as personally threatening. Because we typically act in accordance with our perceptions of people and events, the potential for hostile interactions among spectators and viewers is increased.

The second point involves the notion of catharsis, described briefly in chapter 3. Recall that catharsis concerns the belief that one's aggressive impulses can be released through the observation of or participation in violent activities. One of the major benefits believed to be gained from observing combatant sports is that it allows spectators to discharge or vent their pent-up aggressive impulses. The popularity of these beliefs is seen in the responses of a national sample of almost four thousand 15- to 19-year-old Canadian high school students (Russell, Arms, & Bibby, 1995). Fully 51 percent of boys and 38 percent of girls expressed support for the view that "watching violent TV shows tends to make people less aggressive." Among U.S. college students, 39 percent believed that a cathartic discharge of aggression results from watching aggressive sports in person, while 13 percent felt that similar benefits result from observing aggressive sports on television (Wann, Carlson, Holland, et al., 1999). Interestingly, it was those students who were most involved with violent sports who expressed the strongest belief in catharsis. These figures underestimate the level of support for cathartic beliefs in the general population. Reviews indicate that approximately two-thirds of North Americans believe in some form of cathartic mechanism (see Russell, 1983, 1993).

As popular and intuitively plausible as the notion of a catharsis may be, the belief simply does not stand up under careful scrutiny. Study after study has shown that viewing aggression either does not affect the viewer's aggressive state or, even more likely, leads to an increase in aggression (e.g., Gilbert & Twyman, 1984; Goranson, 1980; see Russell, 1993, chap. 9, for a review). It is pure fiction that spectators watching combatant sports on television or from the stands are miraculously drained of their aggressive impulses.

The View from the Couch While spectators often fill the stands at major sporting events, greater numbers will watch the competition on television sets in public lounges, in bars, and at home. Indeed, a recent study makes clear the fact that followers of a sport typically spend far more time on a couch in front of a television screen than they do in the stands. In this research, university men reported attending an average of fourteen hockey games each season. However, they reported watching an average of fifty-nine games on television during the same period (Russell & Arms, 1998). Public health authorities and others have speculated that some individuals may be harmed as a result of televised images of violence. In fact, it has been claimed by some that domestic violence and even homicides can be traced to television programming featuring combatant sports. As we will shortly see, there is merit in these speculations.

Consider first the plight of women in the vicinity of Washington, D.C., on game day. The admission records of emergency wards in D.C. area hospitals were examined for the hours surrounding home and away games of the NFL Washington Redskins. The analysis revealed that Redskins' victories at home were shortly followed by an increase in the number of women treated for assaults, stabbings, "accidental" falls, and gunshot wounds. Admissions remained unchanged following losses (G. F. White, Katz, & Scarborough, 1992). The authors attributed the rise in interpersonal aggression to an increase in power motivation. As has been shown elsewhere (Tesler & Alker, 1983), fans watching their favorite team triumph over their rivals experience an increase in their sense of personal power. Seemingly, that increased sense of power finds violent expression in interpersonal relationships. Disputes that might normally be resolved by negotiation or compromise are instead settled by force.

A study by Drake and Pandey (1996) offers a ray of hope that any harmful effects arising from major professional sporting events do not extend to child abuse. Based on official government records in Missouri, there was no evidence of an increase in male-perpetrated child abuse on either the day of national playoff games in baseball, basketball, football, and hockey or the day following the contest. Similarly, neither wins nor losses by the hometown St. Louis Blues hockey club were associated with levels of child abuse.

Media coverage of combatant sports can have lethal consequences for those in the viewing area. G. F. White (1989) tested the hypothesis that important football games are followed by an increase in local homicide rates. All NFL playoff games from 1973 to 1979 were examined, as were the homicide rates for the metropolitan areas in which the franchises were based. An increase in homicides was found, but the increase occurred six days after the playoff game and only in those cities whose teams were eliminated from the playoffs. The reason offered for the jump in homicides is intriguing. The sixth day following a playoff game falls on the eve of the next round of the playoffs. For fans of last week's winner, their team is still in contention. By contrast, fans of losing teams are forced to confront the realization that their season is over—there will be no game tomorrow. The investigators speculated that disputes arising from gambling losses might also have contributed to the increase in homicides.

Other evidence demonstrates that being physically distanced from the sport site fails to buffer the dangerous effects of witnessing violence. For instance, consider the research program initiated by Phillips (1986). He tested the notion that heavyweight championship boxing matches are followed by a rise in national homicide rates. His measure of lethal aggression was derived from the registry of U.S. national death certificates that record several key bits of information, including, age, sex, race, and cause of death. Homicide rates were examined for ten days following all title bouts from 1973 to 1978. As predicted, homicides rose 12.5 percent on the third day following the fights and 6.6 percent on the fourth day. The impact of the media was quite evident as the steepest increases occurred following the most heavily televised fights. However, the most intriguing finding of all had to do with the homicide victims themselves. They bore a strong resemblance to the loser of the title fight. That is, if an African-American boxer defeated a Caucasian opponent, there was an increase in homicides among young Caucasian males. Conversely, when a Caucasian fighter defeated an African-American opponent, the increase in homicides occurred in the population of young African-American men.

The View from the Stands Archival investigations suggest that riotous behavior by spectators may be partially the result of violence on the field of play. Reports of sport riots appearing in the *Toronto Globe and Mail* from 1963 to 1973 were analyzed, leading to the identification of sixty-eight serious riots. The riots were typically found at soccer and ice hockey contests. Most interesting was the fact that fully 74 percent of the riots were "ignited by player violence" (M. D. Smith, 1976, p. 127). Similarly, of seventeen major soccer riots reported in the *New York Times*, over half were preceded by threats and assaults by players, fans, or the police. Equally suggestive is a finding by Semyonov and Farbstein (1989) that Israeli soccer teams whose rosters include the most violent players also tend to have the most violent fans.

In addition to the aforementioned archival research, investigators have also employed field research methodologies to examine the effects of observing player aggression. For example, women attending a boxing card at the University of Notre Dame became increasingly angry over the course of the evening while men showed no change in anger (Sloan, 1989). Spectators attending regular season basketball games at the University of Arizona and Notre Dame exhibited increased hostility from before to after the contests (Leuck, Krahenbuhl, & Odenkirk, 1979; Sloan, 1989). A similar increase was found at Notre Dame football games (Sloan, 1989). Finally, Harrell (1981) reported pre- to postseason increases in hostility among World Hockey Association spectators who report they attend games on an infrequent basis.

Goldstein and Arms (1971) provided evidence that the relationship between player violence and spectator hostility is causal. Their classic field experiment was conducted on the occasion of the Army-Navy football game held annually in Philadelphia. Its design deserves close attention. First, it provided for a test of three rival theoretical positions: the frustration-aggression hypothesis, social learning theory, and a cathartic prediction. If supporters of the losing team showed an increase in hostility, the frustration-aggression view would be supported. Should an increase be found among fans of both Army and Navy, social learning theory would be the sole beneficiary. A general reduction in hostility would, of course, favor a cathartic view.

In keeping with sound experimental design, men were approached on a random basis before and after the contest. Serving as a control, the same procedure was followed at an equally competitive but nonviolent sporting event (an intercollegiate gymnastics meet). Participants were asked to complete a hostility inventory and answer biographical and background questions (e.g., were they rooting for Army or Navy). The results were clear. Regardless of team allegiances, men witnessing the football game experienced an overall increase in hostility from before to after the games whereas there were no changes at the gymnastics event. Of the three theoretical viewpoints pitted against each other, only social learning theory was consistent with the results. Seemingly, the observation of aggression led to a general reduction in the strength of inhibitions against the expression of aggression. However, it is seldom the case that a single experiment is the final word on a question.

A number of rival explanations for the results surfaced. Perhaps men grew increasingly hostile in having to sit through a dull, lopsided contest in which Navy trounced Army 27–0. Equally reasonable was the suggestion that alcohol brought about the result. Could it be that some men arrived a little tipsy and became increasingly so as the game wore on? These and other plausible, alternative explanations (e.g., indoor vs. outdoor, time of day, differences in crowd composition) pointed to the need for a replication designed to rule out these alternative explanations.

Such an investigation was conducted at the University of Lethbridge in Canada by Arms, Russell, and Sandilands (1979). Male and female university students were randomly assigned to one of three events: ice hockey, professional wrestling, and a control event—a provincial swim meet. Pro wrestling was chosen as a violent sport because it represents a category of fictional aggression in which most see the violence as a spoof. Once again, the results were straightforward. Men and women showed increases in aggression at both the hockey game and the wrestling card with no changes reported at the swimming competition. These findings strengthen the Philadelphia results. For example, alcohol can be ruled out as a rival explanation because the students were essentially sober. Similarly, the final bout on the wrestling card was anything but boring. The outcome was in doubt until the final minutes of the featured match when the "forces of good" triumphed over the "forces of evil." Thus, the success of the replication allows us to generalize the previous results to include females and different combatant sports.

It warrants mention that most major sport contests take several hours to complete. While comparisons of spectator hostility from before to after these events may reveal increases (or decreases) in aggression, they provide no information about the course of hostility during the contest. Thus, in a unique follow-up study, Russell (1981) administered a hostility measure to hockey spectators at four points in time: before, at the end of the first and second periods, and after the contest. This procedure was conducted at an especially violent game and a relatively peaceable (control) contest. In the case of the violent game, spectator hostility followed an inverted course. That is, hostility rose from pregame levels to peak at the end of the second period, declining slightly thereafter. The peak of the distribution was centered over the second intermission, a major player brawl having erupted moments before as the period drew to a close. No changes in spectator hostility were observed at the nonviolent contest. What we see in this study is that levels of spectator hostility closely track on-ice player violence.

SOCIOLOGICAL APPROACHES TO UNDERSTANDING SPECTATOR AGGRESSION

Having just explored fan violence from a psychological perspective where the focus was on individual differences and specific situational factors, we now turn our attention to sociological approaches to the phenomenon. Sociological perspectives of fan violence tend to emphasize "the effect of crowd members on each other, how spectators interact and influence each other within the crowd" (Mann, 1979, p. 365). In so doing, our focus is shifted toward group factors such as anonymity, conformity, normative pressures, and communication among the crowd members. We begin our examination of these and other social factors by briefly exploring three theories of crowd behavior that have relevance for spectator violence. Later, we explore spectator aggression as a social issue-related phenomenon as well as a response to structural factors unique to particular kinds of sporting events.

Theories of Collective Behavior

We now turn briefly to three classical viewpoints to further our understanding of crowd misbehavior. These theories help identify the dynamics of collective action, that is, how normally mild-mannered, nondemonstrative spectators become involved in episodes of crowd violence. As we shall see, although these approaches have their limitations, they are valuable to the extent that they introduce the reader to several concepts that underscore the importance of the social environment in explaining fan violence.

Contagion and Convergence Theories Contagion theory, originating from the work of Le Bon (1946), argues that ideas, moods, attitudes, and behaviors can become rapidly communicated and uncritically accepted by crowd members (see Polansky, Lippitt, & Redl, 1950). According to the theory, one aroused person in the crowd, by word or deed, arouses another who, in turn, arouses another, and so on. This "circular action" has the effect of stimulating the first person to an even greater extent, as well as other members in the "circle of influence." Because the arousal has no specific focus or outlet, the collectivity is very suggestible, and especially vulnerable to a leader's cues.

Contagion theory assists in our understanding of how both social (e.g., the wave, rhythmic clapping, loud, organized cheering) and antisocial behaviors (e.g., booing, throwing missiles, invading the pitch) can take hold within a large crowd. What appears to be key is the presence of a leader, usually of high status, to instruct and direct others in violent or destructive actions. While contagion theory does help explain how particular crowd behaviors are self-developed and manifested, it is not without its shortcomings (Simons & Taylor, 1992). For instance, the theory fails to account for the initial source of arousal. Further, the theory does not adequately explain how the circular reaction process actually occurs nor how the leader specifically impacts the process.

Similar to contagion theory, convergence theory suggests that "crowd behavior stems from the convergence of likeminded persons who are already predisposed to act in certain ways" (Simons & Taylor, 1992, p. 210; see Wright, 1978). Increases in crowd homogeneity (i.e., similarity in values, norms, motives, and interests) lead to lowered inhibitions and, ultimately, collective actions. Convergence theory predicts that greater numbers of similar people in a crowd lead to higher levels of arousal and lessened inhibitions, thereby increasing the likelihood of collective behavior. Unfortunately, this theory also leaves several important processes unexplained. For instance, the size of the critical mass of like-minded crowd members remains unspecified and the exact mechanism by which arousal lessens inhibitions is not fully explained.

Emergent-Norms Theory   Emergent-norms theory involves group conformity, that is, the process by which crowd membership influences individual members to conform to new norms developed within the group (Turner & Killian, 1972). Deviant behaviors such as spectator aggression become increasingly likely when crowds adopt antisocial standards of behavior they consider appropriate for a particular situation. Soon, many in the crowd are behaving in a particular way, leading others to join in as they assume that it is proper and acceptable. For example, if everyone in a crowd feels that an umpire missed a call, it takes only a few fans to express their displeasure by shouting obscenities before others are joining in the hostile behavior. In this situation, a norm has emerged encouraging abusive behavior.

As with the first two theories, important questions remain about emergent-norms theory. For instance, the approach does not adequately detail the process by which the new norm actually develops, nor does it describe how the norm operates despite long-held personal rules of conduct (Simons & Taylor, 1992). Indeed, research suggests that emergent-norms theory is less able than other theories to account for spectator aggression (Mann, Newton, & Innes, 1982).

Value-Added Theory   No theoretical discussion of fan violence would be complete without mention of Smelser's (1968) value-added theory. In explaining an episode of collective behavior, Smelser identifies several "determinants," each of which is viewed as a necessary but insufficient condition for an episode to occur. However, when all are present, the probability of collective behavior occurring is much more likely. What follows is a brief discussion of each determinant, accompanied by appropriate examples. The reader is encouraged to consult J. M. Lewis (1989) for an informative real-world application of Smelser's theory to the Heysel Stadium riot that occurred on May 29, 1985, in Brussels, Belgium.

One important determinant—structural conduciveness—refers to the ecological setting in which the potential behavior may occur. Smelser's (1968) point here is that, as noted earlier in this chapter, some structural factors facilitate aggressive responses (e.g., close and cramped seating, hot temperatures, noisy arenas, etc.). A second determinant—structural strain—refers to a generalized sense of deprivation or conflict. Structural strain may also involve hostile feelings provoked by an antagonistic group or a particular situation, such as a general dislike for authority and authority figures.

The growth of a generalized belief is a third determinant. This factor refers to a perceived threat that has been exaggerated or is seen as being imminent. According to Smelser, the result, in the case of panic, is the belief that a disaster is about to occur. A sport-related example would include spectators' perceptions that the referee is biased toward the home team. A fourth determinant concerns the occurrence of a precipitating factor that confirms or reinforces the generalized belief (e.g., the base runner is "out by a mile" but the home plate umpire calls him or her safe).

A fifth determinant involves the mobilization of participants for action. This is the final stage of the process, and typically involves the emergence of a leader who is able to mobilize the others. For instance, in our previous example of the umpire's poor call, an individual may mobilize others by yelling "Kill the umpire!" while encouraging them to express their displeasure by throwing missiles at the official.

And finally, the operation of social controls (or the lack thereof) serves as the sixth determinant. This factor refers to strong threats of force discouraging the display of hostile actions. Thus, social controls function as a counterdeterminant. Staying with the previous example, this determinant is represented by stadium security who confront the loud fan and escort him or her out of the stadium before a collective action takes place.

While Smelser's (1968) theory has value (e.g., there is strong empirical support for the impact of structural factors and social controls), it also has weaknesses that the author himself was quick to acknowledge. For example, the theory does not assign any importance to psychological factors that might explain why, in the presence of the first five determinants and the absence of social controls, most spectators fail to participate in a hostile collective action. Further, the theory assumes that the five determinants combine in the spectator's mind in some fashion, yet fails to describe the exact process by which this occurs. The theory also fails to adequately explain different gradations in involvement in a collective action as participants are drawn into the violent episode.

Issue-Relevant versus Issue-Irrelevant Factors in Spectator Aggression

Earlier, we discussed several psychologically related environmental factors that can facilitate spectator aggression. Now, we examine several sociological or "group-level" factors that play a role in spectator aggression. These factors have been classified into two categories: issue-relevant and issue-irrelevant. Issue-relevant factors assume that the roots of spectator violence lie outside the stadium or arena. That is, the violence manifested at sporting events is merely reflective of major stresses, strains, and problems extant within the larger society (e.g., a lack of educational opportunities, unemployment, racism, identity problems, failure to achieve status, delinquency, etc.). Conversely, issue-irrelevant factors are to be found inside the walls of the stadium or arena. From this perspective, it is the immediate social environment that holds the key to understanding the etiology of spectator misbehavior (Eitzen, 1979). What needs to be appreciated, say the proponents of this position, is the contribution that group and event factors have on fan behavior.

Issue-Relevant Factors   Described below are four issue-relevant factors intended to account for fan violence: failure of negative sanctions, incivility, absence of fathers, and societal violence.

Failure of negative sanctions • Although no longer popular within the academic community, instinct theory proposed that human aggression is caused by an innate predisposition to act violently—it can be neither created nor extinguished by learning (Freud, 1920, 1961; Hall & Lindzey, 1968; Lorenz, 1966). According to this viewpoint, all human beings have a propensity (i.e., are "hardwired") for aggressive, violent behavior. What keeps humans from giving expression to these instinctual urges are an effectively working conscience and the presence of strong social support to maintain it (Cheren, 1981). If we are witnessing more fan violence at sporting events today (which is merely speculation at this point), instinct theorists would argue that it is due to weakened negative sanctions and the public's failure to condemn the violence. Perhaps the fan violence we see today at sporting events is related to a general normative malaise in the larger society. Although strictly conjecture, one has to wonder whether some of the fan violence observed at sporting events today is related to a general breakdown in societal norms and a growing disrespect for cultural values. While instinct theory has been thoroughly discredited over the years (see Berkowitz, 1969), the possible failure of negative sanctions to discourage violent behavior remains a viable explanation, one certainly worthy of our consideration.

Incivility • Related to the previous point is the observation that the boorish behavior observed in some social settings, such as spectator sports, is not so much a disregard for normative structures, but rather, stems from a general lack of concern for the well-being of others—one measure of a civil society. Is civil society on the decline (Etzioni, 1993; Putnam, 1995; Walzer, 1991)? Is incivility becoming the norm rather than the exception? Harris (1998) suggests that moral codes of conduct centered around individual self-interest have penetrated our social institutions, including the family, community, and education. For many fans, it would be appropriate to add sport fandom to the list. For example, one can see evidence at the ballpark of an individual ethos sometimes out of control. Some sport fans appear to deliberately seek their own personal pleasure and entertainment at the expense of others. For instance, many do not seem to worry that their cheering is too loud, that their handmade sign is blocking the view of the person behind them, that their sloppy drinking is objectionable, or that their foul language is offensive to the ears.

What is being suggested is that one fallout of the "decline of civil society" is a rise in incivility as reflected in poor manners in public places. This problem is difficult to solve because it lies largely outside government control (Boldt, 1998). How to successfully address the issue in the classroom, the restaurant, the movie theater, the department store, and at sporting events remains a formidable challenge.

Absence of fathers • Statistics show that 36 percent of all children in the United States live apart from their fathers and that fatherlessness is at an all-time high. According to Blankenhorn (1995), author of *Fatherless America*, this is a major social problem because fatherlessness plays a major role in the etiology of male violence. For example, Blankenhorn notes that, compared to children living with their fathers, those with absent fathers are more likely to be suspended from school, to exhibit emotional and behavioral problems, and to run into trouble with police (Yonda, 1998). What Blankenhorn is calling for is a reaffirmation of the "norm of parental obligation," that is, a recognition by biological fathers that they must accept their social responsibility to serve as guardian and protector of their children.

Because the vast majority of fan violence is initiated by males against other males, fatherlessness may possibly play a role in spectator aggression. Certainly, with respect to fan violence, Blankenhorn's provocative thesis raises some interesting research possibilities. For example, it would be valuable to learn more about the family backgrounds and family dynamics of persistent, violent male sport fans. We might hypothesize that adolescent males who did not have the benefits of being raised by their biological fathers would be overrepresented among the most rowdy and disorderly. If this was indeed the case, alternative explanations focusing on the mediating influence of race/ethnicity, socioeconomic status, and the quality of the parent-child relationship would also be tested.

Our violent society • One of the more popular issue-relevant sociological explanations of sport fan violence is societal violence. Social institutions such as sport are seen as microcosms of the larger society—their vales, norms, and belief systems mirroring the larger sociocultural context (M. Real, 1975). According to this perspective, if we lived in a less violent society, then we would see less violence at sporting events. Increases in disorderly behavior at sport venues simply reflect the fact that our society has become more violent. Bok makes the case that we do indeed live in a "culture of violence" when she writes: "It's a culture where people can make a lot of money by producing violent entertainment, violent books, or certainly selling drugs. People also benefit a lot from buying and selling weapons.

People see so much violence on television, in the newspapers and in their neighborhoods. Even there's domestic violence [sic]. All of these factors work together" (cited in Reynolds & Benedetto, 1990, p. 13A). Sipes (1996) extends this point further by offering a "cultural pattern model" to explain violent behavior. He observed: "We learn our individual patterns of behavior, and that our culture supplies us with these patterns. . . . We can decrease unwanted violence and other aggressive behavior by reducing the aggressive component of culture patterns wherever this component is found" (p. 155).

Any number of statistics support the contention that we live in a very violent society. For instance, consider the following:

- The American Psychological Association estimates that by the time the average American child leaves elementary school, he or she will have viewed 8,000 murders and 100,000 acts of violence on television ("Senators Seek 'Report Card,'" 1995).
- Homicide is the tenth leading cause of death in the United States ("CDC: Americans Live Longer," 1994).
- Private violence (e.g., child abuse, wife beating, rape), while difficult to accurately assess, is believed by law enforcement and social service professionals to be endemic (Dowd, 1983).
- The American Academy of Pediatrics, which represents 48,000 pediatricians, has concluded that violence in entertainment makes some children more aggressive, desensitizes them to real-life violence, and makes them feel they live in a mean and dangerous world (Kane, 1996).

Issue-Irrelevant Factors Eitzen (1979) is of the opinion that the very structure of a sporting event promotes fan violence. Eitzen's perspective argues in support of issue-irrelevant factors in explaining spectator aggression. Two such factors will be explored here: the crowd and the event.

The crowd factor • Crowding and the presence of others can facilitate aggression (Baron & Richardson, 1994; Berkowitz, 1993). With respect to sport spectators, this implies that fans are more likely to exhibit violent behaviors while spectating with others than when watching alone. There are a number of psychosocial phenomena present in large sport crowds that are related to fan violence. Jaffe and Yinon (1983) believe that four such phenomena are particularly relevant: anonymity, lack of fear of retaliation, diffusion of responsibility, and deindividuation.

Anonymity concerns the extent to which individuals feel their identity is hidden from others. Large crowds enhance a person's perception that he or she is anonymous by serving as a "human fog." Because the individual spectator is just one among many, he or she is nameless, unknown, and less likely to accept authorship of his or her own aggressive actions.

Anonymity also plays a key role in one's fear of retaliation. For instance, if a spectator does engage in some type of antisocial behavior (e.g., throws a missile on the field), there is often little reason for him or her to fear retaliation given the difficulty of affixing individual blame in a very large crowd. For example, Dewar (1979) monitored spectator fights at forty regular season MLB games of a single team and found that about 70 percent of the fights occurred at night games, when anonymity would be greater and fear of retaliation less.

Crowd members also feel secure knowing that they can diffuse responsibility for their behavior onto other members of the crowd. Violent fans know that it is virtually impossible to be singled out for censure in a large crowd. This realization, coupled with the knowledge that if any punishment is meted out it will fall upon everyone in the crowd, leads the individual spectator to feel more emboldened. Because stadium management is unwilling to risk punishing the innocent along with the guilty, individual acts of misbehavior often do go unpunished.

Finally, as a consequence of the combined influence of these three group factors, the individual spectator is likely to experience deindividuation. Deindividuation is a mental state characterized by membership in a group, feelings of anonymity, and a loss of self-awareness (Diener, 1980; Festinger, Pepitone, & Newcomb, 1952; Mann et al., 1982). When individuals are in a deindividualized state, they tend to focus their attention on the group, the result of which is a diminution of self-awareness. This loss of self-awareness, coupled with anomynity, allows some crowd members to give free reign to their otherwise inhibited aggressive inclinations.

The event factor • The four group-related processes just described are not just characteristic of sport crowds, but rather, are evident wherever large numbers of people come together (e.g., rock concerts, political rallies, and parades). Yet individual misbehavior seems to be more likely to occur at sporting events than at other large social gatherings. To understand violent sport crowds, sociologists suggest we consider an additional factor that renders sporting events more vulnerable to antisocial behaivor: the event itself.

The ecological setting of a sporting event, while similar in some respects to other large gatherings, is also very different. Today sporting events are presented and packaged as "entertainment events."

Management spares no expense to ensure that the spectator's arousal level is maximized. The "Cheer Meter," the wave, mascots of all kinds and descriptions, scantily clad cheerleaders, exhortations on the message board, fireworks, and loud rock music are all designed to excite and entertain the crowd. Management typically invites the fan to become an "extra player"—the twelfth man (or woman) in football—and join the action. This strategy is not without problems because if support for the home team (in-group) is encouraged too strongly, it can engender very negative, potentially dangerous, feelings toward the opposing team (out-group) and its supporters (Wann, 1993). Given sufficient provocation, what was an innocent rivalry between opposing teams and fans can give way to serious intergroup conflict (M. J. Lee, 1985).

According to Eitzen (1979), the game is presented to the spectator as a festive, carnival-like event, as an opportunity to cast aside personal restraints and "party"—"Viva la celebration!" When you add alcohol and player violence to the mix, there is always the possibility the party can get out of control and turn ugly. The combination of high arousal level, alcohol, aggressive models, and management's invitation to "have a good time" make some sport contests more vulnerable to violence than other social events.

ALCOHOL

Sometimes the academic community is accused of overanalyzing and overtheorizing the simple and obvious. Some would argue that such is the case with fan violence. Indeed, if you were to stop someone on the street and ask what causes spectators to act violently while watching their favorite sporting events, the answer is almost certain to involve alcohol consumption. Certainly, not all acts of spectator violence are fueled by alcohol, but surely many are. The fact is, spectators who overindulge and become bellicose and belligerent are primed for antisocial behavior that runs the gamut from profanity to throwing a beer can on the field to picking a fight with another spectator. In this section we examine the potential role alcohol plays in the violence exhibited by sport fans. The topic is being addressed here rather than in the psychological or sociological sections presented earlier because the alcohol consumption of sport fans has been of concern to both sport psychologists and sport sociologists alike.

Before proceeding with our analysis of the relationship between alcohol and spectator aggression, it warrants mention that alcohol is not the only substance that has implications for spectator violence.

TABLE 6.1

Effect of Selected Drugs on Human Aggression

DRUG	EFFECT ON AGGRESSION	SAMPLE REFERENCE
Alcohol	Increase	Bushman and Cooper (1990)
Barbiturates	Negligible	Chermack and Taylor (1993)
Caffeine	Increase	De Freitas and Schwartz (1979)
Cocaine	Increase	Licata, Taylor, Berman, and Cranston (1993)
Diazepam (valium)	Increase	Gantner and Taylor (1988)
Marijuana	Negligible	Myerscough and Taylor (1985)
Morphine	Increase	Berman, Taylor, and Marged (1993)
Steroids	Increase	Pope and Katz (1990)

Rather, an indeterminate number of spectators may have used, or be in possession of, a variety of drugs, legal or otherwise. The effects of common drugs on aggression are presented in table 6.1. The studies cited are representative of the findings in investigations of each drug's effect on aggression.

The Alcohol-Aggression Relationship

Certainly, alcohol is central to the carnage we see on our highways as well as the tragedy of alcoholism. However, the relationship between alcohol and human aggression is not always clear-cut; some early studies found a relationship while others did not. More recently, reviews of the literature have utilized meta-analysis techniques, a research procedure that takes into account all findings on a topic (positive and negative) in reaching an overall conclusion. The results of these analyses point to a positive relationship between alcohol and aggression (Bushman & Cooper, 1990; Ito, Miller, & Pollock, 1996). Bushman and Cooper concluded in their review that "alcohol does indeed facilitate aggressive behavior" and that it "appears to influence aggressive behavior as much or more than it influences other social and nonsocial behaviors" (p. 350).

Alcohol and Spectator Aggression

Although preliminary research has failed to establish a relationship between alcohol consumption and level of sport fandom (Koss & Gaines, 1993; Wann, 1998a), it is more than obvious that many fans become intoxicated while watching sporting events. In fact, it was recently estimated that approximately 8 percent of male fans leaving MLB games are legally drunk (O'Brien & Hersch, 1998). Given a modest Saturday afternoon crowd of twenty-five thousand spectators, this means that approximately two thousand intoxicated individuals are roaming about the ballpark and parking lot, a sobering thought indeed.

While empirical studies are few, we do have anecdotal data to support a linkage between alcohol and fan violence. When the New England Patriots management decided to only sell low-alcohol beer at the concession stands a few years ago, violence diminished noticeably. When regular beer was returned to these professional football fans later in the season, the violence returned (Sullivan, 1986).

Soccer hooliganism is a worldwide problem, and several solutions have been introduced to deal with it (see chapter 7 for additional discussion of hooliganism). For example, former British prime minister Margaret Thatcher once argued for a general prohibition on selling alcoholic beverages during soccer matches after the 1985 European Cup final between Liverpool and Juventus turned to tragedy when British fans charged the Italian fans leaving 38 dead and 250 injured. A total ban on alcohol at football games in England and Wales was in fact introduced for the 1985–86 season. Coupled with the use of closed-circuit television and good policing, arrests dropped 51 percent between the 1984–85 and 1985–86 seasons (Spackman, 1986).

The Importance of Situational Factors in the Alcohol-Induced Aggression of Sport Spectators Whether or not alcohol increases the aggression of a user is in large measure determined by the situation in which it is consumed. We have all attended social functions where drinks flowed freely but tempers were not frayed and the partygoers did not come to blows. All in all, it was probably a relatively subdued environment in which alcohol acted as a social lubricant rather than a trigger for aggression among the guests. The situation in our party example can be characterized as congenial and nonthreatening. Obviously, other situations involving alcohol may be less friendly. Research by Taylor, Gammon, and Capasso (1976) points to the importance of the situation in determining the influence of alcohol on aggression. In this experiment, sober and intoxicated respondents in nonthreatening circumstances did not differ in their levels of aggression. However, when threat was introduced into the situation, the aggression of sober participants increased slightly whereas that of intoxicated individuals soared! The implications for spectator violence are straightforward. Sport conducted in an atmosphere that is perceived as personally threatening by spectators (e.g., taunting from rival fans) is especially likely to invite hostile outbursts from intoxicated viewers.

Alcohol Policies and Spectator Aggression In the United States every professional team has its own set of alcohol control policies to deal with excessive drinking. These policies include some combination of the following: alcohol-free seating, no vending in the seats, vendor training to recognize drunkenness, early termination of sales, limits on purchases, and smaller servings. However, Buikhuisen (1986) believes that the control of alcohol at sporting events to curb disorderly behavior is, in the long run, likely to meet with limited success. His pessimism is based on two lines of logic.

First, behavior is the product of the interaction of two factors: the person and the situation. Although alcohol may be eliminated from the situation, the person may still be "primed" for antisocial behavior. For example, to understand the behavior of British hooligans, one must acknowledge that the most persistent offenders: (1) come from the very rough, lower strata of society; (2) are undereducated and underemployed; (3) have a need for danger and thrill-seeking behavior; and (4) have an inordinate need to prove their masculinity (Dunning, Murphy, & Williams, 1986). These personality factors are present in these individuals even when they are not intoxicated. Consequently, although alcohol may exacerbate a potentially flammable situation, it is not a necessary component for the aggressive actions of these persons. Rather, because they possess a personality profile and a life history that predisposes them to act violently, hooligans often exhibit highly aggressive behaviors in the absence of alcohol.

Second, Buikhuisen (1986) notes that there are great differences in the way people react to alcohol. Some become violent, others react in an euphoric way, some turn very quiet, and still others have a tendency toward depression. Thus, because there are multiple reactions to alcohol consumption, it is difficult to predict the impact of limiting alcohol sales at sporting events (although some past attempts have appeared to be successful; e.g., Spackman, 1986).

Cognitive Functioning and Alcohol Consumption

In concluding, we would be remiss if we did not clear up a common misconception. Intoxicated individuals are perfectly able to process information. That is, they can foresee the consequences of their actions and can readily show restraint in response to social cues (Jeavons & Taylor, 1985). Furthermore, a third party can successfully reason with an intoxicated person to reduce his or her aggression. Even under conditions of extreme provocation, inebriated people are responsive to the "coaxing, cajoling, and reasoning" of a peacemaker (Taylor & Gammon, 1976, p. 928).

SOME FINAL THOUGHTS

At several points in this text we call for additional work on topics related to the psychological and sociological implications of sport fandom and spectating. These pleas for additional research are a response to the limited number of empirical studies assessing the phenomena. However, such is not the case with sport spectator aggression. Rather, social scientists have been very active in examining the micro- and macrolevel factors that facilitate displays of fan violence. One conclusion that is quite clear from this research is that any comprehensive explanation of fan violence must forge a synthesis between sociological determinants and psychological considerations. While the social environment may well provide the opportunity, even encourage an episode of individual or group misbehavior, "some individuals are more or less completely 'programmed' psychologically to 'act out' in collective episodes" (Smelser, 1968, pp. 101–102). In other words, when it comes to understanding the aggressive actions of sport spectators, both psychological viewpoints and sociological perspectives are necessary pieces of the puzzle.

Chapter Seven | SPORT SPECTATOR RIOTS

O ne of the authors of this text recently bought his first newspaper in several years (he lives on a tiny island). In separate articles, details were provided of a full-scale soccer riot in Rotterdam, a riot following a water polo tournament in Greece, and riotous behavior by cricket fans in Barbados (*Vancouver Sun*, April 26, 1999). It is unlikely that the day was typical for reporting riots. However, it does remind us that sport riots are not a rarity, nor are they confined to particular sports or cultures. In this chapter, we take a critical look at the occurrence and form of these crowd disturbances. Our examination includes reviews of typology schemes for classifying sport riots, a discussion of those persons most likely to become involved in a riot, and a look at those most likely to intervene to stop a riot. In conclusion, we take a brief look at the phenomenon of soccer hooliganism.

DEFINITIONS AND TYPOLOGY OF RIOTOUS BEHAVIOR

Similar to the construct of aggression, there is considerable diversity among definitions of riots. To illustrate, Darrow and Lewinger (1968) define riots simply as "aimless behavior involving disturbances or turmoil" (p. 2). Riots have also been described as "relatively spontaneous group violence contrary to traditional norms" (Marx, 1972, p. 50). Other scholars have attempted to define riots as they occur in the context of sport. For instance, Simons and Taylor (1992) define riots as "purposive destructive or injurious behavior by partisan spectators of a sporting event that may be caused by personal, social, economic, or competitive factors" (p. 213). These divergent definitions highlight an important facet of riotous behavior, namely, that riots come in many different forms. Consequently, we begin our analysis of sport riots by examining several typologies that have been proposed as schemes for classifying sport riots.

Classifying sport riots is important because, as Mann (1979, 1989) points out, "the usual stereotype of the sports riot, as a wild, uncontrolled outburst following defeat, is not the major or only form" (p. 352). Thus, typologies assist in the recognition and categorization of particular kinds of collective behavior. A typology is also important because it has implications for understanding (1) the causes of hostile outbursts, (2) when they are most likely to occur (e.g., before, during, or after a game), (3) the types of individuals most likely to participate, and (4) those most likely to be targeted (Mann, 1979).

Two useful typologies of sport riots have been proposed: Mann's (1979) FORCE model and M. D. Smith's (1983) issue-relevant versus issue-irrelevant riots.

Mann's FORCE Typology

Mann (1979, 1989) developed a typology for classifying sport riots based on an analysis of case materials and archival records. Assigned the acronym FORCE, this typology identifies five types of riots, each based on the dominant characteristics of the rioters. A brief description of the riot categories included in this model are presented in table 7.1.

Frustration Sport Riots The frustration riot is caused by bitterly disappointed fans who wish to retaliate for what they regard as an illegitimate or unacceptable action. Berkowitz (1982) refers to their disappointment as "a bitter, painful experience," the primary antecedent of hostile aggression. The frustration riot can be precipitated when fans are deprived of a service (e.g., access to a sporting event) or when they perceive a gross injustice (e.g., a referee's bad call).

Considered within the North American context, frustration riots are a rare occurrence. Efficient, well-organized, and well-managed ticket distribution systems are unlikely to result in a sporting event being oversold. Further, the quality of officiating across all competitive levels is generally very good. Of course, even the best game officials will occasionally miss a call or two, but even their harshest critics are likely to agree that the officials are well-trained, competent, and usually call a fair game. This is not to say that North American spectators never express their frustration toward officials

TABLE 7.1

Mann's (1979) FORCE Typology of Sport Riots

Frustration riots	Riots caused by disappointed fans who wish to retaliate against the perceived source of frustration.
Outlawry riots	Riots caused by delinquent groups who assemble at sporting events for the purpose of engaging in threatening and destructive behavior.
Remonstrance riots	Riots that represent protests from groups who wish to use the sport stadium to express their political or ideological grievances.
Confrontational riots	Riots involving opposing fan groups with a history of hostility and resentment.
Expressive riots	Riots directly related to the euphoria or anger and depression spectators feel in response to the outcome of a sporting event.

who miss important calls. For instance, during the 1999 American League Championship Series, the Boston Red Sox (and their fans) found themselves on the wrong end of several questionable calls. Finally, the frustration became so great for the Red Sox faithful that they felt compelled to display their displeasure by throwing missiles on the field, causing a lengthy delay.

Outlawry Sport Riot When the game becomes an opportunity for delinquent groups to assemble and engage in threatening or destructive acts, we have an outlawry riot. According to Mann, the game and outcome are inconsequential to the violence as the participants have neither an emotional nor a social attachment to the contesting teams or the sport itself. Rather, the game event merely provides them with an opportunity to act out and cause others grief.

Again, judged within the North American sport context, it is rare for youth gangs to seek out high school, college, or professional sporting events to engage in destructive behavior. The fact that high school events are geographically more accessible to delinquent gangs probably makes them more vulnerable to this type of riot, although few have been reported in the mass media. But there are exceptions. For example, the principal of a suburban Los Angeles high school forfeited a football game to an urban school because he feared gang violence made the game too dangerous to play or watch ("High School Team Opts to Take Forfeit," 1991).

Remonstrance Sport Riots The remonstrance riot is essentially an ideological protest in which a group uses a sporting event to express a political grievance or advance a particular ideology. Hartmann (1996) notes that the popularity and availability of cultural arenas like sport are especially appealing to powerless racial and ethnic minorities who wish to draw attention to a particular cause. Typically, these sport-related demonstrations are carefully planned and organized by those seeking a forum for their views. On occasion, they can turn ugly and confrontational. For example, the Stop The Seventy Tour Committee waged a very successful protest campaign in Great Britain in 1970 to stop a tour by a "whites only" South African cricket team. For eight months the British public watched in amazement as antitour groups aggressively expressed themselves against the racial discrimination policies of the South African sport system. Police ringed the pitches to stop demonstrators from running onto the field and interfering with the matches. Cricket fields were surrounded by barbed wire in preparation for the visit by the Apartheid cricketers. Demonstrations, confrontations, and fixed battles were commonplace at these sport venues (Hain, 1971).

While occasional protest groups appear at North American sporting events, these demonstrations are almost always peaceful and nondisruptive. For example, Native-American groups have protested against teams (e.g., the NFL Washington Redskins, the MLB Atlanta Braves) whose symbols (e.g., the Tomahawk Chop, Chief Wahoo) are seen as demeaning to their culture. Also, antismoking groups have protested outside sport facilities where smoking advertisements are prominently displayed (e.g., Doctors Against Smoking protested against the Marlboro Man billboard inside Ralph Wilson Stadium, home of the NFL Buffalo Bills). More recently, the first baseball game played between Cuba and the Baltimore Orioles in the United States attracted two groups of protestors. One supported an end to the U.S. embargo against Cuba, the other opposed the game and closer ties with the Fidel Castro regime (Dodd, 1999).

Confrontational Sport Riots Confrontational riots involve opposing fan groups with a history of hostility and resentment toward each other. On this point King (1995) has observed that while a negative "historical background between two factions does not automatically

cause disorder, this background nevertheless has a degree of deter-
mination over the actualization and interactional levels since it limits the horizon of possible practices, in which fans can engage" (p.
649). Basically, King is suggesting that, all things being equal, intergroup violence is more likely to occur between supporters of rival
teams than between fan groups who have no history of confrontation.
For example, an NFL game between the Buffalo Bills and the Miami
Dolphins is likely to place security on greater alert than a game
between the Bills and the San Diego Chargers, a nonconference game
involving two teams that seldom meet. The same can be said about a
baseball game between the New York Yankees and the Cleveland
Indians, as opposed to a game between the Yankees and the
California Angels. In the former instance, both teams are in the same
division, play each other several times, and have faced each other in
the playoffs on more than one occasion.

The origin of the hostility between rival groups can be racial, ethnic, religious, class, or regional in nature (Wahl, 1999). For instance,
when visiting Roman Catholic soccer fans from Belfast arrived in the
Protestant town of Portadown to see a game, they were met by a rock-
throwing mob of pro-British, Protestant supporters of the local team
("Protestant Mob," 1996). Further, an exhibition soccer game between
England and Ireland played in Dublin had only begun when some
4,500 English fans reacted to an Irish goal by attacking the home
team fans, subsequently forcing the termination of the game. The
violence led to more than 40 arrests, and two people required hospi-
tal treatment ("Rioting Fans," 1995).

While serious confrontation riots at North American sporting
events are infrequent, racial and ethnic differences between opposing teams and fans have caused some problems. For example, when
a predominantly white high school team from the suburbs plays a
predominantly black high school team from the inner city, history
shows that disturbances are more likely to occur.

Expressive Sport Riots Expressive riots are directly related to expressions of extreme euphoria or deep depression and anger. Referred to
as "victory riots" and "sore loser riots," respectively, these crowd disturbances are typically postgame phenomena. It is hypothesized that
the emotional arousal engendered by the outcome of a game, be it joy
and ecstasy or grief and anger, leads to a loss of normal restraint, or
disinhibition. Disinhibition involves the expression of behavior
"which is usually restrained by fear of adverse consequences mediated externally (punishment) or internally (guilt). Conditions that

reduce anticipated risk or punishment or guilt disinhibit aggressive actions" (Jaffe & Yinon, 1983, p. 267). The probability of expressive riots occurring at sporting events is more likely because of the emotionally charged atmosphere in which they are conducted, the fact that there are winners and losers, and the anonymity spectators enjoy in a large crowd.

Although there are certainly exceptions, fans of the losing team at a North American sporting event generally respond with cold silence and a hasty retreat from the venue. On the other hand, the victory or celebratory riot has become quite frequent—there were eleven major victory riots in North America between 1968 and 1993. In fact, these crowd disturbances are often anticipated following a championship victory by the home team. In anticipation of a sixth NBA title, the city of Chicago used a new computer mapping system that allows police to identify trouble spots and quickly dispatch officers (the same type of system used by the CIA, Scotland Yard, and U.S. Border Patrol; see Howlett, 1998). In addition, the police department's 13,500 officers were placed on alert, some freeway ramps were closed, traffic was rerouted away from trouble spots, and bar owners were asked to close early if they saw their patrons getting rowdy.

Two distinct forms of victory riots • Mann's celebratory riot category needs to be subdivided because there appear to be two different kinds of victory riots. The first form typically takes place in the host city immediately after the game, usually under nightfall, and has little to do with sport fandom. The celebration merely provides a cover for criminal types to loot, rob, and maim. The motive behind their actions is straightforward: destroy what's not valuable and steal what is. Celebratory riots also become an opportunity for the socially and economically disadvantaged to take out their frustration on a social system that "doesn't work for them." For example, the riots associated with Chicago Bulls NBA championships may well have constituted a form of economic protest by socially and economically marginalized groups (Rosenfeld, 1997).

The second type of victory riot is closer to what Mann (1979) describes. These riots result from the sense of euphoria fans feel when their team has won a championship. For example, on October 30, 1993, seven people were critically hurt and dozens more were injured when thousands of celebrating fans poured onto the football field following Wisconsin's 13–10 victory over Michigan. Approximately 12,000 spectators among the sellout crowd of 77,745 scrambled out of five student sections in an attempt to reach the field. The injured fans were trampled in the rush (Telander, 1993).

The euphoria of the surging crowd was understandable given the fact that it was the first Badger victory over Michigan in twelve years. More importantly, the victory raised Wisconsin's record to 7–1, giving the school an excellent chance to win the Big Ten Conference, something it had not done in thirty-one years, and a trip to the Rose Bowl. Couple the crowd's excitement with weak, ineffective physical barriers separating the student sections from the end zone, a grossly undermanned security force, and Halloween weekend, and you have a potentially deadly situation.

Smith's Issue-Relevant versus Issue-Irrelevant Typology

A different but equally useful spectator violence typology was developed by M. L. Smith (1983). The components of Smith's scheme are shown in table 7.2. In Smith's typology, riots are classified as either

---

TABLE 7.2

M. D. Smith's (1983) Typology of Sport Riots

ISSUE-ORIENTED (I.E., ISSUE-RELEVANT) RIOTS

↑	Structural sources	**Demonstration riots**: Relatively organized attempts to disrupt an event and draw attention to a cause.
		Confrontation riots: Relatively spontaneous clashes between traditional enemies.
	Situational sources	**Entry riots**: Relatively spontaneous reaction to being denied admission to a sporting event.
		Defeat riots: Relatively spontaneous reactions to being denied a victory.
		Victory riots: Semi-institutionalized revelry following a victory; minimal social control.
↓		**Time out riots**: Institutionalized revelry; minimal social control.

ISSUELESS (I.E., ISSUE-IRRELEVANT) RIOTS

Note: Adapted from M. D. Smith (1983).

---

issue-relevant or issue-irrelevant. Recall from chapter 6 that issue-relevant riots have their origins outside the stadium or arena while the causes of issue-irrelevant fan violence are found inside sport venues. For issue-relevant violence, it is a variety of societal strains that are believed to be the cause of fan misbehavior. Conversely, issue-irrelevant riots are related to the specific social environment in which the event occurs (Eitzen, 1979).

Thus, the origin of issue-relevant riots is to be found beyond the realm of the sporting event itself. Smith further divides these riots into those that arise from structural sources and those that originate with situational sources. Structural issue-relevant riots include demonstration and confrontation riots. Demonstration riots involve the use of a sporting venue to draw attention to a certain cause or issue. These riots are highly organized and similar to Mann's (1979) remonstrance riot. Consistent with Mann's typology, confrontation riots involve clashes between historical rival factions. Situational issue-relevant riots include entry riots and defeat riots. Entry riots occur when spectators are denied entrance to a sporting event. This form of riot would serve as an example of a frustration riot in the FORCE typology. As the title suggests, defeat riots result from the disappointment spectators feel after their team has suffered a loss. Defeat riots are consistent with the "sore loser" expressive riots in Mann's framework.

Finally, M. D. Smith's (1983) typology of spectator riots includes two forms of issue-irrelevant riots: time out and victory. Time out riots involve institutionalized revelry and minimal social control—similar to the outlawry riot category found in Mann's (1979) typology. Similar to time out riots in form and control, victory riots occur following successful team performances. Clearly, these riots represent the "victory" or "celebration" expressive riots in the FORCE classification scheme.

Although M. D. Smith's (1983) typology is similar to Mann's (1979) FORCE framework in many respects, Smith's system is different in one important way. Smith's typology emphasizes a continuum with overlapping rather than discrete categories. The various forms of riotous behavior fall on a continuum ranging from completely issue-relevant riots at one end to completely issue-irrelevant riots at the other. Conversely, Mann's typology involves discrete sport riot categories.

THOSE WHO WOULD PARTICIPATE IN AND ESCALATE A SPORT RIOT

You may be surprised to learn that we know a great deal about those individuals who are at the center of a riot, trading punches, destroying property, and/or throwing missiles of one sort or another. Specifically, we know something about their demographics, the impact of group processes on their behavior, the ways in which they process information, and their personality profile. Each of these topics is discussed in this section.

Demographic Characteristics of Rioters

Several decades of research, primarily by European sociologists, present us with a picture of the typical rioter as a young, single male. Beyond that, he can be described as marginalized, poorly educated, often unemployed, and alienated from the mainstream of society (e.g., Dunning et al., 1986; Kerr, 1994; Pilz, 1989; Zani & Kirchler, 1991). This profile is also accurate for North America, where it is young males who appear most eager to participate in sport crowd disturbances (e.g., Russell & Arms, 1998) and who also commit the bulk of the violent crimes (Reiss & Roth, 1993).

Group Processes and Riotous Behavior

Those bent on trouble run in packs. An official inquiry by Harrington into British hooliganism observed that "most misbehavior at soccer matches involves small or large groups; rarely does it involve a single spectator" (cited in Mann & Pearce, 1978). Evidence pointing to higher levels of aggression on the part of group members is seen in several studies. For example, Mann found that groups of spectators attending Australian football league matches scored higher on a hostility measure than those attending alone (cited in Mann & Pearce, 1978). Also, not only do groups of young male hockey spectators score higher on anger and physical aggression scales, they also have a history of repeated and recent fighting (e.g., Russell & Arms, 1998). More to the point, men attending in the company of other men rate the likelihood of their escalating a riot higher than do solitary spectators.

Social Cognition and Riotous Behavior

Turning now to studies of cognitive processes, we get a glimpse of how would-be rioters perceive events inside the arena or stadium. Spectators are often sharply divided in their explanations of competitive outcomes on the field of play. A critical factor is whether "their team" won or lost the contest. The impact of fan cognitions was highlighted in research by Mann (1974). He found that fans supporting the losing side in Australian Rules Football matches saw the result as due to dirty play, inept officiating, and bad luck. What is important to note here is that these are *external* attributions for their team's downfall. Internal causes are not offered, such as poor preparation or a lack of skill or effort. Internal attributions are more likely to be offered by fans who support the winning team, such as "we were well prepared," "we displayed superior skill," or "we exerted greater effort." As noted earlier, Mann (1974, 1979) described these external attributions as "sore loser" reactions, suggesting that they underlie at least one type of crowd disturbance, namely, expressive riots.

These self-serving explanations were also seen in a study of Italian football supporters (Zani & Kirchler, 1991). Those involved in violent incidents attributed their misconduct to an external cause, in this case violence in Italian society. External attributions of this sort allow spectators to legitimize their violence. From their perspective, their violence is an understandable response to societal forces over which they have no control. As a consequence, they may see themselves as having little choice but to behave as they do.

A second cognitive bias, the "false consensus effect," may also underlie the hostile outbursts of some spectators. The phenomenon involves the tendency of people "to see their own behavioral choices and judgments as relatively common and appropriate to existing circumstances while viewing alternate responses as uncommon, deviant, or inappropriate" (L. Ross, Greene, & House, 1977, p. 280). Consider an example of how it might work in practice. An acknowledged expert on sexual behavior addresses a large gathering of students informing them of a new male contraceptive. She points out the advantages of this innovative means of birth control as well as its easy (free) availability at the Student Health Center. Following her departure, the men are surveyed and asked whether or not they intend to obtain the new product and whether or not they believe other men will take advantage of the free offer. Were this study to be conducted, a prediction based on the false consensus effect would be confirmed if those men planning to obtain the contraceptive provided higher percentage estimates of other men who will do as they. In short, people generally believe that others in similar circumstances will behave much as they do.

This perceptual bias is evident among hockey spectators. For example, those expressing a strong likelihood of joining a fight that erupts in the stands estimate that a higher percentage of others would do likewise, compared to those who would not get involved. Similarly, those attending because they like to watch players fight believe that a disproportionately larger number of other spectators are attending for the same reason (Russell & Arms, 1995). What does this have to do with crowd disturbances? We believe it sets the stage for some spectators to engage in violence. Those wavering in their decision to join in a fight may be emboldened by their belief that an inflated number of other spectators would tacitly approve of their intervention, and indeed, are poised to follow them into battle.

A Personality Profile of Rioters

Our everyday observations of those around us bring us quickly to the realization that some people are more volatile, more aggressive, and quicker to take offense than others. It is this question of individual differences as it applies to rioters that is at the heart of a recent line of inquiry. Research on the personality of rioters was begun by Meier and his colleagues in 1941. These investigators presented college students with a scenario describing a kidnapping and the later arrest of those involved. Shortly after the arrests a mob began to assemble outside the county jail. Based on a rudimentary analysis, the investigators concluded that those who would join the lynch mob tended to be freshmen, extroverted, low on self-sufficiency, and without ties to organized religions (N. C. Meier, Mennenga, & Stoltz, 1941).

It was not until the 1960s that investigators again formally explored the relationships between individual difference variables and spectators' involvement in riotous behavior. Ransford (1968) conducted interviews with men who had participated in the Los Angeles riots of 1965. It was the combination of three variables that provided the strongest prediction of men most prone to violence: "Negroes who are isolated, who feel powerless, and who voice a strong disaffection because of discrimination appear to be an extremely volatile group" (p. 590).

More recently, a series of field studies were undertaken in Canada, Finland, and the Netherlands using spectators attending ice hockey and, in the Dutch case, a football match (e.g., Mustonen, Arms, & Russell, 1996; Russell, 1995; Russell & Goldstein, 1995). An extensive battery of personality measures was administered to spectators over the course of nine studies. To no one's surprise, men who are angry and physically aggressive are more likely than others to become involved in a riot.

However, the researchers found that other less obvious traits also characterized the rioters. Individuals apt to involve themselves in crowd disorders exhibit strong sensation seeking tendencies (e.g., Dunning et al., 1986; Mustonen et al., 1996). For example, given choices between exciting activities (e.g., surfing and sky diving) and less exciting pastimes (e.g., chess or reading a book), they choose the former. Sensation seekers express a "need for varied, novel, and complex sensations and experiences and the willingness to take physical and social risks for the sake of such experience" (M. Zuckerman, 1979, p. 10). A crowd disturbance, containing as it does an element of risk, would understandably act like a magnet for these people.

Another interesting facet of the personality of would-be rioters is their tendency to act impulsively (Arms & Russell, 1997). Faced with a social situation that calls for action, they jump in without reflecting on the consequences. In the case of a nearby disturbance, they may well join in, giving little thought to the physical harm and legal consequences that might await them. The means by which impulsive individuals become involved in crowd violence was shown in an early experiment (Wheeler & Caggiula, 1966). Impulsive individuals were found to exhibit more aggression following exposure to aggressive models than were individuals lacking impulsive tendencies. Seemingly, they had fewer inhibitions against violating social norms and as a consequence were more easily influenced by peers to act on their deviant inclinations.

A final characteristic that appears related to riotous behavior is psychopathology, or antisocial tendencies (e.g., Russell, 1995). This syndrome involves a lengthy list of symptoms and is not adequately diagnosed by personality inventories alone (see Hare, 1993, for a review). However, inventories do provide a rough approximation, capturing an individual's tendency to be manipulative, unremorseful, and deceitful. The motivation underlying the antisocial behaviors of these individuals is glimpsed in the inventory item, "I often do things just for the hell of it" (Levenson, 1990).

There are additional indicators of which individuals are most likely to be drawn into a crowd disturbance. Most notably, such individuals are males who have a history of fighting. Specifically, they report having been involved in fights with other men during the past year. Interestingly, an even stronger indication of men's readiness to join a riot is how long it has been since they last got into an altercation. In an overarching study that included the cognitive, personality, and social measures described above, this recency measure and attending an event because they "like to watch the fights" emerged as the two strongest predictors of violent behavior (Russell & Arms, 1998).

THOSE WHO WOULD QUELL A SPORT RIOT: THE PEACEMAKERS

If you look closely at scenes of sport riots, you will see that only a handful of people are in fact rioting. Most are milling around watching, apparently not centrally involved in the violence. It has been noted that there are basically five options open to spectators when a disturbance breaks out. They can join the fight, applaud and incite the combatants, leave the facility, or hang back and merely observe the proceedings. Those who exercise the remaining option are in many ways the most interesting of all. They are the peacemakers, the ones who intervene in a disturbance with the intention of verbally and/or physically dissuading those involved.

How numerous are peacemakers in a crowd of spectators? For that matter, how plentiful are rioters and those who egg them on? Several studies have recently attempted to answer these questions. Russell and Mustonen (1998) intercepted men (mean age 30 years) attending a hockey game in Finland and asked them to indicate their response to a hypothetical disturbance in the stands. Two other studies subsequently asked the same question of younger American (Russell & Wann, 1999) and Canadian (Russell & Arms, 1999) university-aged males. As shown in figure 7.1, the evidence suggests that peacemakers easily outnumber those in a sport crowd who are bent on violence (estimates of those likely to join in as combatants range as high as 13 percent; Mustonen et al., 1996). Similar results are noted in other sit-

FIGURE 7.1

Males' responses to a fight erupting nearby

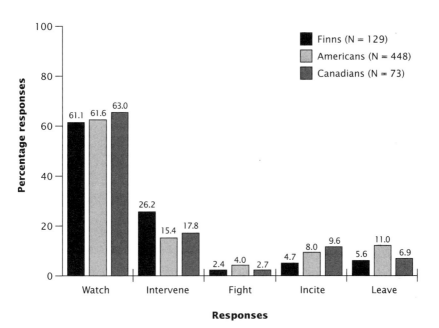

uations where the intervention of a peacemaker is called for. For example, 30 percent of girls will intervene to defend a victim of bullying (Salmivalli, Lagerspetz, Bjorkqvist, Osterman, & Kaukiainen, 1996). Equally impressive is the 26 percent of adult bystanders who would step in to stop a child being physically abused in public (Christy & Voigt, 1994) and the 29 percent of adult bystanders who would attempt to deter a lynch mob (Meier et al., 1941).

A Profile of Peacemakers

As with rioters, we have also begun to piece together a profile of peacemakers. Yes, as you might have guessed, they are of greater stature than rioters, being generally taller and heavier. Regarding their personality traits, peacemakers are less angry, physically aggressive, and more impulsive than those they try to restrain (Russell & Mustonen, 1998). Also in contrast to rioters, peacemakers are low on measures of sensation seeking. Their motives appear to stem from a high regard for the rule of law and the importance of orderliness in a civil society (Russell & Arms, 1999; Russell, Arms, & Mustonen, 1999; Russell & Wann, 1999).

It is something of a truism to note that what people will do in the future is frequently indicated by what they have done in the past. Those who have tried to stop fights in the past, especially those who see their efforts as having been in some ways "successful," are foremost among those most likely to intervene in the future. Finally, high self-esteem is also strongly predictive of spectators who would attempt to stop a fight in progress, a trait also shown to be characteristic of those who intervene on behalf of victims of bullies (Salmivalli et al., 1996).

Peacemakers and rioters do share one commonality, though. They both clearly display the false consensus effect. That is, similar to rioters, peacemakers also believe that a disproportionately large number of other spectators would act as they (i.e., as peacemaker) when a disturbance erupts. Their interventions, although taken precipitously, are bolstered by the belief that others are poised to follow their lead.

Peacemakers as a Source of Crowd Control

If peacemakers are plentiful among the spectators at a sporting event, they represent a large, untapped force for crowd control. As noted elsewhere (Russell & Mustonen, 1998), they are already on the scene, often know the instigators, and are familiar with the events leading up to the hostile outburst. As a result, peacemakers are ideally positioned to control or even snuff out a disturbance before it escalates.

It is unfortunate that spectators with the most honorable of motives and acting on the best of intentions find themselves in physical and legal jeopardy. When security personnel and police eventually arrive on the scene, arrests are likely. And who gets arrested? Sadly for peacemakers, they and the rioters will likely be sharing accommodations in the local lockup, and there is little hope that the judge will be sympathetic to their explanation.

Understandably, police are hard pressed to distinguish peacemakers from rioters in the dangerous and confusing turmoil that surrounds a riot. A recent study makes this very point (Stott & Reicher, 1998). Experienced and highly trained British police officers typically "perceive crowd members as homogeneous in terms of the danger that they represent to public order and to the officer's well-being" (p. 522). That is, police seemingly do not distinguish the various actors and the roles they play in a crowd disturbance. From the officers' perspective "it is impossible to distinguish crowd members from each other behaviourally or physically" (p. 522). A worthy challenge for crowd control specialists then is to devise means of mobilizing peacemakers in a preemptive capacity as an effective complement to existing security arrangements.

SOCCER HOOLIGANISM

Much has been written in recent years about the exploits and violent behaviors of soccer hooligans. Consequently, no discussion of spectator riots would be complete without reference to these persons. The word "hooligan" traces back more than one hundred years to London, home to a hoodlum named Patrick Hooligan (McCallum & O'Brien, 1998c). Often referred to as "the English disease," hooliganism has come to be most closely identified with soccer-crazed English lads and their propensity for antisocial behavior, like lewd chants and songs, pitch invasions, and "no-holds-barred" battles with opposing fans and security personnel. There appear to be no temporal or spatial constraints on hooligan behavior; it can occur before (e.g., at a rest stop along a motorway), during (e.g., at a stadium concession stand), or after a game (e.g., when opposing fans are boarding their buses to return home). At the very least, hooligan behavior is distasteful, disruptive, and dispiriting for those who care about the game and civil order.

While soccer hooliganism is viewed as a decidedly British phenomenon, the behavior can be found all over the world. For example, at the 1996 Soccer World Cup, French officials had to contend not only with overly rabid English fans, but also with German neo-Nazi and French-Tunisian die-hards. Scattered outbreaks of fan violence were everywhere. Riot troops fought pitched battles in Marseille, and newspaper headlines proclaimed "Hooligans Sour World Cup" (1998).

While an analysis of this very complex, multilayered behavior is well beyond the purposes of the chapter, the reader interested in the subject has a plethora of excellent resources from which to choose, depending on whether he or she is interested in Argentinean (Duke & Crolly, 1996), Scottish (Centre for Leisure Research, 1984; Giulianotti, 1995), Italian (Zani & Kirchler, 1991), Israeli (Semyonov & Farbstein, 1989), or English soccer fans (Armstrong, 1998; Buford, 1990; Dunning et al., 1986; Giulianotti, Bonney, & Hepworth, 1994; Kerr, 1994; Marsh, Rosser, & Harre, 1978; Melnick, 1986; Morris, 1981).

Where Are the American Hooligans?

An interesting question regarding hooliganism concerns the apparent lack of the behavior among North American sport spectators. A quick scan of the North American spectator sport scene reveals nothing even remotely resembling soccer hooliganism, European style. To best answer the question "Where are the American hooligans?" the work of Roadburg is instructive (1980). Roadburg identified a number of precipitating factors associated with fan violence and noted their presence or absence at professional soccer games in Britain and the United States. Table 7.3 provides an adaptation of his findings applied to professional team sports in general. It appears that his insightful analysis is just as relevant today as it was two decades ago. It warrants mention that there are exceptions to the descriptions offered under the U.S. sports column. They are presented as "ideal types," that is, the description offered is based on numerous observations but may not correspond to any single empirical instance.

Based on the information presented in table 7.3, we see that the typical British soccer fan's relationship to his favorite team and his actual experience at the sporting event are very different from those of his American counterpart. Personal, psychosocial issues especially related to territoriality, possession, loyalty, and sectarianism, as well as "class cultural conflict over ways of living in English society" (Maguire, 1986) set the British soccer fan apart from the American baseball, hockey, football, or basketball fan. Why no American hooligans? Roadburg's (1980) answer two decades ago is still appropriate today: "Due to differences in the historical development and present day physical and social conditions within which the game is played, soccer in Britain lends itself to crowd violence whereas soccer [basketball, football, hockey, baseball] in North American does not" (p. 265).

TABLE 7.3

Comparison of English Soccer and U.S. Sports

ENGLISH SOCCER	U.S. SPORTS (NBA, NFL, NHL, MLB)
1. Most British stadia were built at the end of the nineteenth century; amenities are very limited.	1. Approximately 84 percent of all stadia and arenas were built since 1960; they are modern, clean, and comfortable.
2. Thousands of fans walk to the soccer grounds because they are centrally located and many fans lack their own transportation; there are many opportunities to engage opposing fans on the way to the game.	2. Spectators drive to games in small groups; they generally do not come in contact with one another until they are at the facility.
3. Strong feelings of solidarity, excitement, and anticipation build on the way to the game.	3. Lead-up activities to the game are not as conducive for generating arousal, excitement, and solidarity.
4. Approximately 35 percent of the spectators are seated, the rest stand on the terraces located at both ends of the pitch; more conducive to developing camaraderie and unity.	4. All spectators are seated with the exception of a few who purchase standing-room-only tickets.
5. Considerable amount of movement among standing fans; changing positions to get a better view of the action.	5. Fixed seats mean fans have no control over their space, hence, little movement among spectators.
6. The game is the culmination of an entire day of preparation, a single event in a sequence of events; anticipation level is very high.	6. The game is typically the only event of the day; when the game is over, the day is over.
7. Plenty of time for drinking before the game because a popular starting time for Saturday soccer games is 3:00 P.M.	7. Less time available for drinking because a popular starting time for NFL and MLB games is 1:00 P.M.

continued on the next page

ENGLISH SOCCER	U.S. SPORTS (NBA, NFL, NHL, MLB)
8. Because of the relatively short distances between home grounds, large numbers of fans follow their favorite teams to rival grounds.	8. Few fans follow their favorite team to away games because of the great distance involved; presence of rival fans is unlikely.
9. Absence of women and small children in the crowd; essentially a male, working-class entertainment; terrace seats are relatively inexpensive.	9. Although middle-class males are usually in the majority, many women and children are present; average cost of admission to NBA, NHL, and NFL games is approximately $45.00 to $48.00.
10. Team identification runs deep because it is often based on religion and/or class; fans are much less likely to change affiliations because they are less geographically mobile.	10. Team identifications not as strong because they are based on proximity; affiliations susceptible to change because of greater geographical mobility.
11. Fans have fewer sports and teams with which to identify; soccer is by far the most popular professional sport; only twenty-two teams in Premier League; interest in favorite team more likely to be intense and passionate.	11. The sport fan has well over a hundred professional teams from which to choose; interest in favorite team not likely to be as intense and passionate.
12. Fan loyalty confined to a single professional soccer team—the local side.	12. Loyalty diffused among several favorite teams within a single geographical region (e.g., the New York Knicks, Rangers, Islanders, Mets, and Yankees).
13. Working class youth have a strong sense of team possession and territoriality; few have substantial possessions so team and local ground are viewed as "mine"; quick to defend threats to their property.	13. No real sense of "possession"; a multimillionaire owns the team and the city owns the facility; enjoy many more "possessions" (e.g., home, car, land, etc.).

continued on the next page

ENGLISH SOCCER	U.S. SPORTS (NBA, NFL, NHL, MLB)
14. Sectarianism often plays a major role in team affiliation; games frequently pit teams representing different religions against one another.	14. No evidence of sectarianism in selection of favorite teams.
15. Limited schedules mean each game takes on greater significance; typically teams play each other only twice, home and away (e.g., the Premier League).	15. Depending on the sport, two teams may play each as many as a dozen times or more each season (e.g., the New York Yankees and Boston Red Sox).
16. Many working class males reaffirm their identities by openly aggressive forms of "macho masculinity"; swearing, posturing, and fighting at soccer games gains them status and prestige from their peers (Dunning et al., 1988).	16. Limited evidence that the middle-class fans who support the professional sports industry have an inordinate need to assert their masculinity at games.

SOME FINAL THOUGHTS

Riots are perhaps the most unfortunate consequence of sport spectating. Almost anyone who has survived such a chaotic and terrifying experience is sure to be haunted by it for quite some time as well as think twice before venturing into another sport stadium or arena. Most certainly, riots give sport fandom a "black eye," tarnishing this leisure pursuit. Consequently, a firm understanding of the factors that precipitate these crowd disturbances is warranted. Similar to comments made at the conclusion of the previous chapter, such an understanding can only be accomplished by combining the efforts of those working from psychological and sociological perspectives. In other words, a complete understanding of sport spectator riots can only be achieved through an analysis of the personalities of the rioters and the social and contextual factors that predispose certain groups toward such behaviors.

However, it is not enough to simply describe and explain sport spectating riots. Although these are highly valuable research goals, in the name of safety and civility, those interested in the sanctity of sport must also strive for the final goal, namely, control. Sport administrators and managers must begin to utilize the information generated by social scientists to control (i.e., reduce and eliminate) the occurrence of riotous behaviors among fans. Thankfully, some organizations have recently begun to do just that. For instance, organizers recently staged a mock riot in Rotterdam in preparation for the 2000 European Soccer Championships. Alas, their efforts were thwarted and they had to end the exercise when real hooligans arrived, armed with stones! It seems that this incident serves notice that the ultimate control of sport spectator riots will require a great deal of effort, patience, and persistence.

PART III

The Functions of Sport Fandom for Individuals and Society

| **THE PSYCHOLOGICAL CONSEQUENCES OF SPORT FANDOM**

Social scientists have debated the virtue of sport fandom and sport spectating for many decades. For instance, consider the thoughts of G. E. Howard, who as early as 1912 stated that sport fandom and spectating were: "A singular example of mental perversion, an absurd and immoral custom tenaciously held fast in mob-mind, has its genesis in the partisan zeal of athletic spectator-crowds. I refer to the practice of organized cheering, known in college argot as 'rooting.' From every aspect it is bad" (G. E. Howard, 1912, p. 46). Granted, this negative perception of sport fandom is almost a century old. However, several contemporary social scientists hold similarly negative views of the pastime (e.g., Beisser, 1967; Lazarsfeld & Merton, 1948; K. V. Meier, 1989), including Reese (1994), who argued that "no human being on this Earth either has to or needs to attend any professional sports events" (p. 12A). In fact, Zillmann et al. (1989) write that there is "nearly a universal condemnation of sport spectatorship" on the part of social scientists (p. 246). Hughes (1987) agreed with this viewpoint and argued that everyone seems to like sport except the social scientists who comment about it.

In contrast to the detractors, some early authors had a more positive impression of sport fandom. For example, in his article titled "The Why of the Fan," Brill (1929, pp. 430, 434) stated:

The average man, for perfectly simple psychological reasons, just will not muster much enthusiasm for the idea of getting out and playing instead of watching the game. On the other hand, through the operation of the psychological laws of identification and catharsis, the thorough-going fan is distinctly benefited mentally, physically, and morally by spectator-participation in his favorite sport. . . . I conclude that the national habit of watching rather than playing games, despite all of the head-shaking of physical culturists and economists, sociologists, and intellectuals, is a salutary habit.

Similarly, in the late 1890s, Roosa (1898) described football crowds as "an orderly, well-dressed, even cultivated and intellectual mass of humanity" (p. 642). Indeed, many other social scientists have viewed sport fandom as a worthwhile pastime (e.g., Guttmann, 1980, 1986; Hemphill, 1995; Lasch, 1989; Melnick, 1993; G. J. Smith, 1988, 1989; G. J. Smith et al., 1981; Zillmann et al., 1989).

So, which of these contrasting views is most accurate? Are sport fans violent beings engaged in a worthless activity that has a negative impact on society and its members? Or, are sport fans similar to non-fans in most respects, with the exception that they have an abiding interest in a worthwhile, socially acceptable pastime? In the next two chapters, we attempt to answer these questions by ascertaining the potential costs and benefits of sport fandom and sport spectating. Our analysis examines the debate from both psychological and sociological perspectives; that is, we review the positive and negative consequences of sport fandom for both the individual fan and for society as a whole. The current chapter focuses on the psychological consequences of fandom, while chapter 9 analyzes its societal consequences.

We begin this chapter with an examination of the criticisms of sport fans and their pastime. Each criticism of sport fandom will be critiqued within a framework of existing data, when possible. We then examine the psychological health of sport fans and the methods they employ to maintain their psychological well-being. The reader is reminded that the current discussion is restricted to the potential psychological costs and benefits of sport fandom and spectating. Possible societal costs and benefits are discussed in the concluding chapter.

PSYCHOLOGICALLY BASED CRITICISMS OF SPORT FANS AND THE PASTIME

Although a number of different psychologically based (i.e., individual-level) criticisms of sport fandom and spectating have been raised, four arguments appear to be most common: (1) fans are lazy, (2) fans are aggressive, (3) sport encourages fans to adopt negative values and maladaptive behaviors, and (4) fans have poor interpersonal relationships. Each of these alleged psychological costs of sport fandom are addressed in this section.

Are Sport Fans Lazy?

One of the most common criticisms of sport fans involves the perception that they are lazy (K. V. Meier, 1989; see Lasch, 1989; G. J. Smith, 1988; Zillmann et al., 1989). Individuals who hold this belief view fans as little more than overweight couch potatoes (these critics are more than happy to point out that approximately three billion potato chips were consumed during the 1998 Super Bowl). However, Guttmann (1980) offered an insightful challenge to this criticism. He suggested, "Although it is unusual to denounce museum-goers for not painting still-lifes and bad form to fault concert audiences for not playing the violin, it is quite common, even for those who are enthusiastic about sports to criticize spectators for athletic inactivity" (p. 275). Likewise, Hemphill (1995) noted that "it would be absurd to insist that all spectators become players, just as it would be absurd to insist that everyone should stop reading books and start writing them, that ballet audiences should take up dancing, that movie goers should make their own films" (p. 52).

The criticism that sport fans are lazy has not held up well to empirical investigation. This conclusion is drawn from two lines of research: (1) the relationship between spectating and athletic participation and (2) the relationship between sport fandom and success/involvement in higher education. With respect to the relationship between spectating and athletic participation, a number of empirical investigations have found that sport fans are as particularly likely to participate in sport as athletes (see chapter 1). If, as claimed, sport fans are lazy, one should find a negative correlation between sport fandom and athletic participation. Clearly, this is not the case.

With respect to higher education, if sport fans are lazy, one would expect them to exhibit poorer academic performances and lower levels of involvement than nonfans. However, once again the data contradict this notion. Instead, research indicates that sport fans perform better in college than nonfans and are more involved with and have better impressions of their university. For example, consider the work of Schurr, Wittig, Ruble, and Henriksen (1993). They compared the six-year college graduation rates and grade point averages (GPAs) of college student fans (i.e., students who had attended one or both of a pair of target games) and nonfans (i.e., students who had not attended either of the two target games). Using the students' high school performance and college entrance scores, the researchers found that the fan (mean predicted college GPA = 2.37) and nonfan groups (mean predicted college GPA = 2.40) were similar in their predicted college performance. However, analysis of actual student performance revealed that the fan group had a higher six-year graduation rate (64 percent versus 48 percent) and higher GPAs (2.55 versus 2.46).

A second study refuting the belief that sport fans are lazy was recently completed by Wann and Robinson (1999; see also Schafer, 1969). These investigators conducted a pair of studies that examined the relationship between university sport team identification and integration into one's university. In the first study, college students completed a questionnaire that assessed their level of identification with the university's men's basketball and football teams. The questionnaire also assessed the students' intentions to graduate from the institution and their involvement in university activities. The data revealed significant correlations between level of identification (for both teams) and graduation intentions and involvement with the university. Participants higher in sport team identification reported greater levels of involvement with the school and were more likely to believe that they would graduate. A second study replicated these effects using students' identification with the university's sport program as a whole.

Are Sport Fans Aggressive?

Another common argument against sport fandom is that sport fans are overly aggressive. When examining the relationship between sport fandom and aggressiveness, it is important to make a distinction between violent actions and violent personalities, that is, the difference between state levels of aggression and trait levels of aggression. State levels of aggression involve temporary shifts in one's aggressive state. Trait levels of aggression, on the other hand, involve an individual's dispositional level of aggression over a long period of time. Thus, trait aggression is similar to a personality variable. The finding that sport fans occasionally report high levels of state aggression and sporadically exhibit violent behaviors does not lead to the conclusion that these individuals also possess high levels of trait aggression (i.e., that fans have an inherently violent disposition). Certainly, the fact that college students have, on occasion, acted violently toward each other and their professors would not lead one to conclude that "college students are aggressive people" (similar arguments can be made for members of the clergy, U.S. postal workers, moviegoers, and a plethora of other groups).

To accurately critique the argument that sport fans are aggressive, one must conduct two separate analyses: one each for the fans' state aggression and trait aggression. With respect to fans' state levels of aggression, on rare occasions sport fans and spectators do become violent (see chapters 5, 6, and 7). But the fact that sport fans occasionally exhibit aggressive behaviors does not make them aggressive individuals per se. Rather, additional research is needed to justify this claim. In one such study (Wann, 1994b; see also Wann, Peterson, Cothran, & Dykes, 1999) college students were asked to indicate their level of identification for their favorite team and to complete the Buss-Durkee Hostility Inventory (Buss & Durkee, 1957). Correlations computed between levels of identification and the various forms of aggression failed to yield any significant relationships.

Wann, Fahl, Erdmann, and Littleton (1999) asked college students to complete a measure assessing their identification with the role of sport fan. The participants were also asked to complete the Buss-Durkee Inventory. Correlational analyses failed to reveal any significant relationships between fandom and trait aggression. Research by Russell and Goldstein (1995; but see also S. Miller, 1976) found similar results. These authors asked Dutch spectators attending a football game and a comparable sample of nonattenders to complete the assault subscale of the Buss-Durkee Inventory. Their results indicated that attenders and those having no interest in sport did not differ in levels of aggressiveness.

A final study on the trait aggression of sport fans was conducted by Koss and Gaines (1993). The researchers examined a number of potential predictors of sexual aggression among college students, including the extent to which they followed sport news and watched televised sport. To test the relationship between the predictor variables and sexual aggression, Koss and Gaines asked several hundred male college students to complete a questionnaire that assessed their self-reported sexual aggression as well as participation in a fraternity or varsity sport team and alcohol consumption. Although some of the predictor variables were positively related to self-reported sexual aggression (including membership in a fraternity, participation in a varsity sport, and alcohol consumption), there was no relationship between sport consumption and sexual aggression.

Based on the research described here, it appears that two conclusions regarding the aggressiveness of sport fans and spectators are warranted. First, fans do exhibit high levels of state aggression, although the occurrence of such outbursts remains quite rare. Second, sport fans neither score unusually high in trait aggression, nor do they differ from nonfans on this personality characteristic. It should be noted that this does not mean that sport fan aggression and personality are unrelated. Rather, as noted previously in this text, there are certain personality traits that may predispose some fans to act violently. In addition, it is possible that the most violent fans possess high levels of trait aggression (i.e., those exhibiting state aggression are also higher in trait aggression). However, even if this were the case, the problem would lie at the individual level of analysis (i.e., the individual's propensity toward violence) rather than with sport fandom because fans and nonfans do not differ in trait aggression.

Does Sport Lead to the Adoption of Negative Values and Maladaptive Behaviors?

Another common criticism of sport fandom is that sport leads to the adoption of negative values and maladaptive behaviors. For instance, it has been argued that sport facilitates beliefs in winning at all costs, strict authoritarianism, and that violence, corruption, cheating, sexism, and racism are acceptable forms of behavior (Brohm, 1978; Cullen, 1974; Hoch, 1972; Schwartz, 1973; Sloan, 1989; G. J. Smith, 1988). This criticism is based on the logic that, because athletes and sport administrators often display questionable values, sport fans may internalize these values. Certainly, it is not difficult to find instances when athletes, coaches, and administrators have exhibited highly questionable behaviors. For instance, the greed and corruption of the International Olympic Committee and academic fraud at the University of Minnesota each received a great deal of media attention in the late 1990s (Patrick, 1999; Swift, 1999). Conversely, others have countered by suggesting that if sport teaches negative values, it must teach positive values as well. For instance, sport may instruct viewers on the importance of fair play and adhering to the rules, teach the value of perseverance and a strong work ethic, and assist in character building (Schafer, 1969; Sloan, 1989; G. J. Smith, 1988; Zillmann et al., 1989).

Which position is correct? To answer this, we must once again consult the available research. Unfortunately, the belief that sport encourages the adoption of negative values is difficult to support or refute empirically because of a scarcity of relevant research. Although it is quite clear that athletes, coaches, and administrators exhibit both positive and negative values and behaviors, it is difficult to document the degree to which these values and behaviors are learned and imitated by fans.

An exception is the work by Wann (1998a, 1998b), who examined the relationship between sport fandom and the use of alcohol and tobacco. Athletes' consumption of alcohol and tobacco are well-known. Sport and tobacco (particularly smokeless tobacco) use have enjoyed a long-term relationship. Professional athletes, and in particular baseball players (D. Snyder & Koenig, 1998), have used and endorsed tobacco products for many decades despite their negative health effects. The relationship between tobacco and sport is also evident at the collegiate level. For instance, the National Intercollegiate Rodeo Association decided to drop Montana State University as the host of the 1999 collegiate rodeo finals when the school refused to allow Copenhagen and Skoal to pass out tobacco samples during the event. With such a clear relationship between sport and tobacco, one might expect fans to report disproportionately high rates of tobacco use. That is, fans (especially younger fans) might imitate the behaviors of their heroes and, consequently, use tobacco products to a larger degree than nonfans do.

There is also a clear connection between sport and alcohol. For instance, most professional and college sports are partially sponsored by alcohol and beer companies. Further, a number of prominent athletes have had well-publicized battles with alcohol addiction and/or DUI arrests. Again, because of the close ties between alcohol and sport, one may expect fans to consume alcohol to a greater extent than nonfans do.

To examine whether or not sport fans tend to adopt the maladaptive behaviors of athletes, Wann examined the relationships between sport fandom and tobacco (1998b) and alcohol consumption (1998a). Sport fandom was operationalized in three ways: a Likert-scale item was used to assess degree of fandom, the amount of money spent on sport consumption, and the amount of time spent on sport consumption. Two forms of tobacco use (cigarettes and smokeless) and two forms of alcohol consumption (beer and liquor) were examined. The results revealed no relationship between sport fandom and the consumption of tobacco or alcohol. Similarly, in their investigation of the behaviors exhibited by sport fans prior to watching sport on television, Wenner and Gantz (1989) found that alcohol consumption was the least common preparatory behavior. Koss and Gaines (1993) also failed to find a positive relationship between sport fandom and the consumption of alcohol and nicotine. Although the aforementioned studies are far from conclusive, they do seriously challenge the position that sport fans adopt the negative and harmful values and behaviors associated with sport. However, it is also clear that additional research is needed before one can fully dismiss this argument against sport fandom.

Do Sport Fans Have Poor Interpersonal Relationships?

In a recent issue of *Reader's Digest* ("Game Plans," 1997), a wife recounted a conversation she had had with her husband as he sat watching football on a Sunday afternoon. When she asked her husband what he intended to do the following evening, he stated that he was planning on watching *Monday Night Football*. When she reminded him that it was their anniversary, he simply said, "Okay, we'll hold hands while we watch the game" (p. 91).

This story speaks to another popular criticism of sport fans, namely, that their interest in sport has a disruptive effect on their interpersonal and intimate relationships. Consistent with this criticism, Quirk (1997) authored a book entitled *Not Now, Honey, I'm Watching the Game*, in which he describes what he calls "sportsaholics." A sportsaholic is someone who has become so addicted to sport that his involvement with the pastime disrupts his relationship with his wife or girlfriend (Quirk believes that the vast majority of sportsaholics are male).

Quirk's book paints a very negative picture of the interpersonal relationships and social skills of sport fans. If one accepts his research data, it appears as though there is strong empirical support for the criticism that sport interferes with fans' close relationships. However, one should be extremely cautious when interpreting Quirk's data because of his research methodology. For instance, rather than relying on standard random sampling techniques, Quirk simply asked individuals to contact him if they felt they were addicted to sport or if they were married to a sportsaholic. Consequently, it is hardly surprising to find that sport fandom had a negative impact on almost everyone described in the book (indeed, Quirk uses the phrase "what to do when sports come between you and your mate" rather than what to do *if* it does). Such a methodology is problematic because it leads to an inaccurate and biased perception of sport fans. Using the same methodology, one could also find individuals whose intimate relationships were disrupted by their significant other's interest in the stock market, world affairs, the opera, and so on. However, this does not mean that all or even most of the individuals with an interest in these activities have problems with their relationships.

Thus, to arrive at a more accurate picture of the impact of sport consumption on interpersonal relationships, one should largely disregard Quirk's survey results and focus instead on quantitative and qualitative data collected in an unbiased fashion. Thankfully, several authors have done just that (incidentally, none of this work was cited or described in Quirk's book). For instance, a detailed examination of the impact of sport fandom on relationship quality was conducted by Roloff and Solomon (1989). They asked college students to list (1) the sports they enjoyed watching on television and attending that their partner did not enjoy watching/attending, (2) the sports their partner enjoyed that they did not enjoy, and (3) the sports they and their partner enjoyed together. The participants were also asked to complete items assessing their satisfaction with their relationship. Roloff and Solomon found greater similarity than conflict in sport interests as 63 percent of the participants listed at least one sport they and their partner enjoyed watching together on television, and 72 percent listed at least one sport they enjoyed attending together. There was no correlation between the number of sports listed that only one partner enjoyed and relationship satisfaction. They concluded that there was "no support for the notion that conflict over sports aversely affects relational quality" (p. 308).

Gantz, Wenner, Carrico, and Knorr (1995a) also published a methodologically sound investigation of the impact of sport fandom on interpersonal relationships (see also Gantz, Wenner, Carrico, & Knorr, 1995b). They conducted several hundred telephone interviews with individuals living in large metropolitan areas. The participants were asked to report their perceptions of how their partner felt about the participants' sport television viewing. The majority of participants (70 percent) believed that their partner thought their television viewing was fine, while an additional 19 percent felt that their partner accepted the behavior. Only 2 percent of the participants believed that their partner was angry or frustrated by their viewing behavior. Similar figures were found when the individuals were asked to evaluate their partner's televised sport viewing behavior. When asked about the role of televised sport in their relationship, 81 percent of the respondents stated that televised sport played a small or very small role. Further, 93 percent of the respondents stated that televised sport had either a positive effect (54 percent) or a neutral effect (39 percent). Similar to the conclusions drawn by Roloff and Solomon (1989), Gantz and his colleagues summarized their findings by stating that "televised sport viewing appears to be a minor and nondisruptive activity in most ongoing relationships" and that "our data appear to refute . . . the much publicized football widow phenomenon" (p. 371).

Based on the research by Roloff and Solomon (1989) and Gantz et al. (1995a, 1995b), claims of sport fandom disrupting interpersonal relationships have been largely overstated. Instead, fandom tends to have either a positive or neutral impact. At this point, the most accurate conclusion suggested by the research is that the vast majority of relationships are not adversely affected by a partner's interest in sport fandom.

PSYCHOLOGICAL WELL-BEING AND SPORT FANDOM

Some social scientists have suggested that there may be psychological benefits associated with sport fandom. For instance, Brill (1929) asked his readers, "Are you a fan? It is altogether to be hoped, for your psychic health and well-being, that you are" (p. 429). Other authors have shared Brill's belief that sport fandom and spectating can enhance psychological well-being and the quality of life (Curtis, Loy, & Karnilowicz, 1986; Giamatti, 1989; S. J. Grove et al., 1982; Iso-Ahola & Hatfield, 1986; G. J. Smith, 1989; G. J. Smith et al., 1981). Here we investigate the psychological well-being of sport fans. We will begin with a review of the empirical research on the subject. We then examine the strategies fans use to maintain their psychological health when it is threatened by their team's poor performance.

The Psychological Health of Sport Fans

It has been argued that identification with sport teams may serve to replace traditional but declining social ties such as religion and the family (e.g., Branscombe & Wann, 1991; Melnick, 1993; Putnam, 1995). Social connections resulting from sport team identification may prove beneficial to one's psychological health by serving as a buffer against depression and alienation while increasing self-esteem (Pan et al., 1997; G. J. Smith, 1988, 1989; Zillmann et al., 1989). Branscombe and Wann (1991) asked college students to complete the Sport Spectator Identification Scale (SSIS) for their university's men's basketball team. The investigators also assessed the participants' self-esteem and depression levels. Correlational analyses revealed a positive correlation between level of identification and self-esteem and a negative correlation between identification and frequency of depression. In a second study, again involving college students, Branscombe and Wann found that higher levels of identification were positively correlated with the frequency of positive emotions and negatively correlated with the frequency of negative emotions and alienation. Similarly, Wann (1994b) demonstrated that team identification was positively correlated with collective self-esteem (i.e., group-level self-esteem; see Crocker & Luhtanen, 1990).

Another examination of the psychological health of sport fans was recently published by Wann, Inman, Ensor, Gates, and Caldwell (1999). These authors used the Profile of Mood States (POMS, J. R. Grove & Prapavessis, 1992; McNair, Lorr, & Droppleman, 1971) to compare the psychological health of highly identified and lowly identified fans. A comparison of the psychological health of fans and nonfans was also undertaken. The POMS assesses seven components of psychological well-being: fatigue, anger, vigor, tension, self-esteem (personal), confusion, and depression. In the first study, Wann and his colleagues asked college students to complete the POMS and the SSIS for their university's men's basketball team. The participants also stated the extent to which they considered themselves a sport fan. The data revealed an "iceberg profile," as highly identified participants exhibited a more healthy psychological profile than lowly identified participants (see figure 8.1). There were no differences in the psychological well-being of fans and nonfans. Thus, Wann et al. found that it was not mere sport fandom that predicted psychological health. Rather, psychological health was related to a high level of team identification with a local university sport team.

In the second study, Wann, Inman, et al. (1999) tested the prediction that high levels of identification with a distant team would not be related to psychological well-being. The hypothesis was based on the argument that the psychological benefits of team identification result from the sense of belongingness associated with ties to nearby teams (Branscombe & Wann, 1991; Eastman & Land, 1997; Melnick, 1993). If a fan is highly identified with a distant team, she will have a difficult time using her identification to gain increased connections with others. Consistent with this logic, the data from the second study revealed no differences in the psychological health of participants high and low in identification with a distant team (see also Wann, Roberts, et al., 1999).

Thus, one can conclude that psychological connections with a geographically close sport team are related to psychological well-being, while simply being a sport fan or being a "displaced" fan with a high level of identification with a distant team is not. However, before concluding this section, several important points warrant mention. First, it should be noted that the previously described research was correlational in nature. Consequently, it is not possible to determine if higher levels of identification cause better psychological health or vice versa. Although the relationship is most likely reciprocal, additional research is needed to pinpoint the exact directionality of the relationship. Second, although highly identified fans

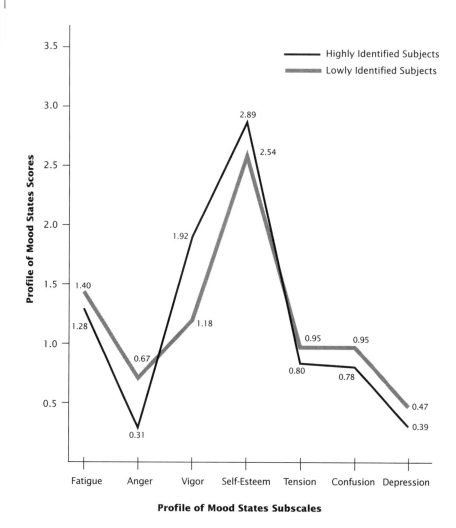

FIGURE 8.1

Profile of Mood States scores for highly and lowly identified sport fans

of a close team do appear to have a healthier psychological profile than lowly identified fans, the magnitude of the effect is quite modest. Although this fact allows one to debate the extent to which highly identified fans are more psychologically healthy than lowly identified fans, one clearly cannot argue that highly identified individuals possess poorer psychological health. And third, because high identification leads to increased social connections, there may be societal benefits associated with sport fandom as well. This possibility is examined in the next chapter.

Highly Identified Fans' Maintenance of Their Psychological Health

The research just described suggests that highly identified sport fans possess a healthy psychological profile. This finding is interesting in light of the fact that highly identified fans often view their team's performances as a reflection of themselves. That is, the team's wins are experienced as personal victories while losses are perceived as personal defeats. Consequently, highly identified fans often experience strong negative reactions to watching their team perform poorly (Bernhardt, Dabbs, Fielden, & Lutter, 1998; Wann et al., 1994). Watching their team lose can make fans feel depressed and negative about life in general (Eastman & Riggs, 1994; Lever, 1969). For instance, consider the following statement of a Pittsburgh Steelers football fan (quoted in Quirk, 1997): "If the Steelers win a big game, I'm happy. I yell, give high-fives and hugs to everyone around me. If they lose and it's a crushing loss I get an empty feeling in my stomach and feel angry and depressed for a month or two" (p. 47).

Several studies have examined the extent to which a team's poor performance negatively affects the psychological state of sport fans. For instance, Schwarz, Strack, Kommer, and Wagner (1987) interviewed German residents immediately prior to and after their country participated in two contests during the 1982 Soccer World Championships. In one game the team was victorious, while the other game ended in a tie (0–0). The results revealed that game outcome had a strong impact on participants' global well-being and satisfaction with work, as both increased after the victory but decreased following the tie.

Schweitzer, Zillmann, Weaver, and Luttrell (1992) examined the impact of a sporting event on expectations of a war erupting between Iraq and the United States and its allies. College student fans of two rival schools were asked to view a football contest between the two universities. After the contest, the participants reported their estimates of the likelihood of war between Iraq and America and, in the event of war, the number of American casualties. The results revealed that supporters of the losing team were more likely to believe that the Gulf War was imminent. In addition, these fans also predicted a greater number of American casualties than did fans of the winning team.

A third study examining the impact of team performance on the mood and outlook of highly identified fans was completed by Hirt and his colleagues (1992). They asked college students to watch a live broadcast of one of their university's men's basketball games. The participants were asked to report the extent to which they felt "depressed" or "elated." They were then given descriptions for a series of additional tasks, including tasks assessing mental skills and social skills. First, the respondents were shown an example of a five-letter anagram in both the scrambled and unscrambled form. They then estimated the number of similar anagrams they could solve in five minutes (this was the "mental skills task"). Next, the respondents were presented with a series of slides depicting attractive members of the opposite sex. Subsequent to viewing each slide, the participants estimated the likelihood that the individual depicted in the slide would accept the participant's invitation to attend a concert (the "social skills task"). The results revealed that the team's performance had a profound effect on the mental state of the participants. Those who watched the team lose were higher in depression (and, consequently, lower in elation) than those who watched the team win. Spectators who witnessed a losing performance also reported significantly lower estimates of their mental skills and social skills (i.e., they estimated completing fewer anagrams and were less likely to believe their invitation to the concert would be accepted). These outcome-based differences in depression/elation and skill estimates were only found among participants with a high level of team identification.

Once again we have a contradiction involving the behaviors and attributes of sport fans. On the one hand, research indicates that highly identified fans (at least those identified with a local team) have a more healthy psychological profile than lowly identified persons. On the other hand, research also suggests that these fans often experience negative affect, a poor outlook on life, and depression subsequent to watching their team lose. To understand this contradiction, one must consider the methods highly identified fans use to handle the threat of their team's poor performance. Research indicates that individuals with high and low levels of identification respond differently to perceived threats (see Dietz-Uhler, 1999, for a review), with those possessing a high level of identification employing a variety of tactics to protect and enhance their psychological health. In the following sections, we examine four such tactics: strategic associations with the team, biased attributions of the team's performance, biased recollections and predictions of the team's performance, and ingroup favoritism toward other fans of the team.

The Maintenance of Psychological Health through Strategic Associations with the Team   One of the most common tactics used by fans to maintain their psychological health is to strategically adjust their associations with their team. These strategies are self-presentational in nature because they involve conscious attempts to alter one's public association with the team (Leary, 1992, 1995). Two of these self-presentational strategies are found in response to success-

---

TABLE 8.2

Self-Presentational Strategies Used by Sport Fans to Enhance or Protect Their Psychological Well-Being

STRATEGY	DESCRIPTION
Strategies following team success	
1. Basking in reflected glory (BIRGing)	Involves increasing one's association with successful teams to enhance psychological health.
2. Cutting off future failure (COFFing)	Involves decreasing one's association with a currently successful team to protect one's future psychological health should the team perform poorly at a later date.
Strategies following team failure	
1. Cutting off reflected failure (CORFing)	Involves decreasing one's association with an unsuccessful team to protect one's psychological health.
2. Blasting	Involves derogating an individual or group to regain one's psychological health.

---

ful team performances and two are used in response to unsuccessful performances. These strategies are briefly described in table 8.2.

Strategies used in response to successful team performance • Researchers have identified two strategic association tactics used following a team's successful performance. One such strategy, termed basking in reflected glory (BIRGing), involves increasing one's association with successful teams to enhance psychological health. The BIRGing phenomenon was first identified in a series of studies conducted by Cialdini and his associates (1976). In one study, these experimenters recorded the proportion of college students who wore clothing that identified their university. As predicted by BIRGing, the proportion of students who wore university-identifying apparel increased following a win by the university's football team. In a second study, Cialdini and his associates telephoned respondents and asked them to describe a recent contest involving their university's football team. Again, consistent with the BIRGing phenomenon, participants were more likely to use the pronoun "we" to describe a recent win and "they" to describe a defeat. A number of other authors have replicated Cialdini's work (Burger, 1985; Cialdini & De Nicholas, 1989; Kimble & Cooper, 1992; McHoul, 1997; Sloan, 1989). Thus, one important method fans use to maintain their psychological health is to increase their relationships with their team when it performs well.

End and his associates (1999) recently suggested that sport fans use BIRGing in a premeditated fashion prior to a season. They argue that fans spontaneously BIRG by supporting teams with a history of successful performances, thereby diffusing damage to their psychological well-being before it occurs. End and his colleagues found strong support for this proactive form of BIRGing in their college student sample. The participants were asked to list their favorite sport teams (in order of first favorite on down) and to report their identification for each team. The researchers then used a variety of indicators of team success (e.g., winning percentage, participation in postseason play) to examine the relationship between team identification and team performance. The results showed that participants were more likely to support successful teams than unsuccessful teams, and that their favorite teams tended to be particularly successful. By engaging in this strategy, these fans were able to increase the likelihood that they could bask in the glory of their team's future successes.

In some situations, supporters of winning teams may be reluctant to bask in their team's victory. For instance, consider a sport fan who is highly identified with his university's men's basketball team, a team that has had a history of poor performances and typically finishes last in its conference. Imagine further that this team somehow manages to gain a home court victory over the conference powerhouse. Research on BIRGing suggests that the fan would increase his association with his team, thereby enhancing his psychological well-being. However, what might happen if the two teams were scheduled to meet a second time at the rival school's home court? Would the fan be as willing to boast about his team's surprising victory? Research by Wann, Hamlet, Wilson, and Hodges (1995) on cutting off future failure (COFFing) suggests that he may not. COFFing is found when individuals resist the urge to bask in a team's success and, instead, distance themselves from the team out of concern the team will be unsuccessful in the future. Although individuals may maintain a private connection to the team, publicly they tend to downplay their association. Thus, COFFing helps one maintain a positive psychological state by avoiding association with a potential loser, even though that team is currently experiencing success.

Strategies used in response to unsuccessful team performance • Researchers have also identified two strategies used in response to a team's poor performance. One such tactic is cutting off reflected failure (CORFing). You may recall that CORFing involves decreasing one's association with an unsuccessful team to protect one's psychological well-being. For instance, C. R. Snyder et al. (1986) had participants complete a cognitive task followed by bogus feedback about their performance (positive, negative, or no feedback). After receiving the feedback, respondents were given the opportunity to take and wear badges identifying their group. In support of the CORFing phenomenon, respondents were reluctant to take and wear team badges after receiving negative feedback. In support of BIRGing, participants were quite willing to take and wear badges following positive feedback.

Thus, following a poor team performance, "fair-weather" fans decrease their association with the team. However, research indicates that this self-presentational strategy may not be available to all fans. Rather, for fans with a high degree of team identification, CORFing is not a viable method for protecting their psychological health (Hirt et al., 1992; Wann, 1993; Wann & Branscombe, 1990a). Because the concept of team follower is such a central component of the self-identity of highly identified fans (see chapter 1), they cannot dissociate themselves from the team when it plays poorly. Rather, these "die-hard" fans stick with the team through thick and thin, maintaining their allegiance even during trying times (e.g., members of the Chicago

Cubs Die-Hard Fan Club). As a consequence of not CORFing follow-ing their team's poor performance, the psychological well-being of highly identified fans is jeopardized. Indeed, as indicated by the lit-erature described earlier in this chapter, highly identified fans may experience depression and an intense negative affective state and adopt a poor outlook on life subsequent to their team's defeat. These problems are less likely among lowly identified fans who simply use CORFing to protect their psychological well-being.

To return to a positive state of psychological well-being, highly identified fans who support a losing team may utilize a second response to poor performance. This strategy, referred to as blasting, involves derogating an individual or group to regain one's psycholog-ical health (Branscombe & Wann, 1994; Cialdini & Richardson, 1980; Wann, 1993). By acting in a hostile manner toward members of the other team, derogating the officials, and so on, highly identified fans can feel they are better than the others, thereby restoring their psy-chological health.

Thus, self-presentational strategies for responding to a team's poor performance vary among fans. Fans with a low level of team identification use CORFing, while highly identified fans use blasting. This does not mean that highly identified fans will always act in a hostile and derogatory manner subsequent to their team's defeat. Rather, blasting is but one alternative available to these persons to help them cope with their team's defeat.

The Maintenance of Psychological Health through Biased Attributions Another common method used by sport fans to help maintain their psychological health involves biased attributions. Previously, we discussed the locus of causality dimension and noted the differences between internal and external attributions. Although this dimension is germane to the current topic, there are other attri-butional dimensions that play a role in the maintenance of psycho-logical health. These dimensions have been termed stability and controllability (Weiner, 1979, 1980).

The stability dimension concerns the extent to which an individ-ual believes that a behavior was due to features that are variant. Stable attributions reflect the belief that a behavior was caused by permanent or near permanent personality traits or environmental features. The belief that an athlete performed well because of his or her ability would be classified as a stable attribution. Unstable attri-butions reflect the belief that a behavior was caused by variable traits or environmental features. The perception that a player performed poorly because he or she had the flu reflects an unstable attribution.

The second dimension, controllability, concerns the extent to which an individual believes that the cause of a behavior was under the voluntary control of the individual. Controllable attributions reflect the belief that the individual had control over the behavior, while uncontrollable attributions reflect the belief that a behavior was beyond the control of the actor. For example, the belief that a player performed poorly because she or he did not exert enough effort would be classified as a controllable attribution (athletes typically have voluntary control over their level of effort). Conversely, the perception that a poor performance was caused by a lack of natural ability would be classified as an uncontrollable attribution (natural ability is a given).

The self-serving bias • Strategic use of the aforementioned attributions may help individuals maintain their psychological well-being. One such strategy, referred to as the self-serving bias (D. T. Miller & Ross, 1975), involves an attributional pattern in which individuals externalize failures (an ego-protecting component) while internalizing successes (an ego-enhancing component). As applied to sport fans and spectators, the self-serving bias implies that fans will often use internal attributions to explain their team's victories (e.g., they won because they are talented, intelligent, put forth a high level of effort, etc.), but assign external causes to account for their team's defeats (e.g., they were defeated because the other team was too skillful, the referees were biased, etc.).

A number of studies have found support for the self-serving bias among sport spectators (Lau, 1984; Lau & Russell, 1980; Mann, 1974; Tanner, Sev'er, & Ungar, 1989; Winkler & Taylor, 1979). Perhaps the most often cited study was conducted by Hastorf and Cantril (1954). In this study, Dartmouth University and Princeton University students were asked to describe a football game involving the two schools. The spectators' descriptions of the game revealed a biased pattern of attributions. For example, while 25 percent of the Dartmouth supporters classified the game as "rough but fair," only 2 percent of the Princeton fans viewed the game in the same way. Instead, the Princeton fans saw the game as "rough and dirty." Further, when asked whether Dartmouth had intentionally injured Princeton's star player, only 10 percent of the Dartmouth supporters agreed with the accusation. Conversely, 55 percent of the Princeton fans reported that the injury was intentional. Hastorf and Cantril concluded that supporters for the two teams observed two different games.

Thus, sport fans may use the self-serving bias to help maintain their psychological well-being by forming internal attributions when the team plays well and external attributions to account for the team's poor play. In this manner, fans can enhance their well-being after victories and protect their well-being after defeats. However, research indicates that the self-serving bias is not found among all spectators. Rather, only those with a high degree of team identification utilize this strategy; lowly identified persons tend not to engage in self-serving attributions (Branscombe, N'gbala, Kobrynowicz, & Wann, 1997; J. R. Grove, Hanrahan, & McInman, 1991; Wann, 1997; Wann & Branscombe, 1993; Wann & Wilson, in press). Because the psychological well-being of highly identified fans is related to their team's performances, these fans have the most to gain through biased beliefs about the causes of an outcome. Indeed, this line of reasoning is consistent with research suggesting that highly identified fans generate a particularly large number of potential explanations for their teams's performance (Wann & Wilson, in press).

Two recent studies highlight the relationship between level of team identification and use of the self-serving bias. In the first study, conducted by Wann and Dolan (1994a), college students met prior to one of two basketball games involving their university's men's team: a home team win and a home team loss. The participants were asked to complete the SSIS and then watched the contest. At the conclusion of the game, the respondents completed a questionnaire assessing their attributions of the game's outcome. The questionnaire assessed both internal attributions (i.e., the outcome was due to the home team or to the home crowd) and external attributions (i.e., the outcome was due to the opponent, the referees, or luck). As expected, spectators formed internal attributions following a win and external attributions after a loss. However, these self-serving attributions were only exhibited by highly identified fans.

Although most work on the self-serving bias has focused on the locus of causality dimension, the stability and controllability dimensions may also be used in a self-serving manner. The self-serving use of these dimensions was demonstrated by Wann and Schrader (in press). College students were asked to attend a win or a loss by their university's men's basketball team. Immediately following the conclusion of the contest, they completed a questionnaire packet that assessed their level of identification with the basketball team and their attributions for the outcome of the game. The attribution items examined the extent to which the participants believed that the outcome was due to internal or external factors (i.e., locus of causality), stable or unstable factors, and controllable or uncontrollable factors. Consistent with past research, the participants reported a self-serving attributional pattern. For instance, when explaining the team's successful performance, the respondents relied on internal, stable, and controllable attributions. However, these self-serving attributions were only reported by highly identified fans. It should also be noted that the self-serving attributions of the highly identified fans were most prevalent after the team was victorious (see also Wann & Dolan, 1994a). This finding suggests that highly identified fans are more likely to use the self-serving bias to enhance rather than protect their self-esteem.

The Maintenance of Psychological Health through Biased Recollections and Predictions of the Team's Performance A third method sport fans employ to help maintain their psychological well-being is to develop biased predictions and recollections of their team's performances (Murrell & Dietz, 1992; Wann, 1996). That is, fans protect and enhance their psychological health by believing that their team performed well in the past and will continue this success in the future. Once again, these biased evaluations of team performance are more common among highly identified fans than those low in team identification (Dietz-Uhler & Murrell, 1999; Hirt et al., 1992; Wann & Branscombe, 1993). For instance, consider the research by Wann and Dolan (1994b). In this study, college students were asked to complete a questionnaire assessing their level of identification with the university's men's basketball team (using the SSIS). The questionnaire also asked the participants to estimate the number of games the team had won during the previous season and the number of games they would win in the current season. Respondents were to base their estimates on a 30-game season. As expected, the highly identified participants were more biased in their estimates than were lowly identified participants. Those high in identification estimated that the team had won 20.4 games during the previous season and that they would win 19.1 games during the current season (both estimates were higher than the actual number of wins, as the team had won 17 games during the previous season and would win 18 during the current season). However, those low in identification estimated the wins to be only 18.7 and 17.6 for the past and current seasons, respectively. Wann (1994a) was able to replicate these biased estimates among highly identified fans of a historically unsuccessful college football team.

The literature cited here is strong evidence that highly identified fans use biased predictions and recollections to help cope with threats to their psychological well-being. However, to fully understand the relationship between performance estimates, team identification, and psychological health, one must also consider the length of time since the team's last contest. The importance of this variable was highlighted in the aforementioned research by Hirt et al. (1992; see also Hirt & Ryalls, 1994). Recall that in this project college students watched one of their school's men's basketball games and then completed a questionnaire assessing their psychological health (e.g., depression, estimates of social skills, etc.). Subsequent to watching the contest, the participants were also asked to estimate the team's future performances. The data revealed that the estimates of highly identified fans were strongly influenced by the team's performance in the game they had just witnessed. The outcome had no effect on the estimates of lowly identified fans. When the team was victorious, highly identified respondents were quite positive about the team's future. Conversely, and in opposition to the data just described (e.g., Wann, 1994a; Wann & Dolan, 1994b), these persons were quite negative about their team's future subsequent to watching them lose. This finding reflects the depression and negative affect highly identified fans experience when their team performs poorly. However, after a certain amount of time has passed (the exact amount of time is not currently known), they begin to adjust their estimates in a manner that is biased in favor of their team. In this way, they get beyond the team's poor performance and return to a positive state of psychological health.

The Maintenance of Psychological Health through Ingroup Favoritism A final method fans utilize to help maintain their psychological health is through biased perceptions of supporters of their team and rival teams. Fans may be able to deflect some of the negative impact of their team's losses by believing that "our team may have lost the game, but our fans are still better than your fans." Certainly, this "ingroup favoritism effect" has been well-documented in general social psychology (e.g., Brewer, 1979; Gerald & Hoyt, 1974; J. W. Howard & Rothbart, 1980). With respect to research on sport fans, a number of authors have found that fans possess a more favorable impression of fellow fans than rival fans (Franco & Maass, 1996; Sabo, Jansen, Tate, Duncan, & Leggett, 1996). In fact, Sage (1996) argues that professional sport teams in the United States often attempt to capitalize on the ingroup bias by marketing their team as "patriotic." For instance, team logos often involve nationalistic colors (i.e., red, white, and blue). Sage notes that this marketing strategy is rather hypocritical in light of the fact that the merchandise used to present these "patriotic" logos is often manufactured in foreign countries!

Research suggests that highly identified fans are especially likely to possess a biased perception of fellow fans (Wann & Branscombe, 1993, 1995a, 1995b; Wann & Dolan, 1994c; but see also Branscombe, Wann, Noel, & Coleman, 1993). Wann and Branscombe (1995a) placed college students into one of two groups based on their responses to the SSIS: highly identified with the university's men's basketball team or lowly identified with the team. The participants were asked to list the positive, negative, and neutral traits, characteristics, and attributes they believed best described fellow fans of the team. The respondents were asked to generate a similar list they believed to be descriptive of fans of a rival team. The findings revealed a rather complex pattern of results. The most favorable descriptions (i.e., the largest percentage of positive traits) were provided by highly identified participants describing fellow fans. The highly identified participants also reported a significantly higher percentage of negative traits when asked to describe the outgroup. This trend was absent among lowly identified fans.

SOME FINAL THOUGHTS

In this chapter, we examined the impact of sport fandom on the psychological well-being of the individual fan. We began by critiquing four microlevel criticisms of sport fans and spectators (i.e., they are lazy, overly aggressive, adopt negative values and maladaptive behaviors, and have poor interpersonal relationships). Using empirical analyses to evaluate the merits of these hypothesized psychological costs of sport fandom, the following conclusions appear warranted. First, each criticism of sport fandom can probably be supported anecdotally. For instance, some fans do consume large amounts of alcohol (W. O. Johnson, 1988; Stainback, 1997; Wolfe, Martinez, & Scott, 1998). Similarly, high levels of sport involvement have led to marital problems for some fans (Quirk, 1997; G. J. Smith et al., 1981). Further, some fans do become violent when watching their favorite team compete. However, the existing data indicate that these problems are the exception rather than the rule—most fans do not have a drinking problem, marital strife, or violent tendencies. Thus, it appears that the pastime is a harmless leisure activity.

We also investigated the possibility that, rather than having a detrimental effect on a fan's psychological health, sport fandom (or, more specifically, identification with a local team) actually facilitates one's psychological well-being. Indeed, recent evidence suggests that strong attachments to a geographically close sport team is positively (albeit modestly) related to a number of indexes of psychological stability, including personal and collective self-esteem, affective expression, alienation, and vigor. In light of the fact that sport fans are often bitterly disappointed by their favorite team's poor performance, the finding that highly allegiant fans generally possess a sound psychological makeup may well be the most compelling paradox in all of sport spectating. It would seem more logical for these persons to possess an unhealthy and perhaps fragile psychological profile. Clearly then, highly identified fans must find ways to protect and even enhance their psychological health in the face of constant threats to a highly valued and central component of their self and their social identity. Although we addressed a number of possible methods employed to maintain a state of psychological well-being, more research is needed before we arrive at a complete understanding of the mechanisms through which highly identified sport fans ensure that their spectating activity is personally beneficial.

| Chapter Nine | # THE SOCIETAL CONSEQUENCES OF SPORT FANDOM |

In the previous chapter our examination of the utility of sport fandom and spectating focused on the individual level of analysis. That is, our concern was with the impact and meaning of fandom for the psychological well-being and mental health of sport fans—the extent to which this is a harmful or beneficial activity for the participant. In the current chapter the focus of the analysis moves from the individual participant to society at large. For students of sport fanship there is perhaps no more compelling nor challenging question than, "What is the relationship between sport fandom and society?" The answer to this question is necessary for a fuller understanding of sport fandom and spectating. Indeed, pursuit of this answer forces us to address several related questions, including: Which societal needs, if any, are satisfied by sport fandom, and would society be any different if we were unable to root for our favorite athletes and teams? Stevenson (1974) was most persuasive in stating the importance of the first question when he observed, "The obvious enormity and the manifest importance of sport in society compels us to ask the question, 'Why?' Why has sport as an element of our society, of our culture, become so pervasive and so visibly central?" (p. 8).

Similar to the issues surrounding the psychological impacts of sport fandom, differences abound with respect to the societal values of sport fandom. Some critics are perfectly comfortable assigning sport fandom to the "toy department of human affairs," regarding it as nothing more than the "pots and pans" of everyday life. Others see sport fandom as a highly valuable activity, one that contributes to society in a multitude of ways. In attempting to address the debate on the societal values of sport fandom, the student of sport spectating has a number of theoretical perspectives available to help guide the way, each with its own particular strengths, weaknesses, and biases. For example, structural-functionalism argues that sport fandom is highly beneficial to society. On the other hand, conflict theory and feminist theory view sport fandom and spectating in much more negative terms. In this chapter, we describe and critique several of these theories in an attempt to better understand the impact of sport on society at large. We begin with structural-functionalism and the argument that sport serves society well. We will then discuss several critiques of the functionalist point of view and conclude with several alternative explanations of the spectator sport-society nexus.

THE STRUCTURAL-FUNCTIONALIST PERSPECTIVE

The functionalist perspective takes the position that for any social institution to exist, it must contribute to the maintenance or survival of the society. If we accept, for argument's sake, that spectator sports satisfy the definition of an institution (see Goodger & Goodger, 1989; Zurcher & Meadow, 1967), then the functionalist challenge is to discover which specific societal objectives sport serves.

Typical of functionalist thinking is the specifying of several "prerequisites" or "imperatives" that every society must successfully address if it wishes to remain a viable entity (Aberle, Cohen, Davis, Levy, & Sutton, 1950; Parsons, 1951; Stevenson, 1974). In the sections that follow, several functions of sport fandom are identified, discussed, and critiqued. Both anecdotal and empirical evidence is cited where available and relevant. A brief description of each function can be found in table 9.1.

Sport Fandom and Affective Expression

The expression of affect is part and parcel of being human. To smile, to laugh, to dream, to experience eustress, and to be joyful is to be alive. While society must guard against the unrestricted expression of some affects lest the social order be seriously disrupted (e.g., anger and rage), other affects need to be encouraged and produced (e.g., excitement and joy). For the functionalist, society must provide its members with structures that produce positive affect in order to survive. Perhaps the ancient Roman satirist Juvenal said it best when he observed, "Duas tantum res anxius optat, panem et circenses," meaning, "Two things only the people anxiously desire—bread and cir-

TABLE 9.1

Potential "Functional Imperatives" Associated with Sport Fandom and Spectating

Spectator sports may:
1. Allow for emotional expression.
2. Provide quality entertainment.
3. Enhance communication.
4. Facilitate national identity.
5. Produce social capital.
6. Contribute to the socialization process.
7. Enhance integration at all levels.
8. Assist in social control.
9. Serve as a form of religion.

cuses" (cited in Preston, 1978, p. 207). In spectator sports we have an institutional structure with a Barnumesque quality, where marching bands, exploding scoreboards, deafening music, cheerleaders, mascots, and colorful pageantry overwhelm the senses. More importantly, sporting events provide an opportunity for spectators and fans to experience a range of euphoric and dysphoric emotions (Ferguson, 1981). Although the affective payoffs are directly mediated by the uncertainty of the outcome, the stakes involved, and the presence or absence of heroic performances (Coakley, 1994), there is always the possibility that each and every contest will provide the spectator with an intense emotional workout. Those events that score exceptionally high on the emotional workout scale (e.g., "buzzer-beaters" and "barnburners") are likely to be remembered for a lifetime.

The act of survival, whether it be at the individual or societal level, depends "not only on living and working, struggling and persevering, but also joking, laughing, cheering and celebrating" (Marcotte, 1989, p. 15A). Sporting events promise all of this and more. By serving as a catalyst for the expression of affect, they help combat the pernicious effects of apathy and the cessation of motivation, a condition that can prove fatal to any social system.

Sport Fandom as Performance-Entertainment

The affective expression engendered by observing sporting events, whether it be in person or watching on television, cannot be fully understood or appreciated without recognizing how it interfaces with spectator behavior. Far from being a passive onlooker, spectators frequently become physically involved in the action on the field, court, or pitch. Even for television sport viewers, their ritualized actions reflect their vicarious participation in the event (Eastman & Riggs, 1994). The habits, traditions, and superstitions of sport spectators suggest that they are anything but passive. Rather, they become active participants, altering and constructing their own sport experiences.

Lancaster (1997) observed that the increasingly active role observed among sport spectators is reflective of a major redefinition taking place in popular culture today as seen in the communal relationships now found between spectators and performers. That is, the demarcation line between who is a performer and who is an audience member is becoming increasingly blurred. U.S. popular culture provides us with a host of "performance-entertainment" examples including movie theme parks, karaoke, television talk shows, participatory theater, and role playing games. According to Lancaster, "these kinds of events demand active participation by spectators, which blur the boundary between the performers' space and the spectators' space, as they create the performance event together" (p. 77).

By transforming sport spectators into performers (e.g., doing the wave, responding to the noise meter, participating in half-time promotions, etc.), the sporting event becomes for the fan a framed arena for his or her physical, social, and emotional involvement. Thus, spectator sports produce necessary and important affects as well as encourage considerable social interaction. Moreover, they offer a beckoning stage to those fans daring enough to seize its opportunities. As Gitlin observed, "A lot of people feel they don't really exist unless they've gone public. . . . A lot of people feel diminished if they haven't been anointed or discovered by the spotlight" (quoted in "Fan Behavior," 1993). Judged from a functionalist perspective, sport fandom can provide an antidote to feelings of apathy, marginalization, and neglect—serious threats to a society's well-being.

Sport Fandom and Communication

No society, however simple, can exist without shared, learned, symbolic modes of communication (Aberle et al., 1950). Communication is absolutely essential because it provides the basis for all social interaction, helps maintain a society's common-value structure, and is indispensable to the socialization and role differentiation processes. To have effective communication in a complex, postmodern society, three essential elements are necessary: (1) language, (2) ways of communicating, and (3) communication channels. Language involves a system of shared, learned sound patterns having standardized meanings. Popular ways of communicating include the spoken, written, and signed word. Communication channels refer to the institutional structures by which information, ideas, meanings, experiences, and traditions are broadly disseminated, such as print and broadcast media, cinema, theater, the Internet, and so forth.

Sport fandom contributes to the communication process in two important ways. First, the language of sport finds its way into almost every aspect of life, be it the military, business, politics, advertising, or even sexual relations (Hardaway, 1976; Segrave, 1994). For example, Palmatier and Ray's (1989) *Sports Talk: A Dictionary of Sports Metaphors* lists a total of 1,700 popular words and expressions in American English derived from terms directly associated with sports, games, and recreation. Many of these terms have become an integral part of our language. Baseball, in particular, provides many popular metaphors. Several such metaphors are listed in table 9.2. As Segrave (1994) pointed out, metaphors are very powerful and important linguistic conventions because they help "explain difficult, complex, and even sensitive and mysterious concepts in familiar images" (p. 99). And, as Lakoff and Johnson (1980) observed, "metaphors structure how we perceive, how we think, and what we do" (p. 1).

Thus, the lexicon of spectator sports makes an important contribution to the communication process. Through the sport metaphor we are able to share our ideas, desires, meanings, and experiences using shared, learned sound patterns ("words") easily understood by others. When a friend asks, "Can you pinch hit for me tonight?" or when your boss instructs you to, "Take the ball and run with it," we know what these individuals mean and expect.

A second way sport fandom contributes to the communication process is by providing a topic for conversation. Although much of everyday conversation focuses on people, sport is also a popular topic, especially among those who follow sport on a regular basis. Because sport talk functions so well as small talk, it has become a very important vehicle for communication in modern society. Sport talk as small talk is a lot more important than people think. Not only does it make individuals feel more comfortable in social situations but it also helps them establish new relationships as well as maintain old ones.

Sport talk takes on even greater importance as societies become increasingly more complex and techno-specialized. As Shenk (1997) notes, we work and live most of our lives in rarefied niche environ-

TABLE 9.2

Metaphors in Contemporary Language Directly Traceable to Baseball

1. He was born with two strikes against him.
2. He couldn't get to first base with that girl.
3. He sure threw me a curve that time.
4. I'll take a rain check on it.
5. He went to bat for me.
6. I liked him right off the bat.
7. He was way out in left field on that one.
8. He's a foul ball.
9. I think you're way off base on that.
10. It was a smash hit.
11. Let's take a seventh-inning stretch.
12. I hope you touch all the bases on this report.
13. Could you pinch hit for me?
14. He doesn't even know who's on first base.
15. I just call 'em like I see 'em.
16. He's only a bush-leaguer.
17. Major league all the way.
18. He was safe by a mile.
19. He has a lot on the ball.
20. No game's over until the last man's out.

Note: Adapted from Spink (1978).

ments. As professions and personal interests become increasingly more specialized, modern society runs the risk of greater and greater fragmentation and factionalization. Sport fandom provides society with a common language ("Sportugese") that many know and understand (Tannenbaum & Noah, 1959; Wann et al., 1997). In those societies that continue to grow more technical and fragmented, sport talk allows members to more comfortably engage both friend and stranger alike. Perhaps this explains the immense popularity of sport talk radio shows (Goldberg, 1998; Mariscal, 1999).

Sport Fandom and National Identity

Because sport allows people to represent themselves or their social groups to others, national sports carry particular psychological and societal significance, even where there is considerable social and cultural heterogeneity (Goodger & Goodger, 1989). The following examples come immediately to mind: baseball in the Dominican Republic, rugby in New Zealand, bull fighting in Mexico, ice hockey in Canada, basketball in the Philippines, skiing in Norway, golf in Scotland, ice skating in the Netherlands, and sumo wrestling in Japan. Goodger and Goodger (see also Zurcher & Meadow, 1967) have argued that national sports operate as social institutions, representing in symbolic form the social identity, nature, and relations of the collective in which they are generated and sustained.

Consider the sport of professional football in the United States. Arguably the most popular of all American spectator sports, the game commands the attention of millions of spectators throughout its sixteen-game season, the playoffs, and the most anticipated event on the sport calendar, the Super Bowl. M. Real's (1975) analysis provides an understanding of the widespread, emotional appeal of this sport and the manner in which it symbolizes American cultural values and ideology. He argues that as mythic spectacle, the Super Bowl strengthens and develops American social structures while at the same time reflecting the dominant tendencies of the culture (i.e., sport serves as a microcosm). Real identified twelve elements embedded in professional football that help sustain American social institutions and lifestyles. These elements are listed in table 9.3. Real concludes that

---

TABLE 9.3

Elements of Professional Football Sustaining American Social Institutions and Lifestyles

1. Personal identification through collective representation.
2. Heroic archetypes.
3. Collective participation with others.
4. Suspension of profane, everyday, secular time and space markers.
5. Veneration of material well-being.
6. Winning territory (property) through competition.
7. Recognition of the limited time for success.
8. Male-dominated labor.
9. Modern corporate management.
10. Physical action.
11. Attractiveness of "packaging."
12. Spectacle.

Note: Adapted from M. Real (1975).

---

the game of professional football resonates strongly with American spectators because it elaborates upon society's most elemental themes (e.g., heroic archetypes, material well-being, and corporate management), speaking to them in the terms of cultural myths that they clearly understand and embrace.

Such is also the case with the NCAA men's college basketball championships, otherwise known in the United States as March Madness. In trying to account for the extraordinary attention and excitement this sixty-four-team tournament engenders, Price (1991) suggested that the competition appeals to the American Dream—it's democratic (e.g., all teams start on equal footing), it appeals to the American underdog mentality, it's monotheistic (i.e., the idea of a single champion is attractive), and it celebrates capitalist competition (i.e., survival of the fittest).

The importance of national sports as collective representations is accentuated when great excitement surrounds a particular contest or event, as is the case with international competition. According to Goodger and Goodger (1989), excitement and collective representation are intrinsically related. Excitement intensifies the symbolic significance of a national sport, while the latter provides a venue for the shared experience of heightened emotionality and tension excitement (i.e., eustress). Thus, national spectator sports have the potential to satisfy two societal imperatives, namely, they strengthen the social fabric and assist in the production of positive affect.

While a strong case can be made for the close link between national sports and collective representation, Bairner (1996) made a very important point when he observed that this association is by no means straightforward. Rather, the exact nature of the relationship depends on the role of nationalism in each societal context. For example, in Scotland and the Republic of Ireland, because of the politics of nationalism, it has proved impossible to "construct a cohesive sportive nationalism" (p. 33). On the other hand, "in Sweden, where national identity is less of a political issue, the development of an inclusive sportive nationalism has been relatively smooth" (p. 332). While some national sports contribute to collective representation and nationalism, others accentuate group differences making it difficult to construct coherent and unified national identities (Bairner, 1996).

Attacks Against National Sport Identities An interesting dilemma is posed when a society's national sport comes under attack. Canadian ice hockey provides such an example. Consider that in 1969 approximately 99 percent of the players in the NHL were Canadian.

Today only 56 percent of the players are Canadian, the lowest national representation in league history; the rest are evenly divided between Americans and Europeans (Allen, 1999). The twenty-six-team league now has just six teams located in Canada. The adverse consequences of these trends were noted by Canadian radio host Roy Green when he observed, "Hockey is our national glue. It defines Canada and Canadians. We have so few people in such a large land. We are left out of the international political process. . . . But hockey holds us together" (quoted in Brady, 1998). Similarly, former Hall of Fame goalie Ken Dryden observed, "It is important for the Canadian people, for dreams and bonds and common stories for new genera- tions, that Canadian teams win the Stanley Cup—at least some of the time" (quoted in Crary, 1998). Thus, a country's loss of its national sport may also result in the loss of its national identity.

Sport Fandom and Social Capital

One of the most controversial and hotly debated sociological essays published in recent years was Putnam's (1995) "Bowling Alone: America's Declining Social Capital." Putnam offers the provocative thesis that social capital in American society (i.e., features of social organization such as networks, norms, and social trust that facilitate coordination and cooperation for mutual profit) has declined over the past several decades. To bolster his argument, Putnam points to the fact that the average number of associational memberships (e.g., church-related groups, labor unions, fraternal-veteran organizations, and school-service groups) has fallen about 25 percent over the last twenty-five years (see chapter 8 for a similar argument). Putnam notes that, to make matters worst, the two most fundamental forms of social capital—the family and the neighborhood—no longer pro- vide the rich social interaction and bonding opportunities they once did. These disturbing trends in social connectedness and civic engagement, and their subsequent toll on social trust, cooperation, and communication, are blamed on several factors, including the movement of women into the labor force, geographical mobility, and technology. Putnam suggests that the latter has been responsible for "privatizing" or "individualizing" our use of leisure time and thus dis- rupting many opportunities for "social-capital formation" (p. 75). Although Putnam dismisses secondary and tertiary networks and associations (e.g., sport fandom) as effective venues for social capital formation, closer inspection of these "social worlds" (Unruh, 1983), "public scenes" (Irwin, 1977), and "third places" (Oldenburg & Brissett, 1982) reveals perhaps a hasty judgment on his part.

Although Putnam (1995) concedes that two fans may root for the same team, he argues that "they are unaware of each other's existence. Their ties, in short, are to common symbols, common leaders, and perhaps common ideals, but not to one another" (p. 71). But is that really the case? We suspect the two die-hard, season-ticket holding, New York Jets football fans seated in Section 111, Row C, seats 7 and 8 would strongly disagree! The fact is, traditional forms of sociability in American life have been changing for some time "from primary associations to secondary ones, from the more intimate to the less intimate, from the realm of stronger affect to weaker affect, and from less monetized forms of social interaction to more monetized ones" (Melnick, 1993, p. 48). What Americans (and similar cultures) have been witnessing is a gradual shift in locale for the satisfaction of their social needs. No longer do traditional institutions such as the family, workplace, and neighborhood fully satisfy our need for social interaction and engagement. Instead, Americans now turn to less intimate, more public locales for association and to connect with one another (e.g., singles bars, personal columns in newspapers and magazines, dating services, cruises, and the Internet). Does this mean that American social capital is declining? Maybe, maybe not. Rather than a decline in social capital, what we appear to be witnessing today is a new stage in its development; that is, it has taken on a different form.

In the sport stadium and sport arena, we have a public place where the play form of association is freely and safely available. What Putnam (1995) fails to fully appreciate is that sport locales are venues alive with communal, Gemeinschaft possibilities. To say that two NFL season-ticket holders seated thigh-to-thigh for eight home games are "unaware of each other's existence" (Putnam, 1995, p. 71), that they share no personal ties, is to underappreciate the quasi-intimacy and social connectedness that sport fans can and do share.

It would appear that the social forces of urbanization, individualism, interpersonal competition, technology, and geographical mobility have conspired to deny Americans their traditional forms of sociability (Denney, 1979). As a result, they are forced to satisfy their need for social interaction and civic engagement in less personal, less intimate, less private ways. This does not necessarily mean that a decline in American social capital is under way. The counterargument is offered that a tertiary social network provided by something like sport fandom satisfies an important social imperative in postmodern society by serving as a unique urban structure whereby strangers assemble not only to be entertained but to "engage the other" in meaningful dialogue.

Sport Fandom and Socialization

Perhaps no functional imperative is more important to a society's survival than successfully teaching its "structure of action" to each generation of new members, as well as individuals of any age who seek new social roles or societal intergration. Parsons, the father of structural functionalism, referred to this imperative as "pattern maintenance." Each individual must be taught the appropriate modes for dealing with everyday life circumstances and situations. This socialization process involves teaching each of the following: (1) shared cognitive orientations, (2) articulated sets of goals, and (3) the prescription of means for attaining those socially formulated goals (Aberle et al., 1950). It is absolutely essential for the members of any society to become effectively integrated into its core belief system and acquire the appropriate behavioral patterns (Stevenson, 1974).

For the current discussion, we are interested in what role, if any, spectator sports play in teaching members of a society the "structure of action" they should follow to successfully navigate their way through the vicissitudes of everyday living. That is, we are concerned here with the extent to which sport fandom contributes to the adoption of shared cognitions, articulated goals, and opportunities for receiving those goals. Edwards (1973) was of the opinion that sport effectively performs this socializing function. He observed that: "sport is a social institution which has primary functions in disseminating and reinforcing the values regulating behavior and goal attainment and determining acceptable solutions to problems in the secular spheres of life" (p. 90). Directing his attention specifically to sport fans, Edwards also noted, "As an institution having primarily socialization and value maintenance functions, sport affords the fan an opportunity to reaffirm the established values and beliefs defining acceptable means and solutions to central problems in the secular realm of everyday societal life" (p. 243).

Shared Cognitive Orientations Perhaps the most critical cognitions taught by the socialization process are cultural values. As discussed in chapter 8, a number of authors have suggested that following spectator sports may lead to adopting the value systems of favorite athletes (see Sloan, 1989; G. J. Smith, 1988). However, sport fandom may also encourage consumers to internalize those values that society most tenaciously embraces. This distinction between the adoption of an athlete's personal value system and socialization into the value complex of the larger society is admittedly subtle, but very important just the same. For example, consider a young, North American spectator who, because his favorite player has exhibited poor sportspersonhip and a sexist attitude, may be tempted to adopt these values for himself. Certainly, these are not the values encouraged by society at large. Thus, in addition to teaching these athlete-specific values, sport spectating may also teach the young fan prosocial values that constitute the sport ethos and mirror the American creed.

Indeed, although the hard-core realities of sport sometimes suggest otherwise, sport has the potential to model several values regarded as crucial to a democratic and humane society, such as legitimization of authority, honesty, justice, equality, respect for the rule of law, respect for the rights of others, cooperation, competition, and fair play, to name just a few. Clearly, sport is far from a perfect social institution, and exceptions to each of these values can be cited (e.g., when former Baltimore Orioles second baseman Roberto Alomar spit in the face of an umpire over a disputed call). However imperfect, sport typically offers spectators and fans demonstrable evidence of the ideological elements that constitute the dominant value structure in American society (Loy, 1978). In fact, even those watching sport on television can access the important value lessons sport teaches. For instance, Bailey and Sage (1988) conducted a content analysis of the sportscasters' commentary during a Super Bowl football game and found that the dominant values communicated were the prototypical American values of individualism and achievement. They concluded that "the salience of the sportscasters' specific comments provides a vehicle for value transmission" (p. 126).

Shared and Articulated Sets of Goals With respect to shared and articulated sets of goals, Loy (1978) makes the case that the most compelling lesson sport teaches both the participant and spectator alike is the importance of success. For example, the cultural system of American sport contributes to the propagation of a success ideology by extolling the value of high aspiration (e.g., "Show me a good loser, and I'll show you a loser") and stigmatizing athletes as lazy and worthless if they do not accept the goal of high aspiration with unquestioned commitment (e.g., "He/she just doesn't want it badly enough"). In many instances, it is the drive to succeed and the material well-being it brings that American spectator sports most dramatically symbolize for those sitting in the stands rooting for their favorite teams and players (e.g., Stiles, Gibbons, Sebben, & Wiley, 1999).

Other goals reflected on the field of play that are likely to have a lasting impression on spectators include striving to improve one's skills and abilities, performing up to one's full potential, and always giving a maximum effort. These are the goals embraced by football, basketball, ice hockey, and baseball players, to be sure, but they are also the goal expectations many sport fans encounter every day in the workplace.

Prescription of Means for Attaining the Goals   Having identified success as an important goal to be aggressively pursued within the American sociocultural context, let us now turn our attention to the prescription of means for attaining it. Here, the playing field provides the sport spectator with several unambiguous messages, most prominent of which is the importance of hard work (e.g., "Success is 90 percent perspiration, 10 percent inspiration"). The lesson couldn't be more clear—work hard and you will succeed! For example, when Americans are asked what they consider the most effective ways to get rich, working hard typically heads the list. When one compares standard workloads and minimum vacation time cross-culturally, the United States finishes relatively high on both counts among industrialized nations. For example, the modal U.S. workweek of 40 hours with 2 weeks vacation time per year clearly exceeds Belgium's 38 hours and 4 weeks, Denmark's 37 hours and 5 weeks, and Germany's 35 hours and 6 weeks ("Work and Play," 1996).

Not only does sport subliminally manipulate the spectator to associate hard work with success, but several other approved means for achieving success are transmitted as well. For example, other behaviors that are likely to be modeled by one's favorite players include acts of courage, self-discipline, self-control, confidence, altruism, confidence, competitiveness, ambition, sacrifice, and loyalty.

A Final Comment on Sport Fandom as an Agent of Socialization   One would have to be incredibly naive to believe that all is right with sport today. Even someone who doesn't follow sport closely is probably aware of several serious problems that need to be addressed (e.g., player violence, gender inequity, racial discrimination, poor sportspersonship). Interestingly, although the general public still endorses the belief that sport contributes to the well-being of society, it is beginning to question whether sport can alleviate social problems, help participants become good citizens, or promote fair play (Martin & Dodder, 1993). Nonetheless, there is still reason to believe (to hope?) that by mirroring and reinforcing dominant cultural values, by articulating a set of desired goals, and by identifying the appropriate means for achieving them, spectator sports can and do support the important work of the family, school, and church in teaching society's "structure of action."

Sport Fandom and Integration

Commonly referred to as unification, solidarity, or social cohesion, integration of the collectivity presents every society with a formidable challenge, namely, how to generate common interests, loyalties, and enthusiasms among its members. Lever (1983) suggests that integration is a critically important social imperative because it serves as a counterpoint to the potentially disruptive conflicts, cleavages, and antagonistic factions that are the inevitable consequences of scarce means, unfulfilled expectations, and imperfections in the socialization process.

In spectator sports we have a popular form of mass entertainment with the power to create order amid diversity. According to Lever (1983), the most important and universal social consequence of spectator sports is their ability to help complex modern societies adhere. She argues that the integrative function of spectator sports is due in no small measure to their ability to establish and promote connections between and among people. Evidence of this can be found at each of the following levels of social organization: interpersonal, community, metropolitan, state, national, and global.

Integration at the Interpersonal Level   At the interpersonal level, attending a sporting event can facilitate encounters with strangers and provide opportunities for casual sociability. In analyzing encounters between two strangers at a sporting event, we find a number of potentially positive elements present. For instance, both parties are likely to know and understand the expectations associated with the role of sport fan. Also, the temporal boundaries of the encounter are clear-cut and implicitly understood, thereby guaranteeing the safety of any exchange. Further, both parties are probably willing to share relevant information about players and home teams. And finally, the safety, comfort, and ambience of the ecological setting facilitates attempts at social interaction (Melnick, 1993).

Integration at the Community Level   The notion that sport fandom helps promote connections at the community level has empirical support. Wilkerson and Dodder (1987) tested the proposition that "sport holds the potential to activate collective conscience and group affirmation by linking the identity of individuals to a common community orientation" (p. 36). They surveyed public school teachers in nine different communities and found a significant relationship between attendance at high school football games and scores on a collective conscience scale. Interestingly, the better the team's winning percentage, the higher the scores. The researchers concluded that participation and winning can interact to "provide a basis for shared identity, common focus, and, consequently, collective conscience" (p. 40).

Integration at the Metropolitan Level   At the metropolitan level, there are considerable anecdotal and empirical data to support the proposition that successful teams can unite a city. For example, the success of the Youngstown State (Ohio) Division I-AA football team has had a dramatic impact on the city, currently in the grips of a serious economic slump. As the mayor noted, "The program is vital to our community. Losing the mills took a tremendous psychological toll. We're starting to regain confidence, and YSU football has been a big part of that" (Walters, 1994). Similarly, success of the NFL's Atlanta Falcons during the late 1990s unified that city. According to the team's director of public relations, the team gave the city "a reason to dream" (Bragg, 1998).

Zhang, Pease, and Hui (1996) developed a Community Impact Scale (CIS) to quantify the community impact of a Western Conference NBA team. The eight value dimensions of the scale were positively related to spectator attendance. That is, those spectators who attended games most frequently were more likely to perceive the value of the team to the community. Of special interest was the finding that the team's contribution to promoting community integration was recognized as important and significant.

Integration at the State Level   The Indiana state high school boy's basketball championship tournament provides an excellent example of how sport fandom can unify an entire state. Because high school basketball in Indiana is a central component in the identities of most persons living in the state (K. Johnson, 1996), virtually all Hoosiers turn their attention to basketball at tournament time. Immortalized in the movie classic *Hoosiers* (perhaps the most favorite of all U.S. sport movies) (Brady, 1998), the tournament has, until recently, been open to every school in the state, regardless of enrollment or record. However, beginning with the 1997–98 season, school administrators voted to do away with the one-class tournament in favor of four boys' and four girls' tournaments based on school size. Not surprisingly, in its first year of operation, total attendance was down 22 percent from the previous year. Similarly, profits were down almost 42 percent ("Hoosier Rebellion," 1998). Remarked the Indiana University sports information director, "They are ruining one of the great traditions in the history of Indiana athletics" (cited in C. White, 1996).

Integration at the National Level   The "Do you believe in miracles" U.S.A. men's ice hockey team's gold medal victory in the 1980 Winter Olympic Games clearly demonstrates the integrative powers of sport fandom on the national level. Most Americans can recall what they were doing or where they were on that special day. The one hundred million or more television viewers who tune into the Super Bowl every year provide us with another example of how a major sporting event can integrate an entire country. Scotland provides us with another dramatic example of this point. As the country was about to face off against Brazil in a 1998 World Cup match, the Edinburgh *Evening News* headlined, "Country Grinds to Dead Halt as Game in a Billion Kicks Off" (McCallum & O'Brien, 1998b).

For better or worse, the integrative powers of national sport teams and heroes far exceed those of the most exceptional militarists, politicians, explorers, entertainers, educators, scientists, and clergy men. As "cultural consolidators" (Hoffer, 1998), national sport heroes and heroines, such as Austrian alpine skier Hermann Maier, Norwegian speed skater Johann Koss, French runner Marie-Jose Perec, and Hungarian backstroker Krisztina Egerszegi, exert a profound impact on their societies.

As an example of the manner in which sport heroes can rally and unify a nation, consider the hoopla generated by the Mark McGuire–Sammy Sosa home run race in 1998. As both players chased Roger Maris's all-time, single-season record of sixty-one home runs, Americans followed along with rapt attention. Indeed, as political columnist Sandy Grady (1998) observed, "Just when we were sinking into a national funk, wallowing dismally under White House porn, tapes and impeachment gloom, along came two genuine heroes in a glitzy, gaudy spectacle that has made us laugh, argue and root. Thank you, Mac. Thank you, Sammy. Thank you, Abner Doubleday" (p. 17A).

Integration at the Global Level   Finally, at the global level, it's hard to think of any event, short of a major war, that can capture the world stage like soccer's World Cup. For instance, consider that in 1994, 184 countries were members of the United Nations while during that same year a larger number of countries (191) were members of FIFA, soccer's international governing body. France's 3–0 upset of defending champion Brazil on July 12, 1998, before a stadium crowd of 80,000 in Saint-Denis was watched by a worldwide television audience of 1.7 billion, or approximately 30 percent of the people living on planet Earth!

Given the integrative powers of popular spectator sporting events, it is understandable why scheduled games go on even during times of national crisis. Two U.S. examples come immediately to mind. First, after President John F. Kennedy was pronounced dead from an assassin's bullet on Friday afternoon, November 22, 1963, the NFL had to decide whether to play its Sunday games. Because the general feeling was that the country needed some measure of normalcy, the games were played as scheduled, a decision supported by the Kennedy family. Second, MLB Commissioner Fay Vincent faced a difficult decision after the 1989 World Series was halted when a devastating earthquake struck the Bay Area. He had to consider whether to postpone the series, cancel it, or resume play in another city. He chose the delay option and the games were resumed ten days later. The reasons given were to restore continuity and to not disappoint the one hundred million viewers who were following the games.

Sport Fandom, Integration, and Suicide One of the most intriguing lines of inquiry regarding the integrative possibilities of sport fandom involves the potential relationship between sport fandom and suicide. Durkheim (1951) was one of the first social scientists to propose a relationship between participation in ritualized, ceremonial activities and suicide rates. His thinking is captured in the following syllogism (a syllogism is a logical formula used to test the validity of reasoning and consists of a major premise, a minor premise, and a conclusion):

> *Major Premise:* Participation in collective ceremonies is related to a high degree of integration of the social group.
>
> *Minor Premise:* A high degree of integration of the social group is related to lower suicide rates.
>
> *Conclusion:* Participation in collective ceremonies is releated to lower suicide rates.

This line of deductive reasoning has served as the theoretical basis for most of the research on spectator sports and suicide. That is, it has been hypothesized that the consumption of popular sporting events leads to a sense of greater connectedness and belongingness, which is likely to discourage thoughts of self-destruction, at least in the short term. Curtis et al. (1986) compared two sport ceremonial days, the last day of the World Series and the Super Bowl, and two civil holidays, July 4th and Thanksgiving Day, on suicide incidence rates three days before and after the ceremonial day for the years

1972–78. While net declines in suicides were found for the three days leading up to the two sport days (57.04 fewer suicides), the effect was much stronger for the two civil holidays (131.88 fewer suicides). The researchers concluded that the integrative effects of sport ceremonial days were considerably weaker than those of civil holidays. Lester (1988) replicated the above study but examined a time period (1972–84) twice as long as the one used by Curtis et al. He found, as they did, no significant deviation in suicide rates from chance expectations for the two sport ceremonial days.

Trovato (1998) conducted the most recent examination of the relationship between sport fandom and suicide. This researcher studied the impact of professional ice hockey's Stanley Cup on suicide rates in the Province of Quebec for the years 1951–92. He hypothesized that there would be a reduction in the number of suicides when the Montreal Canadians were engaged in play-off competition and a temporary increase in suicide rates on those occasions when the Canadians lost the Stanley Cup finals. While it appeared to matter little whether the Canadians won or lost the Stanley Cup, there was a rise in self-inflicted deaths for 15- to 34-year-old men if Montreal was eliminated early from the play-offs. The researcher concluded that, after controlling for age, gender, and marital status, there was no convincing evidence "that major sporting events in and of themselves inhibit suicide risk in populations exposed to such occasions" (p. 118). Thus, based on the published research available, ceremonial sport occasions appear to have little if any impact on suicide incidence rates.

A Final Note on the Integrative Function of Sport Fandom Before concluding our discussion of the integrative power of sport fandom, a few caveats are in order. First, functionalism can be criticized for assuming sport serves the needs of all groups in society equally, regardless of age, gender, race, ethnicity, or social class (this point is discussed in greater detail below). If sport fandom does in fact serve an integrative function in society, we need to ask whether it does so for all individuals and all groups. Common sense suggests that it does not. Because males are more voracious sport consumers than females (see chapter 1), sport may integrate males more effectively into a society's core belief system than it does females. The same can also be said about younger members of society as well as those who are more affluent (G. J. Smith, 1978). The latter is certainly the case when discussing attendance at sporting events. For instance, as noted in an earlier chapter, statistics show that while the average annual rate of inflation for consumer goods in the United States since 1991 has been 2.8 percent, the average annual percentage increase in ticket prices for the four major sport leagues has been 7.2 percent (McCallum & O'Brien, 1998d). With ticket prices for professional ice hockey, football, and basketball games averaging $45.00 to $48.00, the fact is, "the high cost of going to sporting events has denied the underclass and even the lower-middle class from attending them" (Eitzen, 1996, p. 98). Addressing the same point, Danielson (1997) observed, "happy images of everyone coming together behind the home team gloss over the role of socioeconomic factors in separating sports fans along class, income, ethnic, and racial lines" (p. 111).

A final point casting some doubt on the integrative role of sport fandom concerns the simple fact that when the contribution of sport team to community cohesion is discussed, it usually occurs in the context of the home team's success. But what about those cities that host perennial losing teams? While the occasional city will rally around a losing team (e.g., the City of Chicago and its Cubs), it seems that "most mediocre teams are communal embarrassments rather than community assets" (Danielson, 1997, p. 111).

Sport Fandom and Social Control

One of the more popular theories advanced to explain the popularity of spectator sports in society is to view them as an opportunity for spectators to vent the full range of their emotions with little fear of retribution. It is argued by some that the net effect of this collective, emotional workout is cathartic; that is, by allowing spectators to release their emotions through the verbalizing or acting out of their frustrations, a lot of potentially dangerous affect is harmlessly dissipated, and society is made safer (Coser, 1956). For instance, although it is doubtful that the Commissioner of MLB is a functionalist, he probably thought he was making a public service announcement when he placed a full-page advertisement in *USA Today* on April 1, 1996, reading, "Today, 597,369 Screaming Lunatics Will Be Off The Streets." He was, of course, referring to the opening day of the season.

Do spectator sports provide society with a "safety-valve" institution, and do they successfully "drain off" hostile and aggressive sentiments? Do umpires, referees, and opposing teams and fans serve as substitute objects for the displacement of hostile affect? Are society's institutions safer and more secure because of spectator sports? As discussed in chapter 6, the general answer to these questions is a resounding "No." Simply put, there is virtually no empirical evidence validating the existence of catharsis in sport (Gilbert & Twyman, 1984; Goranson, 1980; Russell, 1993). The "blowing off steam" theory of sport spectating may be attractive, but it is quite inaccurate.

Although the scientific literature strongly indicates that the catharsis theory is without merit, does this mean that spectator sports make no contribution to social order and control? In the same way that our muscles require regular exercise, so too do human beings need to express and exercise their emotions. Mental health experts tell us that tension resulting from emotional repression can have serious, deleterious health effects (e.g., Gross & Levenson, 1997). Conversely, emotional expression leads to stress reduction and healthier psychosocial functioning. Perhaps one of the underappreciated societal values of spectator sports is their limitless emotional possibilities. Because of the drama, ritual, and excitement of sport, spectators are motivated to give unfettered expression to their feelings. In this sense, spectator sports have much in common with theater. Aristotle observed in 350 BC that theater had a salutary effect on the audience because it helped purge their emotions. Might not the same be true for spectator sports?

The ebb and flow of game action, the point/counterpoint of team success and failure, the spectators' empathic identification with heroes and vilification of villains, the thin line spectators walk between tragedy and ecstasy, all combine to engage them in a type of emotional aerobics, not unlike, and perhaps superior, to classical Greek theater. The pleasant emotional stress that spectator sports offer provides welcome relief from the otherwise routine, dull life patterns many spectators and fans are forced to endure. The point is that although frustration and anger may not be eliminated at the ballpark, other emotions can and do get a vigorous workout. To the extent sport fans choose to express their emotions, freely and openly, they and society are the better for it.

Sport Fandom and Religiosity

The thought that spectator sports are genuinely sacred in nature and share the same societal functions provided by religious institutions is likely to border on blasphemy for some. In spectator sports we have mass entertainment, a fixture of popular culture, that sometimes appears crude, vulgar, and profane. And yet, at least by analogy, the similarities between sport fandom and organized religion are striking. Consider the vocabulary associated with both: faith, devotion, worship, ritual, dedication, sacrifice, commitment, spirit, prayer, suffering, festival, and celebration. Linguistically speaking, we are encouraged to go forward with the comparison. Fortunately, a number of works have been published in recent years that can help inform our efforts (e.g., Higgs, 1995; Hoffman, 1992; Prebish, 1993).

If we begin with a textbook definition of a religious institution, we may be discouraged from exploring the points of articulation between the two. Consider the following:

> A religious institution is a system of social norms and roles organized about the need to answer ultimate questions concerning the purpose of life and the meaning of death, suffering, and fortuitous occurrences. The religious institution answers these questions by defining the supernatural and the nature of man's relationship to the supernatural. In so doing it defines what is sacred and what the proper relationship is between the sacred and the secular. (Theodorson & Theodorson, 1969, p. 345)

Judged strictly by this definition, it is difficult to see how and in what sense sport is "religious." For instance, how does sport answer questions about life and death, assist in defining what is supernatural, address the relationship between the sacred and the secular, or awaken individuals to their social and moral responsibilities?

Faced with these questions, it is difficult to see how spectator sports perform the same functions as organized religion. The analogy appears to be patently false. What is important to remember, however, is that the functions assigned to religious institutions are generally personal in nature and speak to the problems, issues, and states of individuals, not the survival needs of societies (McGee, 1975). When we introduce a societal perspective into the discourse, the relationship between sport and religion comes into sharper focus. According to McGee, the key societal function of the religious institution is to assist in defining, rationalizing, and coping with the crises that people experience (e.g., birth, childbearing, death, etc.). These crises represent organizational problems for society because they threaten to disorganize interpersonal relationships. Thus, one of the key functions of the religious institution from a sociological perspective is to help maintain social cohesion, a critical imperative facing any society. To put it more simply, what the religious institution does for society is bind people together through ritual and belief by offering common values and goals toward which they may strive.

Cannot a similar case be made for the binding, integrating, and organizing functions of sport fandom? When one considers all the major sporting events with which one could identify, the social cohesion function of sport fandom becomes much less problematic. It may not be coincidental that record attendance at U.S. sporting events in recent years has coincided with the lowest levels of attendance at U.S. houses of worship since before World War II. In 1996, 38 percent of U.S. adults reported that they had attended a church or synagogue within the last seven days, the lowest figure since the 37 percent reported in 1940 ("Poll on Weekly Worship," 1997). It may well be that new "houses of worship," sport stadia and arenas, are beginning to challenge the drawing power of traditional houses of worship in American society.

Novak (1976) argues that sport fandom constitutes a type of "natural religion," flowing outward from a deep natural impulse that is radically religious. Dunning (1986) sees sport as a "humanistic religion" in which spectators worship other human beings, their achievements, and the groups to which they belong. Prebish (1993) claims that what sport offers is a type of primitive polytheism in which fans worship favorite players in each of the sports they follow. Similarly, Lever (1983) likens sport stadia and arenas to cathedrals where followers gather to worship their heroes and pray for their success.

Even at the psychological level of analysis, Lever believes that spectator sports and the sporting drama allow fans to transcend their existential existence and experience a type of spiritual transformation. Such thinking is supported by Price (1988), who assigns great meaning to the face painting, hair tinting, and iconographic costuming that have become so commonplace at sporting events throughout the world. He argues that these masking behaviors satisfy three specific religious drives: (1) securing identification with a favorite team, (2) helping the fan escape the structures of confinement and oppression that occur in everyday life, and (3) establishing a sense of community with other faithful fans.

Whether referred to as a civil, secular, natural, or humanistic religion, both analogy and functional analysis suggest that there is much that is religious about sport fandom. As societies grow increasingly more secular and theological beliefs become less salient and all-pervasive (Dunning, 1986), we should expect to see sport fandom assuming greater religious importance at both the individual and societal levels.

SELECTED CRITIQUES OF SPORT FANDOM

While the structural-functionalist view can help us gain insight about the role of sport fandom and spectating in contemporary society, the perspective is not without limitations. Coakley (1998), for example, has articulated three major problems with functionalist theory. First, functionalist theory "leads to exaggerated statements about the positive effects of sports" (p. 34). The fact that an aspect of culture (e.g., sport) is popular doesn't mean, ipso facto, that it is valuable or useful. Just because spectator sports have been around a long time doesn't necessarily mean that they are "functional" or satisfy important societal imperatives.

Second, there is the tendency when using functional analysis to "overlook cases where sports benefit some groups more than others within a community or society" (Coakley, 1998, pp. 34–35). For example, while a case was previously made that sport fandom makes important contributions to affective expression, communication, and integration in American society, a class analysis suggests that it benefits some socioeconomic groups more than others. One cannot ignore evidence of classism in any discussion of sport fandom (Eitzen, 1996). For example, the cost of attending professional sporting events in the United States today strongly discourages the lower and lower-middle socioeconomic classes from participating. If sport fandom is an important contributor to small talk, affect production, and social cohesion, then clearly these positive consequences are not equally distributed among all strata in society.

Third, because functionalists are not especially concerned with how sport might be "created and defined by members of society to promote their own interests and the interests of the groups to which they belong," advocates are likely to overlook how sport "might promote the interests of those with power and wealth, and thereby contribute to disruptive forms of social inequality in societies" (Coakley, 1998, p. 35). Instead of serving the basic needs of society, Coakley argues that sport may actually perpetuate social inequalities based on race/ethnicity, class, and gender.

Thus, although functionalism is helpful in directing our attention to potential benefits of sport fandom for society, its weaknesses and flaws need to be acknowledged (K. V. Meier, 1989). Clearly, alternative explanations for the role of sport in society need to be explored. Below, five critiques of sport fandom are examined, perspectives that, in contrast to the functional analysis previously reviewed, do not paint such a positive picture of the societal impacts of sport fandom. The five critiques are listed and briefly defined in table 9.4.

The Conflict Critique

Viewed from a conflict perspective, sport fandom is seen as maintaining the interests of the power elite of society (Danielson, 1997; Hoch, 1972). Shaped by the needs of capitalist systems, spectator sports serve vested interests as a type of "cultural anesthesia," a form

TABLE 9.4

Critiques of Sport Fandom and Spectating

CRITIQUE	DESCRIPTION
Conflict theorist	Perceives spectator sports as maintaining and consolidating the interests of society's power elite.
Feminist	Sees institutions such as spectator sports supporting the gender order and masculine hegemony.
Cultural elitist	Views sport fandom as a superficial, inferior, brutal, lowbrow form of mass entertainment.
Moralist	Suggests that the moral fiber of society is in decline as evidenced by current television programming, movies, popular music, and spectator sports.
Humanist	Dislikes sport fandom and spectating because they are experienced passively, and passivity is viewed as inherently impoverishing.

of "spiritual masturbation" or "opiate" that distracts, diverts, and deflects attention from the pressing social problems and issues of the day (G. E. Howard, 1912; Lazarsfeld & Merton, 1948; K. V. Meier, 1989; Nash, 1938; Quirk, 1997; see Guttmann, 1980; G. J. Smith, 1988). This perspective argues that by exploiting spectator sports, members of the ruling elite are better able to consolidate their power and privilege. For instance, consider the position taken by K. V. Meier (1989), who argues that sport spectating "depletes the available resources and reservoirs of money, time, and critical thought which could be utilized . . . to attempt to effect productive political and positive, meaningful social transformation" (pp. 113–114).

The "sport spectating as opiate" thesis was strongly articulated by S. J. Harris (1981) when he wrote:

> If Karl Marx, who died 100 years ago, were still alive today, he might be sorely tempted to revise his famous slur, "Religion is the opium of the people." It is no longer true, if it ever was, for something else has taken its place, at least in our country. Today, sport has become the opium of the people. . . . While it may be true that religion, in the past, narcotized many, it also awakened many

others to their social and moral responsibilities. Sport has no such redeeming aspects in our society. . . . It has turned into a passion, a mania, a drug far more potent and widespread than any mere chemical substance. (p. 3B)

Those who agree with this line of reasoning can certainly find instances where sport appeared to be more important to members of the society than their other civic responsibilities. For instance, slightly more than 38,000 voters turned out for the May 1, 1999, mayoral election in Dallas, although later that night well over 45,000 persons attended the Texas Rangers baseball game in Arlington, Texas, a suburb of Dallas (Cook & Mravic, 1999a).

As a second example, consider the media coverage of Micheal Jordan's (second) retirement, which occurred during the same time period as the impeachment trial of President Clinton. The television ratings for CNN's coverage of Jordan's retirement press conference received a rating of 1.6. The next day, during the same time slot, CNN's rating for the impeachment hearings was only 1.3 (Walters, 1999a). Similarly, when the *Chicago Sun-Times* asked local residents to name the greatest Chicagoans of the twentieth century, Jordan placed number one on the list, ahead of several mayors, three governors, and five Nobel Prize winners (Cook & Mravic, 1999b).

If, as the conflict critique purports, spectator sports function as an opiate, fans should be generally apathetic and less involved in the business of society. However, to the contrary, research shows that fans have broader general interests and more active lifestyles than nonfans. Perhaps Lieberman (1991) uncovered what may be the strongest evidence to refute the popular notion that sport fans are passive, single-product consumers. In his national survey on sport fandom, he found that sport fans were more likely than nonfans to report an interest in politics, music, being successful, and being a leader. Additional evidence is provided by the strong positive correlation between sport fandom and athletic particiation (see chapters 1 and 8). Further, in his critique of the neo-Marxist indictment of sport, Guttmann (1980) concluded that there is no evidence to support the notion that sport fans are apolitical; to the contrary, sport fandom may actually heighten class consciousness and intensify class conflict. And Maguire (1986) has observed that soccer hooliganism in England is best understood as a class cultural conflict.

It is one thing to speculate about a power elite exploiting sport for its own ends, but it is quite another matter to identify who they are and provide proof of their conspiratorial activity. Studies of professional sport team ownership show that the wealthiest owners are not linked to any national elite network. Typically, they "represent an approach to business more closely identified with the rugged individualist capitalist entrepreneur" (Flint & Eitzen, 1987, p. 21).

The Feminist Critique

Shuster (1994) made an interesting observation when she noted that "it is fascinatingly coincidental how football has overtaken baseball as the preeminent TV sport for men at the same time women have begun asserting their rights in the arena of sports" (p. 3C). The suggestion that sporting events provide male viewers with something more than diversion and entertainment is worth serious consideration (Nelson, 1994). Judged from a feminist point of view, it is through institutions like sport fandom that male hegemony is constructed and reconstructed (Bryson, 1987). Far from an innocent and innocuous pastime, sport spectating is viewed as reproducing traditional ideas about masculinity and femininity, thereby helping maintain patriarchal rule in the larger society.

According to Bryson (1987), homosocial, hypermasculine cultural rituals (e.g., wrestling, boxing, ice hockey, football) link males with the positively sanctioned use of force and aggression. The net effect of these rituals is to inferiorize females and their activities. Implicit in the feminist analysis is the notion that the celebration of hypermasculinity perpetuates gender inequality, reinforces sexual stereotypes, ensures patriarchal control, and ultimately acts as an agent of women's oppression (Theberge, 1985).

Certainly, the feminist critique of male spectator sports deserves the reader's attention. However, its major weakness is its failure to provide specific guidelines for determining how, when, and where sport reproduce gender relations. For instance, we are left to wonder which sports teach males to embrace notions of domination, suppression, and control of the opposite sex. Are feminists talking about all sports or just a select few? Do they have in mind all male spectators or a smaller group especially vulnerable to sexist messages? And, if so, how can we identify those males who are most susceptible to gender ideology? Given the increasing numbers of female spectators attending professional football (Meyers, 1997) and ice hockey (Mihoces, 1998) games in the United States today (both the NFL and NHL estimate that females constitute approximately 45 percent of their fan base), the future impact of sport fandom on gender relations appears unclear. In fact, one could argue that as more females fill sport stadia and arenas, sport fandom and spectating will serve to weaken the gender order, rather than reinforce it.

The Elitist (Mass Culture) Critique

Higgs (1982) noted, "it is difficult to imagine Socrates, Jesus, Augustine, Leonardo, Newton, Beethoven, Tolstoy or Einstein in the stands cheering a team, which may tell us something about the phenomenon of mass spectacle" (p. 150). Similarly, Pasternak once observed, "Gregariousness is always the refuge of mediocrities; only individuals seek the truth" (cited in Babbage, 1969).

The cultural elitism implicit in these quotes has its roots in Thorsten Veblen's famous put-down of sport spectators. Noted Veblen, spectating "marks an arrested development of man's moral nature" (cited in G. J. Smith, 1988). It goes without saying that sport spectating, as cultural practice, has been traditionally viewed as inferior, brutal, and lowbrow because, according to Smith, "it is for the masses and therefore lacking in refinement. It follows then, that watching a sporting event is several notches below so-called more discriminatory leisure pursuits like visiting an art gallery, attending an opera, or listening to a symphonic concert" (p. 63).

The elitist critique argues that the masses lack taste and refinement. If their tastes are to be satisfied, everything has to be reduced to the lowest common denominator (Strinati, 1995). Judged from this perspective, sport fandom is viewed as a standardized, repetitive, and superficial activity that celebrates the trivial. Because they lack intellectual challenge and stimulation, spectator sports are forced to cater to fantasy and escapism and the denial of thinking.

Elitists can certainly be challenged on their "holier than thou" attitude. However, more telling is the fact that, upon closer inspection, sport spectating is not the trivial, infantile, and superficial activity its critics claim. Rather, sport fans often turn out to be more knowing, active, and discriminating than they are given credit for. Many fans take special pride in their knowledge of individual and team statistics and their ability to strategize. Far from being cultural dolts, the typical sport fan is cognitively engaged in the activity— analyzing individual performances, sharing sport esoteria with others, mulling over game strategies, and critiquing coaching decisions. The intricacies and complexities of the game action allow fans to give expression to their creative and critical thinking skills.

The Moralist Critique

Those identifying with the moralist critique warn that the moral alarm clock is ticking away in the United States and that the nation better pay attention before we are all plunged into a moral abyss. While television programming, movies, and popular music are frequently singled out for specific criticism, spectator sports have not escaped the moralist's critical eye. Boxing, football, ice hockey, and ultimate fighting are viewed as especially barbaric. For example, Mumford (1937) observed, "Sport, in the sense of a mass spectacle, with death to add to the underlying excitement, comes into existence when a population has been drilled and regimented and depressed to such an extent that it needs at least a vicarious participation in difficult feats of skill or heroism to sustain its waning life-sense" (p. 80).

While moralists have been predicting the end of Western civilization for some time, American society continues to defy the predictions of gloom and doom. However, it would be irresponsible to make light of the moralist critique insofar as it is directed at "blood sports" (e.g., Beck, 1995). For example, between 1962 and 1995, twenty-three boxers were killed in fights and hundreds of others have suffered at least some degree of brain damage (e.g., Muhammad Ali). And, what about no-holds-barred ultimate fighting where fans fill arenas or pay $29.95 to their local cable operators for the opportunity to see the mayhem? More like dog and cock fights than anything else, these spectacles are banned in a number of states. Although it may be extreme to argue that sport spectacles such as the Super Bowl, Kentucky Derby, March Madness, and the World Series are debased and immoral, some spectator sports are difficult to defend given their violence and total disregard of basic human values.

The Humanist Critique

Those supporting the humanist critique dislike sport fandom and spectating because they are experienced passively, and passivity is viewed as inherently impoverishing. According to Reich (1970), passivity and its material expression, consumerism, prevent privacy, liberty, sovereignty, performance, taste, self-knowledge, and the ability to create one's own aesthetic standards. Spectator sports are seen as impoverishing because they deny activity and initiative; they teach spectators to rely for their satisfactions on what society provides, rather than help them find their own personal sources of fun and enlightenment. Because passive culture almost completely denies individual performance, the humanist fears that there will come a time when we will be unable to fulfill our own genuine needs.

While one might be inclined to accept the notion that much of U.S. popular culture is designed to be experienced passively, whether sport fandom should be included in the critique can be debated. Whether it is because sport fans are younger, more upscale, or have higher energy levels, research shows that they are more likely to have dinner out, rent a movie cassette, entertain at home, read a paperback, listen to music, and be physically active. Remember, there is no hard evidence that spectator sports socialize fans for consumption, encourage passivity, or rob them of personal initiative (Lieberman, 1991). Rather, as a group, sport fans and spectators tend to embrace highly active, proactive lifestyles.

SOME FINAL THOUGHTS

As one can see from the discussions in this chapter, social scientists have very different views as to the societal impact of sport fandom. The functionalist viewpoint perceives the activity as highly beneficial to society at large. In fact, nine different "imperatives" were identified for sport fandom, each addressing a particular societal function. On the other hand, different opinions about the value of sport fandom were noted in the five critiques of this popular leisure activity. Conflict, feminist, elitist, moralist, and humanist perspectives each challenge the basic assumptions of the functionalist perspective and arrive at very different conclusions about the spectator sports–society relationship. Each critique argues that spectator sports are "dysfunctional," not "functional," although the reasons given vary by perspective.

Although each of the theories and perspectives identified and discussed were supported with the most relevant research available, the fact remains that the formal study of sport spectatorship from institutional and popular-culture perspectives has not received nearly the attention it deserves. Consequently, several of the observations offered must remain informed speculations until such time as more qualitative and quantitative data become available. In the absence of a significant research literature bearing on the question proposed at the beginning of this chapter, the reader is challenged to weigh the strengths and weaknesses of each of the theories and critiques discussed and arrive at his or her own answers to the question, "What is the relationship between sport fandom and society?"

And finally, it seems appropriate to note that there is always the danger of engaging in overanalysis in trying to make sense of something very ordinary, like sport fandom. After all, we're not talking about rocket science! Maybe the importance of sport fandom to a society is more obvious than researchers and theorists would have us believe. The growing popularity and increasing importance of spectator sports throughout the world may simply reflect a collective need on the part of spectators and fans to add a bit of zest to their everyday, lives (Shames, 1989). Sporting events provide followers with an opportunity to take a break from their daily routines and responsibilities, whether to watch a daughter participate in a youth soccer game, attend a minor league baseball game, or take up a comfortable position on the living room couch for a Sunday date with the NFL. Maybe we should view sport fandom as a nutritional supplement, a tropical spice, a spiritual, emotional substitute. In the same way that herbs and spices can improve the taste of a bland main dish, sport fandom can add a dash of eustress, excitement, thrill, and wonder to our lives and society as a whole. Despite all the "socio-babble" the subject attracts, it would truly be ironic if we discover, when all is said and done, that the major societal function of sport fandom is to provide spectators and fans alike with a time-out institution, one that allows them, on occasion, to temporarily reinvigorate their emotional, spiritual, and social lives.

REFERENCES

Aberle, D. F., Cohen, A. K., Davis, A. K., Levy, M. J., & Sutton, F. S. (1950). The functional prerequisites of a society. *Ethics, 60,* 100–111.

Ah, those Sunday victories. (1983, September 3). *Sports Illustrated,* p. 16.

Alderfer, C. P. (1972). *Existence, relatedness, and growth.* New York: Free Press.

Allen, K. (1999, October 12). Canadians in NHL at all-time low 56%. *USA Today,* p. C1.

Alvarez, J. (1997, October). Touchdown internet. *Sportstech,* pp. 46–47, 49, 51.

Anderson, C. A., & DeNeve, K. M. (1992). Temperature, aggression, and the negative affect escape model. *Psychological Bulletin, 111,* 347–351.

Anderson, D. F. (1979). Sport spectatorship: Application of an identity or appraisal of self. *Review of Sport and Leisure, 4*(2), 115–127.

Anderson, D., & Stone, G. P. (1981). Responses of male and female metropolitans to the commercialization of professional sport 1960 to 1975. *International Review of Sport Sociology, 16*(3), 5–20.

Apter, M. J. (1992). *The dangerous edge: The psychology of excitement.* New York: Free Press.

Arms, R. L., & Russell, G. W. (1997). Impulsivity, fight history and camaraderie as predictors of a willingness to escalate a disturbance. *Current Psychology: Research & Reviews, 15,* 279–285.

Arms, R. L., Russell, G. W., Dwyer, R. S., & Josuttes, D. L. (1999). *Females as targets of male aggression in the bungled procedure paradigm.* Manuscript submitted for publication.

Arms, R. L., Russell, G. W., & Sandilands, M. L. (1979). Effects on the hostility of spectators viewing aggressive sports. *Social Psychology Quarterly, 42,* 275–279.

Armstrong, G. (1998). *Football hooligans: Knowing the score.* Oxford, England: Berg.

Aveni, A. F. (1977). The not-so-lonely crowd: Friendship groups in collective behavior. *Sociometry, 40,* 96–99.

Averill, L. A. (1950). The impact of a changing culture upon pubescent ideals. *School and Society, 72,* 49–53.

Baade, R. A., & Tiehen, L. J. (1990). An analysis of major league baseball attendance, 1969–1987. *Journal of Sport & Social Issues, 14*(1), 14–32.

Babbage, S. B. (1969). *The vacuum of unbelief.* Grand Rapids, MI: Zonderan.

Bailey, C. I., & Sage, G. H. (1988). Values communicated by a sports event: The case of the Super Bowl. *Journal of Sport Behavior, 11,* 126–143.

Bairner, A. (1996). Sportive nationalism and nationalist politics: A comparative analysis of Scotland, the Republic of Ireland, and Sweden. *Journal of Sport & Social Issues, 23,* 314–334.

Balswick, J., & Ingoldsby, B. (1982). Heroes and heroines among American adolescents. *Sex Roles, 8,* 243–249.

Bandura, A. (1973). *Aggression: A social learning analysis.* Englewood Cliffs, NJ: Prentice Hall.

Bandura, A. (1986). *Social foundations of thought and action.* Englewood Cliffs, NJ: Prentice Hall.

Barney, R. K. (1985). The hailed, the haloed, and the hallowed: Sport heroes and their qualities—An analysis and hypothetical model for their commemoration. In N. Muller & J. Ruhl (Eds.), *Sport history* (pp. 88–103). Niederhausen, Germany: Schors-Verlag.

Baron, R. A. (1987). Effects of negative air ions on interpersonal attraction: Evidence for intensification. *Journal of Personality and Social Psychology, 52,* 547–553.

Baron, R. A., & Richardson, D. R. (1994). *Human aggression* (2nd ed.). New York: Plenum.

Baron, R. A., Russell, G. W., & Arms, R. L. (1985). Negative ions and behavior: Impact on mood, memory, and aggression among Type A and Type B persons. *Journal of Personality and Social Psychology, 48,* 746–754.

Beck, J. (1995, March 7). A sport that's no longer tolerable. *Democrat and Chronicle,* p. 14A.

Beisser, A. R. (1967). *The madness in sports: Psychosocial observations on sports.* New York: Appleton-Century-Crofts.

Benedict, J., & Yaeger, D. (1998). *Pros and cons: The criminals who play in the NFL.* New York: Warner Books.

Berkowitz, L. (1969). Simple views of aggression: An essay review. *American Scientist, 57,* 372–383.

Berkowitz, L. (1982). Aversive conditions as stimuli to aggression. *Advances in Experimental Social Psychology, 15,* 249–288.

Berkowitz, L. (1989). Frustration-aggression hypothesis: Examination and reformulation. *Psychological Bulletin, 106,* 59–73.

Berkowitz, L. (1993). *Aggression: Its causes, consequences, and control.* Philadelphia: Temple University Press.

Berman, M., Taylor, S. P., & Marged, B. (1993). Morphine and human aggression. *Addictive Behaviors, 18,* 263–268.

Bernhardt, P. C., Dabbs, J. M., Fielden, J. A., & Lutter, C. D. (1998). Testosterone changes during vicarious experiences of winning and losing among fans at sporting events. *Physiology and Behavior, 65,* 59–62.

Bibby, R. W. (1995). *The Bibby report: Social trends Canadian style.* Toronto: Stoddart.

Bird, P. J. (1982). The demand for league football. *Applied Economics, 14,* 637–649.

Blankenhorn, D. (1995). *Fatherless America.* New York: Basic Books.

Bloss, H. (1970). Sport and vocational school pupils. *International Review of Sport Sociology, 5,* 25–58.

Boldt, D. (1998, June 21). U. S. morals under social microscope. *Democrat and Chronicle*, p. A15.

Brady, E. (1998, July 15). Readers rank favorite sports flicks. *USA Today*, pp. 1C-2C.

Bragg, R. (1998, November 30). Awakening from a football slumber. *The New York Times*, p. 3C.

Branscombe, N. R., N'gbala, A., Kobrynowicz, D., & Wann, D. L. (1997). Self and group protection concerns influence attributions but they are not determinants of counterfactual mutations focus. *British Journal of Social Psychology, 36*, 387–404.

Branscombe, N. R., & Wann, D. L. (1991). The positive social and self-concept consequences of sport team identification. *Journal of Sport & Social Issues, 15*, 115–127.

Branscombe, N. R., & Wann, D. L. (1992a). Physiological arousal and reactions to outgroup members that implicate an important social identity. *Aggressive Behavior, 18*, 85–93.

Branscombe, N. R., & Wann, D. L. (1992b). Role of identification with a group, arousal, categorization processes, and self-esteem in sports spectator aggression. *Human Relations, 45*, 1013–1033.

Branscombe, N. R., & Wann, D. L. (1994). Collective self-esteem consequences of outgroup derogation when a valued social identity is on trial. *European Journal of Social Psychology, 24*, 641–657.

Branscombe, N. R., Wann, D. L., Noel, J. G., & Coleman, J. (1993). In-group or out-group extremity: Importance of the threatened social identity. *Personality and Social Psychology Bulletin, 19*, 381–388.

Brawl games. (1988, July 31). *Democrat and Chronicle*, p. D3.

Bredemeier, B. J., Weiss, M. R., Shields, D. L., & Cooper, B. A. B. (1986). The relationship of sport involvement with children's moral reasoning and aggression tendencies. *Journal of Sport Psychology, 8*, 304–318.

Brewer, M. B. (1979). In-group bias in the minimal group situation: A cognitive motivational analysis. *Psychological Bulletin, 86*, 307–324.

Brill, A. A. (1929). The why of the fan. *North American Review, 228*, 429–434.

Brohm, J. M. (1978). *Sport—A prison of measured time*. London: Ink Links.

Brooks, C. M. (1994). *Sport marketing: Competitive business strategies for sports*. Englewood Cliffs, NJ: Prentice Hall.

Brown, B. R., Jr., Baranowski, M. D., Kulig, J. W., Stephenson, J. N., & Perry, B. (1996). Searching for the Magic Johnson effect: AIDS, adolescents, and celebrity disclosure. *Adolescence, 31*, 253–264.

Brummett, B., & Duncan, M. C. (1990). Theorizing without totalizing: Specularity and televised sports. *Quarterly Journal of Speech, 76*, 227–246.

Bryan, C., & Horton, R. (1976). School athletics and fan aggression. *Educational Researcher, 5*, 2–11.

Bryant, J. (1989). Viewers' enjoyment of televised sports violence. In. L. A. Wenner (Ed.), *Media, sports, and society* (pp. 270–289). Newbury Park, CA: Sage.

Bryant, J., Brown, D., Comisky, P. W., & Zillmann, D. (1982). Sports and spectators: Commentary and appreciation. *Journal of Communication, 32*, 109–119.

Bryant, J., Comisky, P. W., & Zillmann, D. (1981). The appeal of rough-and-tumble play in televised professional football. *Communication Quarterly, 29*, 256–262.

Bryant, J., Rockwell, S. C., & Owens, J. W. (1994). "Buzzer beaters" and "barn burners": The effects on enjoyment of watching the game go "down to the wire." *Journal of Sport & Social Issues, 18,* 326–339.

Bryant, J., & Zillmann, D. (1983). Sports violence and the media. In J. H. Goldstein (Ed.), *Sports violence* (pp. 195–211). New York: Springer-Verlag.

Bryson, L. (1987). Sport and the maintenance of masculine hegemony. *Women's Studies International Forum, 10,* 340–361.

Buford, B. (1990). *Among the thugs.* New York: W. W. Norton & Company.

Buikhuisen, W. (1986). Alcohol and soccer hooliganism. *International Journal of Offender Therapy and Comparative Criminology, 30,* ix–xi.

Burger, J. M. (1985). Temporal effects on attributions for academic performances and reflected-glory basking. *Social Psychology Quarterly, 48,* 330–336.

Bushman, B. J., & Cooper, H. M. (1990). Effects of alcohol on human aggression: An integrative research review. *Psychological Bulletin, 107,* 341–354.

Buss, A. H. (1961). *The psychology of aggression.* New York: Wiley.

Buss, A. H., & Durkee, A. (1957). An inventory for assessing different kinds of hostility. *Journal of Consulting Psychology, 4,* 343–349.

Butt, D. S. (1987). *Psychology of sport: The behavior, motivation, personality, and performance of athletes* (2nd ed.). New York: Van Nostrand Reinhold.

Byrne, D. (1971). *The attraction paradigm.* New York: Academic Press.

Byrne, D., Clore, G. L., & Smeaton, G. (1986). The attraction hypothesis: Do similar attitudes attract anything? *Journal of Personality and Social Psychology, 51,* 1167–1170.

Calisch, R. (1954). Spectator problems in secondary school athletics. *Research Quarterly, 25,* 261–268.

Cantor, J. (1998). Children's attraction to violent television programming. In J. H. Goldstein (Ed.), *Why we watch: The attraction of violent entertainment* (pp. 88–115). New York: Oxford University Press.

Castine, S. C., & Roberts, G. C. (1974). Modeling in the socialization process of the black athlete. *International Review of Sport Sociology, 9,* 59–74.

CDC: Americans live longer; Deaths drop from 12 killers. (1994, December 16). *Democrat and Chronicle,* p. A8.

Centre for Leisure Research. (1984). *Crowd behaviour at football matches: A study in Scotland.* Endinburgh, Scotland: Dunfermline College of Physical Education.

Cheren, S. (1981). The psychiatric perspective: Psychological aspects of violence in sports. *Arena Review, 5,* 31–35.

Chermack, S., & Taylor, S. P. (1993). Barbiturates and human physical aggression. *Journal of Research in Personality, 27,* 315–327.

Chorbajian, L. (1978). The social psychology of American males and spectator sports. *International Journal of Sport Psychology, 9,* 165–175.

Christy, C. A., & Voigt, H. (1994). Bystander responses to public episodes of child abuse. *Journal of Applied Social Psychology, 24,* 824–847.

Cialdini, R. B., Borden, R. J., Thorne, A., Walker, M. R., Freeman, S., & Sloan, L. R. (1976). Basking in reflected glory: Three (football) field studies. *Journal of Personality and Social Psychology, 34,* 366–375.

Cialdini, R. B., & De Nicholas, M. E. (1989). Self-presentation by association. *Journal of Personality and Social Psychology, 57,* 626–631.

Cialdini, R. B., & Richardson, K. D. (1980). Two indirect tactics of image management: Basking and blasting. *Journal of Personality and Social Psychology, 39,* 406–415.

Coakley, J. J. (1994). *Sport in society: Issues and controversies* (5th ed.). St. Louis: Times Mirror/Mosby.

Coakley, J. J. (1998). *Sport in society: Issues and controversies* (6th ed.). St. Louis: Times Mirror/Mosby.

Cook, K., & Mravic, M. (1999a, May 17). Go figure. *Sports Illustrated*, p. 24.

Cook, K., & Mravic, M. (1999b, August 16). Go figure. *Sports Illustrated*, p. 28.

Cooper, D., Livingood, A. B., & Kurz, R. B. (1981). Children's choice of sports heroes and heroines: The role of child-hero similarity. *Psychological Documents, 11,* 85 (Ms. No. 2376).

Coser, L. (1956). *The functions of social conflict.* New York: Free Press.

Cramer, J. A., Walker, J. E., & Rado, L. (1980). Athletic heroes and heroines: The role of the press in their creation. *Journal of Sport Behavior, 4,* 175–185.

Crary, D. (1998, April 29). Teams plead for Canada's aid. *USA Today*, p. 6C.

Creedon, P. (Ed.). (1994). *Women, media and sport: Challenging gender values.* Thousand Oaks, CA: Sage.

Crist, S. (1998, January 26). All bets are off. *Sports Illustrated*, pp. 82–86, 88, 90–92.

Crocker, J., & Luhtanen, R. (1990). Collective self-esteem and in-group bias. *Journal of Personality and Social Psychology, 58,* 1–8.

Cullen, F. T. (1974). Attitudes of players and spectators toward norm violation in ice hockey. *Perceptual and Motor Skills, 38,* 1146.

Curtis, J., Loy, J., & Karnilowicz, W. (1986). A comparison of suicide-dip effects of major sports events and civil holidays. *Sociology of Sport Journal, 3,* 1–14.

Danielson, M. N. (1997). *Home team: Professional sports and the American metropolis.* Princeton, NJ: Princeton University Press.

Darrah, E. M. (1898, May). A study of children's ideals. *Popular Science Monthly, 52,* 88–98.

Darrow, C., & Lewinger, P. (1968). The Detroit uprising: A psychological study. In J. Masserman (Ed.), *The dynamics of dissent: Science and psychoanalysis* (Vol. 13). New York: Grune & Stratton.

Deci, E. L. (1971). Effects of externally mediated rewards on intrinsic motivation. *Journal of Personality and Social Psychology, 18,* 105–115.

Deci, E. L., & Ryan, R. M. (1985). *Intrinsic motivation and self-determination in human behavior.* New York: Plenum.

Deford, F. (1969, June 9). What price heroes? *Sports Illustrated*, pp. 33–40.

De Freitas, B., & Schwartz, G. (1979). Effects of caffeine in chronic psychiatric patients. *American Journal of Psychiatry, 136,* 1337–1338.

Demmert, H. G. (1973). *The economics of professional team sport.* Lexington, MA: D. C. Health.

Denney, R. (1979). Feast of strangers: Varieties of social experience in America. In H. J. Gans, N. Glazer, J. R. Gusfield, & C. Jencks (Eds.), *On the making of Americans: Essays in honor of David Riesman* (pp. 251–269). Philadelphia: University of Pennsylvania Press.

Dewar, C. K. (1979). Spectator fights at professional baseball games. *Review of Sport & Leisure, 4,* 14–25.

Didillon, H., & Vandewiele, M. (1985). Individuals whom the youth in Central Africa would like to resemble. *Perceptual and Motor Skills, 61,* 442.

Diener, E. (1980). Deindividuation: The absence of self-awareness and self-regulation in group members. In P. Paulas (Ed.), *The psychology of group influence* (pp. 209–242). Hillsdale, NJ: Erlbaum.

Diener, E., & DeFour, D. (1978). Does television violence enhance program popularity? *Journal of Personality and Social Psychology, 36,* 333–341.

Dietz-Uhler, B. (1999). Defensive reactions to group-relevant information. *Group Processes & Intergroup Relations, 2,* 17–29.

Dietz-Uhler, B., Harrick, E. A., End, C., & Jacquemotte, L. (1999). *Sex differences in sport fan behavior and reasons for being a sport fan.* Manuscript submitted for publication.

Dietz-Uhler, B., & Murrell, A. (1999). Examining fan reactions to game outcomes: A longitudinal study of social identity. *Journal of Sport Behavior, 22,* 15–27.

Dodd, M. (1999, May 3). Security tight at Camden Yards. *USA Today,* p. C3.

Dollard, J., Doob, L. W., Miller, N. E., Mowrer, O. H., & Sears, R. R. (1939). *Frustration and aggression.* New Haven, CT: Yale University Press.

Dowd, M. (1983, September 5). Private violence. *Time,* pp. 18–29.

Doyle, R. C., Lewis, J. M., & Malmisur, M. (1980). A sociological application of Rooney's fan region theory. *Journal of Sport Behavior, 3*(2), 51–60.

Drake, B., & Pandey, S. (1996). Do child abuse rates increase on those days on which professional sporting events are held? *Journal of Family Violence, 11,* 205–218.

Duda, J. L. (1989). Goal perspectives and behavior in sport and exercise settings. In C. Ames & M. Maehr (Eds.), *Advances in motivation and achievement* (Vol. 6, pp.81–115). Greenwich, CT: JAI Press.

Duda, J. L., Smart, A. E., & Tappe, M. K. (1989). Predictors of adherence in the rehabilitation of athletic injuries: An application of personal investment theory. *Journal of Sport and Exercise Psychology, 11,* 367–381.

Duke, V., & Crolly, L. (1996). Football spectator behavior in Argentina: A case of separate evolution. *The Sociological Review, 44,* 272–293.

Duncan, M. C. (1983). The symbolic dimensions of spectator sport. *Quest, 35,* 29–36.

Duncan, M. C., & Brummett, B. (1989). Types and sources of spectating pleasure in televised sports. *Sociology of Sport Journal, 6,* 195–211.

Dunning, E. (1986). The sociology of sport in Europe and the United States: Critical observations from an "Elisian" perspective. In C. R. Rees & A. W. Miracle (Eds.), *Sport and social theory* (pp. 29–56). Champaign, IL: Human Kinetics.

Dunning, E., Murphy, P., & Williams, J. (1986). *The roots of football hooliganism: An historical sociological study.* London: Routledge and Kegan Paul.

Durkheim, E. (1951). *Suicide.* (J. A. Spaulding & G. Simpson, Eds. and Trans.). Glencoe, IL: Free Press. (Original work published 1897)

Eastman, S. T., & Land, A. M. (1997). The best of both worlds: Sports fans find good seats at the bar. *Journal of Sport & Social Issues, 21,* 156–178.

Eastman, S. T., & Riggs, K. E. (1994). Televised sports and ritual: Fan experiences. *Sociology of Sport Journal, 11,* 149–174.

Edwards, H. (1973). *Sociology of sport.* Homewood, IL: The Dorsey Press.

Eisenman, R. (1994). College students say Mike Tyson innocent of rape. *Psychological Reports, 74,* 1049–1050.

Eitzen, D. S. (1979). Sport and deviance. In D. S. Eitzen (Ed.), *Sport in contemporary society: An anthology* (pp. 73–89). New York: St. Martin's Press.

Eitzen, D. S. (1996). Classism in sport: The powerless bear the burden. *Journal of Sport & Social Issues, 20,* 95–105.

Elias, N., & Dunning, E. (1970). The quest for excitement in unexciting societies. In G. Luschen (Ed.), *The cross-cultural analysis of sport and games.* Champaign, IL: Stipes.

End, C. M., Dietz-Uhler, B., Harrick, E. A., & Jacquemotte, L. (1999). *Identifying with winners: Sport fans' tendency to spontaneously BIRG.* Unpublished manuscript, University of Miami, OH.

Etzioni, A. (1993). *The spirit of community: Rights, responsibilities, and communitarian agenda.* New York: Crown.

Evaggelinou, C., & Grekinis, D. (1998). A survey of spectators at the International Stoke Mandeville Wheelchair Games. *Adapted Physical Education Quarterly, 15,* 25–35.

Famighetti, R. (Ed.). (1998). *The world almanac & book of facts, 1998.* Mahwah, NJ: World Almanac Books.

Fan behavior. (1993, November 15). *The NCAA News,* p. 10.

Fan insults spark divided opinions. (1991, March 12). *USA Today,* p. C9.

Fazio, R. H., Powell, M. C., & Williams, C. J. (1989). The role of attitude accessibility in the attitude-to-behavior process. *Journal of Consumer Behavior, 16,* 280–288.

Feather, N. T. (1991). Attitudes towards the high achiever: Effects of perceiver's own level of competence. *Australian Journal of Psychology, 43,* 121–124.

Feather, N. T., Volkmer, R. E., & McKee, I. R. (1991). Attitudes towards high achievers in public life: Attributions, deservingness, personality, and affect. *Australian Journal of Psychology, 43,* 85–91.

Ferguson, J. D. (1981). Emotions in sport sociology. *International Review of Sport Sociology, 16,* 15–23.

Festinger, L., Pepitone, A., Newcomb, T. (1952). Some consequences of deindividuation in a group. *Journal of Abnormal and Social Psychology, 47,* 382–389.

Flint, W. C., & Eitzen, D. S. (1987). Professional sports team ownership and entrepreneurial capitalism. *Sociology of Sport Journal, 4,* 17–27.

Fortier, M. S., Vallerand, R. J., Briere, N. M., & Provencher, P. J. (1995). Competitive and recreational sport structures and gender: A test of their relationship with sport motivation. *International Journal of Sport Psychology, 26,* 24–39.

Foundation for Child Development (1977). *National survey of children.* New York: Foundation for child development.

Franco, F. M., & Maass, A. (1996). Implicit versus explicit strategies of out-group discrimination: The role of intentional control in biased language use and reward allocation. *Journal of Language and Social Psychology, 15,* 35–359.

Freedman, J. L., Levy, A. S., Buchanan, R. W., & Price, J. (1972). Crowding and human aggressiveness. *Journal of Experimental Social Psychology, 8,* 528–548.

Freischlag, J., & Hardin, D. (1975). The effects of social class and school achievement on the composition of sport crowds. *Sport Sociology Bulletin, 4,* 36–46.

Freud, S. (1920). *A general introduction to psycho-analysis.* New York: Boni and Liveright.

Freud, S. (1961). *Civilization and its discontents* (J. Strachey, Trans.). New York: Norton. (Original work published 1930)

Frey, J. H. (1992). Gambling on sport: Policy issues. *Journal of Gambling Studies, 8,* 351–360.

Fromm, E. (1941). *Escape from freedom.* New York: Holt, Rinehart, & Winston.

Fullerton, S., & Merz, G. R. (1982). An assessment of attendance at Major League baseball games. In M. Etzel & J. Gaski (Eds.), *Applying marketing technology to spectator sports* (pp. 77–94). South Bend, IN: University of Notre Dame Press.

Game plans. (1997, September). *Reader's Digest*, p. 91.

Gantner, A. B., & Taylor, S. P. (1988). Human physical aggression as a function of diazepam. *Personality and Social Psychology Bulletin, 14*, 479–484.

Gantz, W. (1981). An exploration of viewing motives and behaviors associated with television sports. *Journal of Broadcasting, 25*, 263–275.

Gantz, W., & Wenner, L. A. (1995). Fanship and the television sports viewing experience. *Sociology of Sport Journal, 12*, 56–74.

Gantz, W., Wenner, L. A., Carrico, C., & Knorr, M. (1995a). Assessing the football widow hypothesis: A co-orientation study of the role of televised sports in long-standing relationships. *Journal of Sport & Social Issues, 19*, 352–376.

Gantz, W., Wenner, L. A., Carrico, C., & Knorr, M. (1995b). Televised sports and marital relationships. *Sociology of Sport Journal, 12*, 306–323.

Gayton, W. F., Coffin, J. L., & Hearns, J. (1998). Further validation of the Sports Spectator Identification Scale. *Perceptual and Motor Skills, 87*, 1137–1138.

Geen, R. G., & McCown, E. J. (1984). Effects of noise and attack on aggression and physiological arousal. *Motivation and Emotion, 8*, 231–241.

Gerald, H. B., & Hoyt, M. F. (1974). Distinctiveness of social categorization and attitude toward in-group members. *Journal of Personality and Social Psychology, 29*, 836–842.

Giamatti, A. B. (1989). *Take time for paradise: Americans and their games.* New York: Summit.

Gibb, C. A. (1969). Leadership. In G. Lindsey & E. Aronson (Eds.), *The handbook of social psychology* (Vol. 4, pp. 205–282). Reading, MA: Addison-Wesley.

Gilbert, B., & Twyman, L. (1984). Violence: Out of hand in the stands. In D. S. Eitzen (Ed.), *Sport in contemporary society* (pp. 112–212). New York: St. Martin's Press.

Giulianotti, R. (1995). Football and the politics of carnival: An ethnographic study of Scottish fans in Sweden. *International Review for the Sociology of Sport, 30*, 191–223.

Giulianotti, R., Bonney, N., & Hepworth, M. (Eds.). (1994). *Football, violence, and social identity.* London: Routledge.

Gmelch, G., & San Antonio, P. M. (1998). Groupies and American baseball. *Journal of Sport & Social Issues, 22*, 32–45.

Goldberg, D. T. (1998). Sports, talk radio, and the death of democracy. *Journal of Sport & Social Issues, 22*, 212–223.

Goldstein, J. H., & Arms, R. L. (1971). Effects of observing athletic contests on hostility. *Sociometry, 34*, 83–90.

Goodger, J. M., & Goodger, B. C. (1989). Excitement and representation: Toward a sociological explanation of the significance of sport in modern society. *Quest, 41*, 257–272.

Goodhart, P., & Chataway, C. (1968). *War without weapons.* London: W. H. Allen.

Goranson, R. E. (1980). Sports violence and the catharsis hypothesis. In P. Klavora (Ed.), *Psychological and sociological factors in sport* (pp. 131–138). Toronto: University of Toronto Press.

Grady, S. (1998, September 28). Mac and Sammy take our minds off gloom and doom. *USA Today*, p. 17A.

Greendorfer, S. L. (1993). Gender role stereotypes and early childhood socialization. In G. L. Cohen (Ed.), *Women in sport: Issues and controversies* (pp. 3–14). Newbury Park, CA: Sage.

Gregg, B. G. (1992, June 16). Ballgames become embattled. *USA Today*, p. C10.

Gross, J. J., & Levenson, R. W. (1997). Hiding feelings: The acute effects of inhibiting negative and positive emotion. *Journal of Abnormal Psychology, 106,* 95–103.

Grove, J. R., Hanrahan, S. J., & McInman, A. (1991). Success/failure bias in attributions across involvement categories in sport. *Personality and Social Psychology Bulletin, 17,* 93–97.

Grove, J. R., & Paccagnella, M. (1995). Tall poppies in sport: Attitudes and ascribed personality traits. *Australian Psychologist, 38,* 95–115.

Grove, J. R., & Prapavessis, H. (1992). Preliminary evidence for the reliability and validity of an abbreviated profile of mood states. *International Journal of Sport Psychology, 23,* 93–109.

Grove, S. J., Pickett, G. M., & Dodder, R. A. (1982). Spectatorship among a collegiate sample: An exploratory investigation. In M. Etzel & J. Gaski (Eds.), *Applying marketing technology to spectator sports* (pp. 26–40). South Bend, IN: University of Notre Dame Press.

Grover, R. (1998, June 1). Online sports: Cyber fans are roaring. *Business Week,* p. 155.

Guttmann, A. (1980). On the alleged dehumanization of the sports spectator. *Journal of Popular Culture, 14,* 275–282.

Guttmann, A. (1986). *Sports spectators.* New York: Columbia University Press.

Guttmann, A. (1996). *The erotic in sports.* New York: Columbia University Press.

Haag, P. (1996). The 50,000-watt sports bar: Talk radio and the ethic of the fan. *South Atlantic Quarterly, 95,* 453–470.

Hain, P. (1971). *Don't play with apartheid: The background to the Stop the Seventy Tour campaign.* London: George Allen & Unwin Ltd.

Hall, C. S., & Lindzey, G. (1968). The relevance of Freudian psychology and related viewpoints for the social sciences. In G. Lindzey & E. Aronson (Eds.), *The handbook of social psychology* (Vol. 1, 2nd ed., pp. 245–319). New York: Addison-Wesley.

Hansen, H., & Gauthier, R. (1989). Factors affecting attendance at professional sport events. *Journal of Sport Management, 3,* 15–32.

Harackiewicz, J. H. (1979). The effects of reward contingency and performance feedback on intrinsic motivation. *Journal of Personality and Social Psychology, 37,* 1352–1363.

Hardaway, F. (1976). Foul play: Sports metaphors as public doublespeak. *College English, 38,* 78–82.

Hare, R. D. (1993). *Without conscience: The disturbing world of the psychopaths among us.* New York: Pocket Books.

Hargreaves, J. (1993). Bodies matter! Images of sport and female sexualization. In C. Brackenridge (Ed.), *Body matters: Leisure images and lifestyles* (pp. 60–66). Eastbourne, UK: Leisure Studies Association.

Harrell, W. A. (1981). Verbal aggressiveness in spectators at professional hockey games: The effects of tolerance of violence and amount of exposure to hockey. *Human Relations, 34,* 643–655.

Harris, J. C. (1986). Athletic exemplars in context: General exemplar selection patterns in relation to sex, race, and age. *Quest, 38,* 95–115.

Harris, J. C. (1994). *Athletes and the American hero dilemma.* Champaign, IL: Human Kinetics.

Harris, J. C. (1998). Civil society, physical activity, and the involvement of sport sociologists in the preparation of physical activity professionals. *Sociology of Sport Journal, 15,* 138–153.

Harris, S. J. (1981, November 3). Sport is new opium of the people. *Democrat and Chronicle*, p. 3B.

Harter, S. (1993). Causes and consequences of low self-esteem in children and adolescents. In R. F. Baumeister (Ed.), *Self-esteem: The puzzle of low self-regard* (pp. 87–116). New York: Plenum.

Hartmann, D. (1996). The politics of race and sport: Resistance and domination in the 1968 African American Olympic protest movement. *Ethnic and Racial Studies, 19,* 548–566.

Hastorf, A. H., & Cantril, H. (1954). They saw a game: A case study. *Journal of Abnormal and Social Psychology, 49,* 129–134.

Hay, R. D., & Rao, C. P. (1982). Factors affecting attendance at football games. In M. Etzel & J. Gaski (Eds.), *Applying marketing technology to spectator sports* (pp. 65–76). South Bend, IN: University of Notre Dame Press.

Heider, F. (1958). *The psychology of interpersonal relations.* New York: Wiley.

Heinegg, P. (1985). Philosopher in the playground: Notes on the meaning of sport. In D. L. Vanderwerken & S. K. Wertz (Eds.), *Sport inside out* (pp. 455–458). Fort Worth: Texas Christian University Press.

Hemphill, D. A. (1995). Revisioning sport spectatorism. *Journal of the Philosophy of Sport, 22,* 48–60.

Higgs, R. J. (1982). *Sports: A reference guide.* Westport, CT: Greenwood Press.

Higgs, R. J. (1995). *God in the stadium: Sports and religion in America.* Lexington: University Press of Kentucky.

High school team opts to take forfeit to protect students. (1991, November 1). *Democrat and Chronicle,* p. D4.

Hill, J. R., Madura, J., & Zuber, R. A. (1982). The short run demand for major league baseball. *Atlantic Economic Journal, 10,* 31–35.

Hirt, E. R., & Ryalls, K. R. (1994). Highly allegiant fans and sports team evaluation: The mediating role of self-esteem. *Perceptual and Motor Skills, 79,* 24–26.

Hirt, E. R., Zillmann, D., Erickson, G. A., & Kennedy, C. (1992). Costs and benefits of allegiance: Changes in fans' self-ascribed competencies after team victory versus defeat. *Journal of Personality and Social Psychology, 63,* 724–738.

Hoch, P. (1972). *Rip off the big game: The exploitation of sport by the power elite.* New York: Anchor Books.

Hoffer, R. (1998, September 14). Come together. *Sports Illustrated,* p. 15.

Hoffman, S. J. (Ed.). (1992). *Sport and religion.* Champaign, IL: Human Kinetics.

Hooligans sour World Cup. (1998, June 23). *Democrat and Chronicle,* p. A1.

Hoop tickets are most expensive. (1999, November 11). *Democrat and Chronicle,* p. D5.

Hoosier rebellion? (1998, May 7). *USA Today,* p. C7.

Howard, G. E. (1912). Social psychology of the spectator. *American Journal of Sociology, 18,* 33–50.

Howard, J. W., & Rothbart, M. (1980). Social categorization and memory for in-group and out-group behavior. *Journal of Personality and Social Psychology, 38,* 301–310.

Howlett, D. (1998, June 12). Chicago cops know the drill for Bulls titles. *USA Today,* p. C4.

Hughes, R. H. (1987). Response to "An Observer's View of Sport Sociology." *Sociology of Sport Journal, 4,* 137–139.

Irwin, J. (1977). *Scenes.* Beverly Hills, CA: Sage Publishers.

Iso-Ahola, S. E. (1980). Attributional determinants of decisions to attend football games. *Scandinavian Journal of Sports Sciences, 2,* 39–46.

Iso-Ahola, S. E., & Hatfield, B. (1986). *Psychology of sports: A social psychological approach.* Dubuque, IA: Brown.

Ito, T. A., Miller, N., & Pollock, V. E. (1996). Alcohol and aggression: A meta-analysis on the moderating effects of inhibitory cues, triggering events, and self-focused attention. *Psychological Bulletin, 120,* 60–82.

Izod, J. (1996). Television sport and the sacrificial hero. *Journal of Sport & Social Issues, 22,* 173–193.

Jaffe, Y., & Yinon, Y. (1983). Collective aggression: The group-individual paradigm in the study of collective antisocial behavior. In H. H. Blumberg et al. (Eds.), *Small groups and social interaction* (pp. 267–275). London: John Wiley & Sons Ltd.

Jeavons, C. M., & Taylor, S. P. (1985). The control of alcohol-related aggression: Redirecting the inebriate's attention to socially approved conduct. *Aggressive Behavior, 11,* 93–101.

Johnson, K. (1996, January 23). Hoosier hoop dreams. *USA Today,* pp. 1A–2A.

Johnson, W. O. (1988, August 8). Sports and suds: The beer business and the sports world have brewed up a potent partnership. *Sports Illustrated,* pp. 68–82.

Jones, I. (1997). A further examination of the factors influencing current identification with a sports team, a response to Wann et al. (1996). *Perceptual and Motor Skills, 85,* 257–258.

Jones, J. C. H. (1969). The economics of the National Hockey League. *Canadian Journal of Economics, 2,* 1–20.

Jones, J. C. H. (1984). Winners, losers and hosers: Demand and survival in the National Hockey League. *Atlantic Economic Journal, 12,* 54–63.

Jones, J. C. H., Ferguson, D. G., & Stewart, K. G. (1993). Blood sports and cherry pie: Some economics of violence in the National Hockey League. *American Journal of Economics and Sociology, 52,* 63–78.

Jones, S. (1993). Body images: The objectification of the female body in sport. In C. Brackenridge (Ed.), *Body matters: Leisure images and lifestyles* (pp. 136–140). Eastbourne, UK: Leisure Studies Association.

Kaelin, E. F. (1968). The well-played game: Notes toward an aesthetics of sport. *Quest, 10,* 16–28.

Kahane, L., & Shmanske, S. (1997). Team roster turnover and attendance in major league baseball. *Applied Economics, 29,* 425–431.

Kalichman, S. C., & Hunter, T. L. (1992). The disclosure of celebrity HIV infection: Its effects on public attitudes. *American Journal of Public Health, 82,* 1374–1376.

Kane, G. P. (1996, August 5). Violence is distinctively American. *Democrat and Chronicle,* p. 11A.

Kelley, H. H. (1967). Attribution theory in social psychology. In D. Levine (Ed.), *Nebraska Symposium on Motivation* (Vol. 15, pp. 192–238). Lincoln: University of Lincoln Press.

Kenyon, G. S. (1969). Sport involvement: A conceptual go and some consequences thereof. In G. S. Kenyon (Ed.), *Sociology of sport* (pp. 77–99). Chicago: The Athletic Institute.

Kenyon, G. S., & McPherson, B. D. (1973). Becoming involved in physical activity and sport: A process of socialization. In G. L. Rarick (Ed.) *Physical activity: Human growth and development* (pp. 303–322). New York: Academic Press.

Kenyon, G. S., & McPherson, B. D. (1974). An approach to the study of sport socialization. *International Review of Sport Sociology, 1*, 127–138.

Kerr, J. H. (1994). *Understanding soccer hooliganism.* Buckingham, England: Open University Press.

Kimble, C. E., & Cooper, B. P. (1992). Association and dissociation by football fans. *Perceptual and Motor Skills, 75*, 303–309.

King, A. (1995). Outline of a practical theory of football violence. *Sociology, 29*, 635–651.

Klapp, O. E. (1969). *Collective search for identity.* New York: Holt, Rinehart & Winston.

Klapp, O. E. (1972). *Currents of unrest: An introduction to collective behavior.* New York: Holt, Rinehart & Winston.

Klausner, S. Z. (1968). The intermingling of pain and pleasure: The stress-seeking personality in its social context. In S. Z. Klausner (Ed.), *Why man takes chances* (pp. 137–168). Garden City, NY: Doubleday/Anchor.

Koss, M. P., & Gaines, J. A. (1993). The prediction of sexual aggression by alcohol use, athletic participation, and fraternity affiliation. *Journal of Interpersonal Violence, 8*, 94–108.

Krohn, F. B., Clarke, M., Preston, E., McDonald, M., & Preston, B. (1998). Psychological and sociological influences on attendance at small college sporting events. *College Student Journal, 32*, 277–288.

Lakoff, G., & Johnson, M. (1980). *Metaphors we live by.* Chicago: University of Chicago Press.

Lancaster, K. (1997). When spectators become performers: Contemporary performance-entertainments meet the needs of an "unsettled audience." *Journal of Popular Culture, 30*, 75–88.

Lane, M., & Lester, D. (1995). Watching televised sports and personality. *Perceptual and Motor Skills, 81*, 966.

Lang, K., & Lang, G. E. (1961). *Collective dynamics.* New York: Crowell.

Lasch, C. (1989). The degradation of sport. In W. J. Morgan & K. V. Meier (Eds.), *Philosophic inquiry in sport* (pp. 403–417). Champaign, IL: Human Kinetics.

Lau, R. R. (1984). Dynamics of the attribution process. *Journal of Personality and Social Psychology, 46*, 1017–1028.

Lau, R. R., & Russell, D. (1980). Attributions in the sports pages. *Journal of Personality and Social Psychology, 39*, 29–38.

Layden, T. (1995, April 3). Bettor education. *Sports Illustrated*, pp. 68–74, 76–78, 80, 82–86, 90.

Lazarsfeld, P. F., & Merton, R. K. (1948). Mass communication, popular taste, and organized social action. In L. Bryson (Ed.), *The communication of ideas: A series of addresses* (pp. 95–118). New York: Harper.

Le Bon, G. (1946). *The crowd: A study of the popular mind.* New York: Macmillan. (Original work published 1896)

Leary, M. R. (1992). Self-presentational processes in exercise and sport. *Journal of Sport & Exercise Psychology, 14*, 339–351.

Leary, M. R. (1995). *Self-presentation: Impression management and interpersonal behavior.* Dubuque, IA: Brown & Benchmark.

Lee, B. A., & Zeiss, C. A. (1980). Behavioral commitment to the role of sport consumer: An exploratory analysis. *Sociology and Social Research, 64*, 405–419.

Lee, M. J. (1985). From rivalry to hostility among sports fans. *Quest, 37*, 38–49.

Leebow, K. (1999). *300 incredible things for sports fans on the Internet.* Marietta, GA: VIP.

Lester, D. (1988). Suicide and homicide during major sports events 1972–1984: Comment on Curtis, Loy and Karnilowicz. *Sociology of Sport Journal, 5,* 285.

Leuck, M. R., Krahenbuhl, G. S., & Odenkirk, J. E. (1979). Assessment of spectator aggression at intercollegiate basketball contests. *Review of Sport & Leisure, 4,* 40–52.

Levenson, M. R. (1990). Risk taking and personality. *Journal of Personality and Social Psychology, 58,* 1073–1080.

Lever, J. (1969). Soccer: Opium of the Brazilian people. *Trans-Action, 7,* 36–43.

Lever, J. (1983). *Soccer madness.* Chicago, IL: The University of Chicago Press.

Lever, J., & Wheeler, S. (1984). The Chicago Tribune sports page, 1900–1975. *Sociology of Sport Journal, 1,* 299–313.

Lewis, G., & Redmond, G. (1974). *Sport heritage: A guide to halls of fame, special collections and museums in the United States and Canada.* New York: Barnes.

Lewis, J. M. (1980). The structural dimensions of fan violence. In P. Klavora & K. A. Wipper (Eds.), *Psychological and sociological factors in sport* (pp. 148–155). Toronto: University of Toronto Press.

Lewis, J. M. (1982). Fan violence: An American social problem. In M. Lewis (Ed.), *Research in social problems and public policy* (pp. 175–206). Greenwich, CT: JAI Press, Inc.

Lewis, J. M. (1989). A value-added analysis of the Heysel Stadium riot. *Current Psychology: Research & Reviews, 8,* 15–29.

Licata, A., Taylor, S. P., Berman, M., & Cranston, J. (1993). Effects of cocaine on human aggression. *Pharmacology Biochemistry and Behavior, 45,* 549–552.

Lieberman, S. (1991, September/October). The popular culture: Sport in America—a look at the avid sports fan. *The Public Perspective: A Roper Center Review of Public Opinion and Polling, 2*(6), 28–29.

Littlefield, B. (1997, September 12–14). When "kill the umpire!" is more than a taunt. *USA Weekend,* p. 14.

Lorenz, K. (1966). *On aggression.* New York: Harcourt Brace Jovanovich.

Loy, John W., Jr. (1978). The cultural system of sport. *Quest, 29,* 73–102.

MacNeill, M. (1996). Networks: Producing Olympic ice hockey for a national television audience. *Sociology of Sport Journal, 13,* 103–124.

Madrigal, R. (1995). Cognitive and affective determinants of fan satisfaction with sporting event attendance. *Journal of Leisure Research, 27,* 205–227.

Madrigal, R. (1999). *Measuring the multidimensional nature of sporting event consumption.* Manuscript submitted for publication.

Maehr, M. L., & Braskamp, L. A. (1986). *The motivation factor: A theory of personal investment.* Lexington, MA: Lexington Books.

Maguire, J. (1986). The emergence of football spectating as a problem 1880–1985: A figurational and developmental perspective. *Sociology of Sport Journal, 3,* 217–244.

Mahony, D. F., & Howard, D. R. (1998). The impact of attitudes on the behavioral intentions of sport spectators. *International Sports Journal, 2*(1), 96–110.

Mann, L. (1969). Queue culture: The waiting line as a social system. *American Journal of Sociology, 75,* 340–354.

Mann, L. (1974). On being a sore loser: How fans react to their team's failure. *Australian Journal of Psychology, 26,* 37–47.

Mann, L. (1979). Sports crowds viewed from the perspective of collective behavior. In J. H. Goldstein (Ed.), *Sports, games, and play: Social and psychological viewpoints* (1st ed., pp. 337–369). Hillsdale, NJ: Erlbaum.

Mann, L. (1989). Sports crowds and the collective behavior perspective. In J. H. Goldstein (Ed.), *Sports, games, and play: Social and psychological viewpoints* (2nd ed., pp. 299–331). Hillsdale, NJ: Erlbaum.

Mann, L., Newton, J. W., & Innes, J. M. (1982). A test between deindividuation and emergent norm theories of crowd aggression. *Journal of Personality and Social Psychology, 42,* 260–272.

Mann, L., & Pearce, P. (1978). Social psychology of the sports spectator. In D. J. Glencross (Ed.), *Psychology and sport* (pp. 173–201). New York: McGraw-Hill.

Marcotte, H. (1989, October 25). Let's play ball. *Democrat & Chronicle,* p. 15A.

Mariscal, J. (1999). Chicanos and Latinos in the jungle of sports talk radio. *Journal of Sport & Social Issues, 23,* 111–117.

Marsh, P., Rosser, E., & Harre, R. (1978). *The rules of disorder.* London: Routledge & Kegan Paul.

Marshall, J. E., & Heslin, R. (1975). Boys and girls together: Sexual composition and the effect of density and group size on cohesiveness. *Journal of Personality and Social Psychology, 31,* 952–961.

Martens, R. (1981). Sport personology. In G. R. F. Luschen & G. H. Sage (Eds.), *Handbook of social science in sport* (pp. 492–508). Champaign, IL: Stipes.

Martin, D. E., & Dodder, R. A. (1993). A reassessment of the psychosocial functions of sport scale. *Sociology of Sport Journal, 10,* 197–204.

Marx, G. T. (1972). Issueless riots. In J. F. Short, Jr., & M. E. Wolfgang (Eds.), *Collective violence* (pp. 46–59). Chicago: Adline-Atherton.

Mashiach, A. (1980). A study to determine the factors which influence American spectators to go see the Olympics in Montreal, 1976. *Journal of Sport Behavior, 3,* 17–26.

Maslow, A. H. (1970). *Motivation and personality* (2nd ed.). New York: Harper & Row.

McCallum, J., & Hersch, H. (1997, December 1). Courtside at the Eagles' game. *Sports Illustrated,* pp. 24, 29.

McCallum, J., & O'Brien, R. (1998a, January 26). Viewer's guide. *Sports Illustrated,* p. 25–26.

McCallum, J., & O'Brien, R. (1998b, June 22). A world gone mad. *Sports Illustrated,* p. 24.

McCallum, J., & O'Brien, R. (1998c, June 29). The English beat. *Sports Illustrated,* p. 23.

McCallum, J., & O'Brien, R. (1998d, July 13). Go figure. *Sports Illustrated,* p. 26.

McDonald, M. G. (1996). Michael Jordan's family values: Marketing, meaning, and post-Reagan America. *Sociology of Sport Journal, 13,* 344–365.

McEvoy, A., & Erickson, E. L. (1981). Heroes and villains: A conceptual strategy for assessing their influence. *Sociological Focus, 14,* 111–122.

McGee, R. (1975). *Points of departure: Basic concepts in sociology.* Hinsdale, IL: The Dryden Press.

McGraw, D. (1998, July 13). Big league. *U. S. News & World Report,* pp. 40–46.

McGuire, M. (1994, June). Baseball played a special role during World War II. *Baseball Digest,* pp. 66–70.

McHoul, A. (1997). On doing "we's": Where sport leaks into everyday life. *Journal of Sport & Social Issues, 21,* 315–320.

McNair, D., Lorr, M., & Droppleman, L. (1971). *Manual for the Profile of Mood States.* San Diego: Educational and Industrial Testing Service.

McNeil, E. B. (1968). The ego and stress-seeking in man. In S. Z. Klausner (Ed.), *Why man takes chances* (pp. 171–192). Garden City, NY: Doubleday/Anchor.

McPherson, B. (1975). Sport consumption and the economics of consumerism. In D. W. Ball & J. W. Loy (Eds.), *Sport and social order: Contributions to the sociology of sport* (pp. 243–275). Reading, MA: Addison-Wesley.

McPherson, B. (1976). Socialization into the role of sport consumer: A theory and causal model. *Canadian Review of Sociology and Anthropology, 13,* 165–177.

Meier, K. V. (1989). The ignoble sports fan. *Journal of Sport & Social Issues, 13,* 111–119.

Meier, N. C., Mennenga, G. H., & Stoltz, H. T. (1941). An experimental approach to the study of mob behavior. *Journal of Abnormal Psychology, 36,* 506–524.

Melnick, M. J. (1986). The mythology of football hooliganism: A closer look at the British experience. *International Review for the Sociology of Sport, 21,* 1–21.

Melnick, M. J. (1989). The sports fan: A teaching guide and bibliography. *Sociology of Sport Journal, 6,* 167–175.

Melnick, M. J. (1993). Searching for sociability in the stands: A theory of sports spectating. *Journal of Sport Management, 7,* 44–60.

Melnick, M. J., & Jackson, S. J. (1998). The villain as reference idol: Selection frequencies and salient attributes among New Zealand teenagers. *Adolescence, 33,* 543–554.

Merton, R. K. (1967). *On theoretical sociology.* New York: Free Press.

Meyers, B. (1997, August 28). Feminine touches planned but blood and guts remain. *USA Today,* pp. A1, A2.

Mihoces, G. (1998, May 7). Women checking in more as NHL fans. *USA Today,* pp. C1, C2.

Miller, D. T., & Ross, M. (1975). Self-serving biases in the attribution of causality: Fact or fiction? *Psychological Bulletin, 82,* 213–225.

Miller, N. E. (1941). The frustration-aggression hypothesis. *Psychological Review, 48,* 337–342.

Miller, S. (1976). Personality correlates of football fandom. *Psychology, 14*(4), 7–13.

Morgan, W. P. (1980). The trait psychology controversy. *Research Quarterly for Exercise and Sport, 51,* 50–76.

Morris, D. (1981). *The soccer tribe.* London: Jonathan Cape.

Mravic, M., & Kennedy, K. (1998, November 30). A chants encounter. *Sports Illustrated,* p. 36.

Mulrooney, A., & Farmer, P. (1996). Managing the facility. In B. L. Parkhouse (Ed.), *The management of sport: Its foundation and application* (2nd ed., pp. 223–248). St. Louis, MO: Mosby.

Mumford, L. (1937). *Ends and means.* New York: Harper.

Murphy, D. (1997, September 22). Building the entertainment experience. *Stadium & Arena Financing News, 1*(7), 4.

Murrell, A. J., & Dietz, B. (1992). Fan support of sports teams: The effect of a common group identity. *Journal of Sport and Exercise Psychology, 14,* 28–39.

Mustonen, A., Arms, R. L., & Russell, G. W. (1996). Predictors of sports spectators' proclivity for violence in Finland and Canada. *Personality and Individual Differences, 21,* 519–525.

Myerscough, R., & Taylor, S. P. (1985). The effects of marijuana on human physical aggression. *Journal of Personality and Social Psychology, 49,* 1541–1546.

Nash, J. B. (1938). *Spectatoritis.* New York: Barnes.

Nelson, M. B. (1994). *The stronger women get, the more men love football.* New York: Harcourt Brace & Company.

Noll, R. G. (1974). Attendance and price setting. In R. G. Noll (Ed.), *Government and the sports business* (pp. 115–157). Washington, DC: The Brooking Institute.

Novak, M. (1976). *The joy of sports.* New York: Basic Books, Inc.

O'Brien, R., & Hersch, H. (1997a, September 1). Go figure. *Sports Illustrated*, p. 16.

O'Brien, R., & Hersch, H. (1997b, September 8). Go figure. *Sports Illustrated*, p. 16.

O'Brien, R., & Hersch, H. (1997c, October 6). Webs vanity. *Sports Illustrated*, p. 18.

O'Brien, R., & Hersch, H. (1998, June 1). Go figure. *Sports Illustrated*, p. 22.

Oglesby, C. A. (1989). Women and sport. In J. H. Goldstein (Ed.), *Sports, games, and play: Social and psychological viewpoints* (2nd ed., pp. 129–145). Hillsdale, NJ: Erlbaum.

Ohanian, R. (1991, February/March). The impact of celebrity spokespersons' perceived image on consumers' intention to purchase. *Journal of Advertising Research*, 46–54.

Oldenburg, R., & Brissett, D. (1982). The third place. *Qualitative Sociology, 5*, 265–284.

O'Neal, E. C., & McDonald, P. J. (1976). The environmental psychology of aggression. In R. G. Geen & E. C. O'Neal (Eds.), *Perspectives on aggression* (pp. 169–192). New York: Academic Press.

Overcrowding causes deaths in gym. (1991, December 30). *Naples Daily News*, p. A10.

Oyserman, D., Gant, L., & Ager, J. (1995). A socially contextualized model of African American identity: Possible selves and school persistence. *Journal of Personality and Social Psychology, 69*, 1216–1232.

Page, R. A., & Moss, M. K. (1976). Environmental influences on aggression: The effects of darkness of proximity of victim. *Journal of Applied Social Psychology, 6*, 126–133.

Palmatier, R. A., & Ray, H. L. (1989). *Sports talk: A dictionary of sports metaphors.* Westport, CT: Greenwood Press.

Pan, D. W., & Baker, J. A. (1999). Mapping of intercollegiate sports relative to selected attributes as determined by a product differentiation strategy. *Journal of Sport Behavior, 22*, 69–82.

Pan, D. W., Gabert, T. E., McGaugh, E. C., & Branvold, S. E. (1997). Factors and differential demographic effects on purchases of season tickets for intercollegiate basketball games. *Journal of Sport Behavior, 20*, 447–464.

Papazian, E. (Ed.). (1998). *TV dimensions '98* (16th ed.). New York: Media Dynamics.

Parsons, T. (1951). *The social system.* New York: The Free Press.

Patrick, D. (1999, March 12). Minn. loss first fallout in academic scandal. *USA Today*, p. 1A.

Pease, D. G., & Zhang, J. J. (1996). Differentiation of fan psychology with respect to sociodemographic backgrounds of NBA spectators. *Research Quarterly for Exercise and Sport, 67*, A100.

Penner, L. A., & Fritzsche, B. A. (1993). Magic Johnson and reactions to people with AIDS: A natural experiment. *Journal of Applied Social Psychology, 23*, 1035–1050.

Petty, R. E., & Cacioppo, J. T. (1985). *Communication and persuasion: Central and peripheral routes to attitude change.* New York: Springer-Verlag.

Petty, R. E., & Cacioppo, J. T. (1986). The elaboration likelihood model of persuasion. In L. Berkowitz (Ed.), *Advances in experimental social psychology* (Vol. 19, pp. 123–205). New York: Academic Press.

Phillips, D. P. (1983). Mass media violence and U.S. homicides. *American Sociological Review, 48*, 560–568.

Phillips, D. P. (1986). Natural experiments on the effects of mass media violence on fatal aggression: Strengths and weaknesses of a new approach. In L. Berkowitz (Ed.), *Advances in experimental social psychology* (Vol. 19, pp. 207–250). New York: Academic Press.

Pilz, G. A. (1989). Social factors influencing sport and violence: On the "problem" of football fans in West Germany. *Concilium-International Review of Theology, 5,* 32–43.

Player charged with murder after stabbing at basketball game. (1992, April 15). *Democrat and Chronicle,* p. D6.

Polansky, N., Lippitt, R., & Redl, F. (1950). An investigation of behavioral contagion in groups. *Human Relations, 3,* 319–348.

Poll on weekly worship finds 62% like to sleep in. (1997, April 18). *Democrat and Chronicle,* p. 4A.

Pope, H. G., Jr., & Katz, M. D. (1990). Homicide and near-homicide by anabolic steroid users. *Journal of Clinical Psychiatry, 5,* 28–31.

Prebish, C. S. (1993). *Religion and sport: The meeting of sacred and profane.* Westport, CT: Greenwood Press.

Preston, F. W. (1978). Hucksters at the circus. *Urban Life, 7,* 205–212.

Price, J. L. (1988, November). *Masking and transformation: The religious significance of masks for Super Bowl fans.* Paper presented at the ninth Annual Conference of the North American Society for the Sociology of Sport, Cincinnati, Ohio.

Price, J. L. (1991). The final four as final judgment: The cultural significance of the NCAA basketball championship. *Journal of Popular Culture, 24,* 49–58.

Prisuta, R. H. (1979). Televised sports and political values. *Journal of Communication, 29,* 94–102.

Protestant mob attacks Catholics at soccer game. (1996, October 20). *Democrat and Chronicle,* p. 7.

Putnam, R. D. (1995). Bowling alone: America's declining social capital. *Journal of Democracy, 6,* 65–78.

Quirk, K. (1997). *Not now, honey, I'm watching the game.* New York: Fireside.

Rainey, D. W. (1994). Magnitude of stress experienced by baseball and softball umpires. *Perceptual and Motor Skills, 79,* 255–258.

Rainey, D. W., & Duggan, P. (1998). Assaults on basketball referees: A statewide survey. *Journal of Sport Behavior, 21,* 113–120.

Rainey, D. W., & Winterich, D. (1995). Magnitude of stress reported by basketball referees. *Perceputal and Motor Skills, 81,* 1241–1242.

Ransford, H. E. (1968). Isolation, powerlessness, and violence: A study of attitudes and participation in the Watts riot. *The American Journal of Sociology, 73,* 581–591.

Real, M. (1975). Super Bowl: Mythic spectacle. *Journal of Communication, 25,* 31–43.

Real, M. R., & Mechikoff, R. A. (1992). Deep fan: Mythic identification, technology, and advertising in spectator sports. *Sociology of Sport Journal, 9,* 323–339.

Reese, C. (1994, November 5). Game's over if sports fans stop playing the fools. *Democrat and Chronicle,* p. 12A.

Reich, C. A. (1970). *The greening of America.* New York: Bantam Books.

Reifman, A. S., Larrick, R. P., & Fein, S. (1991). Temper and temperature on the diamond: The heat-aggression relationship in major league baseball. *Personality and Social Psychology Bulletin, 17,* 580–585.

Reiss, A. J., & Roth, J. A. (Eds.). (1993). *Understanding and preventing violence* (Vol. 1). Washington, DC: National Academic Press.

Reynolds, B., & Benedetto, W. (1990, December 12). Violence is everywhere, at every level of society. *Democrat and Chronicle*, p. A13.

Rinehart, R. (1996). Dropping hierarchies: Toward the study of a contemporary sporting avant-garde. *Sociology of Sport Journal, 13*, 159–175.

Rinehart, R. (1998). Inside of the outside: Pecking orders within alternative sport at ESPN's 1995 "The eXtreme Games." *Journal of Sport & Social Issues, 22*, 398–415.

Rioting fans put end to English-Irish game. (1995, February 16). *Democrat and Chronicle*, p. D10.

Roadburg, A. (1980). Factors precipitating fan violence: A comparison of professional soccer in Britain and North America. *The British Journal of Sociology, 31*, 265–275.

Roberts, S. (1997, October). Building the American pyramids. *Sportstech*, pp. 34–37.

Roloff, M. E., & Solomon, D. H. (1989). Sex typing, sports interests, and relational harmony. In L. A. Wenner (Ed.), *Media, sports, and society* (pp. 290–311). Newbury Park, CA: Sage.

Roosa, D. B. St. John. (1898). Are foot-ball games educative or brutalizing? *Forum, 16*, 634–642.

Rosenberg, M. (1973). Which significant others? *American Behavioral Scientist, 16*, 829–860.

Rosenfeld, M. J. (1997). Celebrating, politics, selective looting and riots: A micro level study of the Bulls riot of 1992 in Chicago. *Social Problems, 44*, 483–502.

Ross, L. (1977). The intuitive psychologist and his shortcomings: Distortions in the attribution process. In L. Berkowitz (Ed.), *Advances in experimental social psychology* (Vol. 10, pp. 173–220). New York: Academic Press.

Ross, L., Greene, D., & House, P. (1977). The "false consensus effect": An egocentric bias in social perception and attributional processes. *Journal of Experimental Social Psychology, 13*, 279–301.

Ross, M. (1975). Salience of reward and intrinsic motivation. *Journal of Personality and Social Psychology, 32*, 245–254.

Rotton, J., Frey, J., Barry, T., Milligan, M., & Fitzpatrick, M. (1979). The air pollution experience and physical aggression. *Journal of Applied Social Psychology, 9*, 397–412.

Rowdies spoil fun for real sports fans. (1988, May 6). *USA Today*, p. A12.

Rowdy Detroit fans sentenced harshly. (1995, June 3). *Democrat and Chronicle*, p. D3.

Russell, G. W. (1979). Hero selection by Canadian ice hockey players: Skill or aggression? *Canadian Journal of Applied Sport Sciences, 4*, 309–313.

Russell, G. W. (1981). Spectator moods at an aggressive sports event. *Journal of Sport Psychology, 3*, 217–227.

Russell, G. W. (1983). Psychological issues in sports aggression. In J. H. Goldstein (Ed.), *Sports violence* (pp. 157–181). New York: Springer-Verlag.

Russell, G. W. (1986). Does sports violence increase box office receipts? *International Journal of Sport Psychology, 17*, 173–183.

Russell, G. W. (1993). *The social psychology of sport*. New York: Springer-Verlag.

Russell, G. W. (1995). Personalities in the crowd: Those who would escalate a sports riot. *Aggressive Behavior, 21*, 91–100.

Russell, G. W., & Arms, R. L. (1995). False consensus effect, physical aggression, anger, and a willingness to escalate a disturbance. *Aggressive Behavior, 21*, 381–386.

Russell, G. W., & Arms, R. L. (1998). Toward a social psychological profile of would-be rioters. *Aggressive Behavior, 24,* 219–226.

Russell, G. W., & Arms, R. L. (1999). *Calming troubled waters: Peacemakers in a sports riot.* Manuscript submitted for publication.

Russell, G. W., Arms, R. L., & Bibby, R. W. (1995). Canadians' belief in catharsis. *Social Behavior and Personality: An International Journal, 23,* 223–228.

Russell, G. W., Arms, R. L., & Mustonen, A. (1999). When cooler heads prevail: Peacemakers in a sports riot. *Scandinavian Journal of Psychology, 40,* 153–155.

Russell, G. W., Di Lullo, S. L., & Di Lullo, D. (1989). Effects of observing competitive and violent versions of a sport. *Current Psychology: Research & Reviews, 7,* 312–321.

Russell, G. W., & Goldstein, J. H. (1995). Personality differences between Dutch football fans and nonfans. *Social Behavior and Personality, 23,* 199–204.

Russell, G. W., & McClusky, M. G. (1985, May). *The exemplars of adolescents: Their influence and quality.* Paper presented at the meeting of the Banff Annual Seminar in Cognitive Science, Banff, Alberta, Canada.

Russell, G. W., & Mustonen, A. (1998). Peacemakers: Those who intervene to quell a sports riot. *Personality and Individual Differences, 24,* 335–339.

Russell, G. W., & Wann, D. L. (1999). [Peacemakers and law and order]. Unpublished raw data.

Ryan, A. J. (1984 February). Fans need protection. *The Physician and Sportsmedicine, 12,* 43.

Sabo, D., Jansen, S. C., Tate, D., Duncan, M. C., & Leggett, S. (1996). Televising international sport: Race, ethnicity, and nationalistic bias. *Journal of Sport & Social Issues, 21,* 7–21.

Sage, G. H. (1996). Patriotic images and capitalist profit: Contradictions of professional team sports licensed merchandise. *Sociology of Sport Journal, 13,* 1–11.

Salmivalli, C., Lagerspetz, K., Bjorkqvist, K., Osterman, K., & Kaukiainen, A. (1996). Bullying as a group process: Participant roles and their relations to social status within a group. *Aggressive Behavior, 22,* 1–15.

Sandiford, K. A. P. (1982). English cricket crowds during the Victorian age. *Journal of Sport History, 9,* 5–22.

Sapolsky, B. S. (1980). The effect of spectator disposition and suspense on the enjoyment of sport contests. *International Journal of Sport Psychology, 11,* 1–10.

Sargent, S. L., Zillmann, D., & Weaver, J. B., III. (1998). The gender gap in the enjoyment of televised sports. *Journal of Sport & Social Issues, 22,* 46–64.

Schafer, W. E. (1969). Some social sources and consequences of interscholastic athletics: The case of participation and delinquency. In G. S. Kenyon (Ed.), *Aspects of contemporary sport sociology* (pp. 29–44). Chicago: The Athletic Institute.

Schofield, J. A. (1983). Performance and attendance at professional team sports. *Journal of Sport Behavior, 6,* 196–206.

Schurr, K. T., Ruble, V. E., & Ellen, A. S. (1985). Myers-Briggs Type Inventory and demographic characteristics of students attending and not attending a college basketball game. *Journal of Sport Behavior, 8,* 181–194.

Schurr, K. T., Wittig, A. F., Ruble, V. E., & Ellen, A. S. (1988). Demographic and personality characteristics associated with persistent, occasional, and non-attendance of university male basketball games by college students. *Journal of Sport Behavior, 11,* 3–17.

Schurr, K. T., Wittig, A. F., Ruble, V. E., & Henriksen, L. W. (1993). College graduation rates of student athletes and students attending college male basketball games: A case study. *Journal of Sport Behavior, 16,* 33–41.

Schwartz, J. M. (1973). Causes and effects of spectator sports. *International Review of Sport Sociology, 8,* 25–45.

Schwarz, N., Strack, F., Kommer, D., & Wagner, D. (1987). Soccer, rooms, and the quality of your life: Mood effects on judgments of satisfaction with life in general and with specific domains. *European Journal of Social Psychology, 17,* 69–79.

Schweitzer, K., Zillmann, D., Weaver, J. B., & Luttrell, E. S. (1992). Perception of threatening events in the emotional aftermath of a televised college football game. *Journal of Broadcasting & Electronic Media, 36,* 75–82.

Segrave, J. (1994). The perfect 10: "Sportspeak" in the language of sexual relations. *Sociology of Sport Journal, 11,* 95–113.

Semyonov, M., & Farbstein, M. (1989). Ecology of sports violence: The case of Israeli soccer. *Sociology of Sport Journal, 6,* 50–59.

Senators seek "report card" on TV violence. (1995, May 10). *Democrat and Chronicle,* p. A11.

Shames, L. (1989, January 2). America's icon. *Sports inc.,* p. 52.

Shank, M. D., & Beasley, F. M. (1998). Fan or fanatic: Refining a measure of sports involvement. *Journal of Sport Behavior, 21,* 435–443.

Shenk, D. (1997, June 17). No one mingles in "global village." *USA Today,* p. 11A.

Shuster, R. (1994, June 15). Female athletes, fans need not justify passion. *USA Today,* p. 3C.

Silva, J. M., III (1984). Personality and sport performance: Controversy and challenge. In J. M. Silva & R. S. Weinberg (Eds.), *Psychological foundations of sport* (pp. 59–69). Champaign, IL: Human Kinetics.

Simons, Y., & Taylor, J. (1992). A psychosocial model of fan violence in sports. *International Journal of Sport Psychology, 23,* 207–226.

Sipes, R. (1996). Sports as a control for aggression. In D. S. Eitzen (Ed.), *Sport in contemporary society* (pp. 154–160). New York: St. Martin's Press.

Sloan, L. R. (1989). The motives of sports fans. In J. D. Goldstein (Ed.), *Sports, games, and play: Social and psychosocial viewpoints* (2nd ed., pp. 175–240). Hillsdale, NJ: Lawrence Erlbaum Associates.

Smelser, N. J. (1968). Social and psychological dimensions of collective behavior. In N. J. Smelser (Ed.), *Essays in sociological explanation* (pp. 92–121). Upper Saddle River, NJ: Prentice Hall.

Smith, E. R., & Henry, S. (1996). An in-group becomes part of the self: Response time evidence. *Personality and Social Psychology Bulletin, 22,* 635–642.

Smith, G. J. (1976). An examination of the phenomenon of sports hero worship. *Canadian Journal of Applied Sport Sciences, 1,* 259–270.

Smith, G. J. (1978). Use of the mass media for sports information as a function of age, sex and socioeconomic status. In F. Landry & W. A. Orban (Eds.), *Sociology of sport* (pp. 137–146). Miami, FL: Symposia Specialists.

Smith, G. J. (1988). The noble sports fan. *Journal of Sport & Social Issues, 12,* 54–65.

Smith, G. J. (1989). The noble sports redux. *Journal of Sport & Social Issues, 13,* 121–130.

Smith, G. J., Patterson, B., Williams, T., & Hogg, J. (1981). A profile of the deeply committed male sports fan. *Arena Review, 5,* 26–44.

Smith, M. D. (1976). Precipitants of crowd violence. *Sociological Inquiry, 48,* 121–131.

Smith, M. D. (1983). *Violence in sport*. Toronto: Butterworth.

Smith, R. H., Turner, T. J., Garonzik, R., Leach, C. W., Urch-Druskat, V., & Weston, C. M. (1996). Envy and Schadenfreude. *Personality and Social Psychology Bulletin, 22,* 158–168.

Smith, T. W. (1986). The polls: The most admired man and woman. *Public Opinion Quarterly, 50,* 573–583.

Snyder, C. R., Lassegard, M., & Ford, C. E. (1986). Distancing after group success and failure: Basking in reflected glory and cutting off reflected failure. *Journal of Personality and Social Psychology, 51,* 382–388.

Snyder, D., & Koenig, B. (1998, April 8). Baseball's tobacco war. *Baseball Weekly,* pp. 32–35.

Snyder, E. E. (1991). Sociology of nostalgia: Sport halls of fame and museums in America. *Sociology of Sport Journal, 8,* 228–238.

Snyder, M. A. (1993). The new competition: Sports careers for women. In G. L. Cohen (Ed.), *Women in sport: Issues and controversies* (pp. 264–274). Newbury Park, CA: Sage.

Snyder, M. L., & Jones, E. E. (1974). Attitude attribution when behavior is constrained. *Journal of Experimental Social Psychology, 10,* 585–600.

Spackman, A. (1986, May 18). Hooliganism halves by police crackdown. *The Sunday (London) Times,* p. 3.

Spink, C. C. (1978, June 10). We believe. *The Sporting News,* p. 2.

Spreitzer, E., & Snyder, E. (1975). The psychosocial functions of sport as perceived by the general population. *International Review of Sport Sociology, 3-4,* 87–95.

Stainback, R. D. (1997). *Alcohol and sport.* Champaign, IL: Human Kinetics.

Stevenson, C. L. (1974). Sport as a contemporary social phenomenon: A functional explanation. *International Journal of Physical Education, 11,* 8–13.

Stewart, M. J., & Ellery, P. J. (1996). Amount of psychological stress reported by high school volleyball officials. *Perceptual and Motor Skills, 83,* 337–338.

Stiles, D. A., Gibbons, J. L., Sebben, D. J., & Wiley, D. C. (1999). Why adolescent boys dream of becoming professional athletes. *Psychological Reports, 84,* 1075–1085.

Stotler, D. K. (1989). *Successful sport marketing.* Dubuque, IA: W. C. Brown.

Stott, C., & Reicher, S. (1998). Crowd actions as intergroup processes: Introducing the police perspective. *European Journal of Social Psychology, 28,* 509–529.

Straub, B. (1995). Die Messung der Identifikation mit einer Sportmannschaft: Eine deutsche adaptation der "Team Identification Scale" von Wann und Branscombe [A measure of identification with a sport team: A German adaptation of the "Team Identification Scale" by Wann and Branscombe]. *Psychologie und Sport, 4,* 132–145.

Strinati, D. (1995). *An introduction to theories of popular culture.* London: Routledge.

Su-Lin, G., Tuggle, C. A., Mitrook, M. A., Coussement, S. H., & Zillmann, D. (1997). The thrill of a close game: Who enjoys it and who doesn't? *Journal of Sport & Social Issues, 21,* 53–64.

Sullivan, R. (1986, January 6). Foxboro flow. *Sports Illustrated,* p. 7.

Sumser, J. (1992). Campus knowledge of AIDS before and after "Magic" Johnson announced his infection. *SSB, 76,* 182–184.

Swift, E. M. (1999, February 1). Breaking point. *Sports Illustrated,* pp. 32–37.

Tajfel, H. (1981). *Human groups and social categories.* Cambridge: Cambridge University Press.

.ier, J. (1979). An integrative theory of intergroup conflict. In W. Worchel (Eds.), *The social psychology of intergroup relations* (pp. .nterey, CA: Brooks/Cole.

ı, P. H., & Noah, J. E. (1959). Sportugese: A study of sports page .iication. *Journalism Quarterly, 36,* 163–170.

, Sev'er, A., & Ungar, S. (1989). Explaining the steroid scandal: How ıto students interpret the Ben Johnson case. *International Journal of ıt Psychology, 20,* 297–308.

Taylor, S. P., & Gammon, C. B. (1976). Aggressive behavior of intoxicated subjects: The effect of third party intervention. *Journal of Studies on Alcohol, 37,* 917–930.

Taylor, S. P., Gammon, C. B., & Capasso, D. R. (1976). Aggression as a function of the interaction of alcohol and threat. *Journal of Personality and Social Psychology, 34,* 938–941.

Tedeschi, J. T., & Felson, R. B. (1994). *Violence, aggression, and coercive actions.* Washington, DC: American Psychological Association.

Telander, R. (1993, November 8). Violent victory. *Sports Illustrated,* pp. 60–64.

Tesler, B. S., & Alker, H. A. (1983). Football games: Victory, defeat, and spectators' power preferences. *Journal of Research in Personality, 17,* 72–80.

Theberge, N. (1985). Toward a feminist alternative to sport as a male preserve. *Quest, 37,* 193–202.

Theodorson, G. A., & Theodorson, A. G. (1969). *A modern dictionary of sociology.* New York: Crowell.

Thomas, R. M. (1986, June 4). Seven of 10 in survey say they're fans. *The New York Times,* p. 89.

Trail, G. T., James, J. D., & Madrigal, R. (1998). *An examination of the Sport Fan Motivation Scale.* Manuscript submitted for publication.

Trovato, F. (1998). The Stanley cup of hockey and suicide in Quebec. *Social Forces, 77,* 105–127.

Turco, D. (1996). The X factor: Marketing sports to Generation X. *Sport Marketing Quarterly, 5,* 21–26.

Turner, R. H., & Killian, L. M. (1972). *Collective behavior* (2nd ed.). Englewood Cliffs, NJ: Prentice Hall.

Uemukai, K., Takenouchi, T., Okuda, E., Matsumoto, M., & Yamanaka, K. (1995). Analysis of the factors affecting spectators' identification with professional football teams in Japan. *Journal of Sport Sciences, 13,* 522.

Ungar, S., & Sev'er, A. (1989). "Say it ain't so, Ben": Attributions for a fallen hero. *Social Psychology Quarterly, 52,* 207–212.

Unruh, D. R. (1983). *Invisible lives: Social worlds of the aged.* Beverly Hills, CA: Sage.

Vander Velden, L. (1986). Heroes and bad winners: Cultural differences. In L. Vander Velden & J. H. Humphrey (Eds.), *Psychology and sociology of sport* (pp. 205–220). New York: AMS Press.

Violence and high school sports. (1992, June 16). *USA Today,* p. C10.

Wachs, F. L., & Dworkin, S. L. (1997). "There's no such thing as a gay hero": Sexual identity and media framing of HIV-positive athletes. *Journal of Sport & Social Issues, 21,* 327–347.

Wahl, G. (1999, May 17). "Holy war." *Sports Illustrated,* pp. 54–57.

Wakefield, K. L. (1995). The pervasive effects of social influence on sporting event attendance. *Journal of Sport & Social Issues, 19,* 335–351.

Wallis, C. (1999, July 5). The kids are alright. *Time,* pp. 26–28.

Walters, J. (1994, October 17). Town pride. *Sports Illustrated*, pp. 86–87.

Walters, J. (1999a, January 25). SI view: The week in TV sports. *Sports Illustrated*, p. 31.

Walters, J. (1999b, February 1). SI view: The week in TV sports. *Sports Illustrated*, p. 17.

Walzer, M. (1991). The idea of civil society: A path to social reconstruction. *Dissent, 38*, 293–304.

Wann, D. L. (1993). Aggression among highly identified spectators as a function of their need to maintain positive social identity. *Journal of Sport & Social Issues, 17*, 134–143.

Wann, D. L. (1994a). Biased evaluations of highly identified sport spectators: A response to Hirt and Ryalls. *Perceptual and Motor Skills, 79*, 105–106.

Wann, D. L. (1994b). The "noble" sports fan: The relationships between team identification, self-esteem, and aggression. *Perceptual and Motor Skills, 78*, 864–866.

Wann, D. L. (1995). Preliminary validation of the Sport Fan Motivational Scale. *Journal of Sport & Social Issues, 19*, 377–396.

Wann, D. L. (1996). Seasonal changes in spectators' identification and involvement with and evaluations of college basketball and football teams. *The Psychological Record, 46*, 201–215.

Wann, D. L. (1997). *Sport psychology.* Upper Saddle River, NJ: Prentice Hall.

Wann, D. L. (1998a). A preliminary investigation of the relationship between alcohol use and sport fandom. *Social Behavior and Personality: An International Journal, 26*, 287–290.

Wann, D. L. (1998b). Tobacco use and sport fandom. *Perceptual and Motor Skills, 86*, 878.

Wann, D. L. (2000). Further exploration of seasonal changes in sport fan identification: Investigating the importance of fan expectations. *International Sports Journal, 4*, 119–123.

Wann, D. L. (in press). Preliminary validation of a measure for assessing identification as a sport fan: The Sport Fandom Questionnaire. *Journal of Sport Behavior*.

Wann, D. L., Bilyeu, J. K., Brennan, K., Osborn, H., & Gambouras, A. F. (1999). An exploratory investigation of the relationship between sport fan motivation and race. *Perceptual and Motor Skills, 88*, 1081–1084.

Wann, D. L., & Branscombe, N. R. (1990a). Die-hard and fair-weather fans: Effects of identification on BIRGing and CORFing tendencies. *Journal of Sport & Social Issues, 14*, 103–117.

Wann, D. L., & Branscombe, N. R. (1990b). Person perception when aggressive or nonaggressive sports are primed. *Aggressive Behavior, 16*, 27–32.

Wann, D. L., & Branscombe, N. R. (1993). Sports fans: Measuring degree of identification with the team. *International Journal of Sport Psychology, 24*, 1–17.

Wann, D. L., & Branscombe, N. R. (1995a). Influence of identification with a sports team on objective knowledge and subjective beliefs. *International Journal of Sport Psychology, 26*, 551–567.

Wann, D. L., & Branscombe, N. R. (1995b). Influence of level of identification with a group and physiological arousal on perceived intergroup complexity. *British Journal of Social Psychology, 34*, 223–235.

Wann, D. L., Brewer, K. R., & Royalty, J. L. (1999). Sport fan motivation: Relationships with team identification and emotional reactions to sporting events. *International Sports Journal, 3*, 8–18.

Wann, D. L., Carlson, J. D., Holland, L. C., Jacob, B. E., Owens, D. A., & Wells, D. D. (1999). Belief in symbolic catharsis: The importance of involvement with aggressive sports. *Social Behavior and Personality: An International Journal, 27,* 155–164.

Wann, D. L., Carlson, J. D., & Schrader, M. P. (1999). The impact of team identification on the hostile and instrumental verbal aggression of sport spectators. *Journal of Social Behavior and Personality, 14,* 279–286.

Wann, D. L., & Dolan, T. J. (1994a). Attributions of highly identified sport spectators. *The Journal of Social Psychology, 134,* 783–792.

Wann, D. L., & Dolan, T. J. (1994b). Influence of spectators' identification on evaluation of the past, present, and future performance of a sports team. *Perceptual and Motor Skills, 78,* 547–552.

Wann, D. L., & Dolan, T. J. (1994c). Spectators' evaluations of rival and fellow fans. *The Psychological Record, 44,* 351–358.

Wann, D. L., Dolan, T. J., McGeorge, K. K., & Allison, J. A. (1994). Relationships between spectator identification and spectators' perceptions of influence, spectators' emotions, and competition outcome. *Journal of Sport & Exercise Psychology, 16,* 347–364.

Wann, D. L., & Ensor, C. L. (1999a). Further validation of the economic subscale of the Sport Fan Motivation Scale. *Perceptual and Motor Skills, 88,* 659–660.

Wann, D. L., & Ensor, C. L. (1999b). *Further investigation of the relationship between family motivation and preferences for aggressive sports.* Manuscript submitted for publication.

Wann, D. L., Fahl, C. L., Erdmann, J. B., & Littleton, J. D. (1999). The relationship between identification with the role of sport fan and trait levels of aggression. *Perceptual and Motor Skills, 88,* 1296–1298.

Wann, D. L., & Hamlet, M. A. (1995). Author and subject gender in sports research. *International Journal of Sport Psychology, 26,* 225–232.

Wann, D. L., Hamlet, M. A., Wilson, T., & Hodges, J. A., (1995). Basking in reflected glory, cutting off reflected failure, and cutting off future failure: The importance of identification with a group. *Social Behavior and Personality: An International Journal, 23,* 377–388.

Wann, D. L., Inman, S., Ensor, C. L, Gates, R. D., & Caldwell, D. S. (1999). Assessing the psychological well-being of sport fans using the Profile of Mood States: The importance of team identification. *International Sports Journal, 3,* 81–90.

Wann, D. L., Lane, T. M., Duncan, L. E., & Goodson, S. L. (1998). Family status, preference for sport aggressiveness, and sport fan motivation. *Perceptual and Motor Skills, 86,* 1319–1422.

Wann, D. L., Metcalf, L. A., Adcock, M. L., Choi, C. C., Dallas, M. B., & Slaton, E. (1997). Language of sport fans: Sportugese revisited. *Perceptual and Motor Skills, 85,* 1107–1110.

Wann, D. L., Peterson, R. R., Cothran, C., & Dykes, M. (1999). Sport fan aggression and anonymity: The importance of team identification. *Social Behavior and Personality: An International Journal, 27,* 597–602.

Wann, D. L., Roberts, A., & Tindall, J. (1999). The role of team performance, team identification, and self-esteem in sport spectators' game preferences. *Perceptual and Motor Skills, 89,* 945–950.

Wann, D. L., & Robinson, T. N., III. (1999). *The relationship between sport team identification and integration into and perceptions of a university.* Manuscript submitted for publication.

Wann, D. L., & Rochelle, A. R. (1999). *Using sport fandom as an escape: Searching for relief from under-stimulation and over-stimulation.* Manuscript submitted for publication.

Wann, D. L., Royalty, J., & Roberts, A. (1999). *The self-presentation of sport fans: Investigating the importance of team identification and self-esteem.* Manuscript submitted for publication.

Wann, D. L., & Schrader, M. P. (1996). An analysis of the stability of sport team identification. *Perceptual and Motor Skills, 82,* 322.

Wann, D. L., & Schrader, M. P. (1997). Team identification and the enjoyment of watching a sporting event. *Perceptual and Motor Skills, 84,* 954.

Wann, D. L., & Schrader, M. P. (in press). Controllability and stability in the self-serving attributions of sport spectators. *Journal of Social Psychology.*

Wann, D. L., Schrader, M. P., & Adamson, D. R. (1998). The cognitive and somatic anxiety of sport spectators. *Journal of Sport Behavior, 21,* 322–337.

Wann, D. L., Schrader, M. P., & Carlson, J. D. (in press). The verbal aggression of sport spectators: A comparison of hostile and instrumental motives. *International Sports Journal.*

Wann, D. L., Schrader, M. P., & Wilson, A. M. (1999). Sport fan motivation: Questionnaire validation, comparisons by sport, and relationship to athletic motivation. *Journal of Sport Behavior, 22,* 114–139.

Wann, D. L., Tucker, K. B., & Schrader, M. P. (1996). An exploratory examination of the factors influencing the origination, continuation, and cessation of identification with sports teams. *Perceptual and Motor Skills, 82,* 995–1101.

Wann, D. L., & Wilson, A. M. (1999a). The relationship between aesthetic fan motivation and preferences for aggressive and nonaggressive sports. *Perceptual and Motor Skills, 89,* 931–934.

Wann, D. L., & Wilson, A. M. (1999b). Variables associated with sports fans' enjoyment of athletic events. *Perceptual and Motor Skills, 89,* 419–422.

Wann, D. L., & Wilson, A. M. (in press). The relationship between the sport team identification of basketball fans and the number of attributions generated to explain a team's performance. *International Sports Journal.*

Weiller, K. H., & Higgs, C. T. (1997). Fandom in the 40's: The integrating functions of All American Girls Professional Baseball League. *Journal of Sport Behavior, 20,* 211–231.

Weiner, B. (1979). A theory of motivation for some classroom experiences. *Journal of Educational Psychology, 71,* 3–25.

Weiner, B. (1980). A cognitive (attribution)—emotion—action model of motivated behavior: An analysis of judgments of help-giving. *Journal of Personality and Social Psychology, 39,* 186–200.

Weiner, B. (1989). *Human motivation.* Hillsdale, NJ: Erlbaum.

Weisman, L. (1995, August 30). Patriots' fans must play by the rules, too. *USA TODAY,* p. C6.

Wenner, L. A., & Gantz, W. (1989). The audience experience with sports on television. In L. A. Wenner (Ed.), *Media, sports, and society* (pp. 241–268). Newbury Park, CA: Sage.

Wertz, S. K. (1985). Artistic creativity in sport. In D. L. Vanderwerken & S. K. Wertz (Eds.), *Sport inside out* (pp. 510–519). Fort Worth: Texas Christian University Press.

West, D. (Ed.). (1998). *Broadcasting & Cable Yearbook, 1998* (Vol. 12). New Providence, NJ: Bowker.

Wheeler, L., & Caggiula, A. R. (1966). The contagion of aggression. *Journal of Experimental Social Psychology, 2,* 1–10.

White, C. (1996, April 30). Multiclass opponents consider strategy. *USA Today,* p. 4C.

White, G. F. (1989). Media and violence: The case of professional football championship games. *Aggressive Behavior, 15,* 423–433.

White, G. F., Katz, J., & Scarborough, K. E. (1992). The impact of professional football games upon violent assaults on women. *Violence and Victims, 7,* 157–171.

Whitney, J. D. (1988). Winning games versus winning championships: The economics of fan interest and team performance. *Economic Inquiry, 26,* 703–724.

Wilkerson, M., & Dodder, R. A. (1987). Collective conscience and sport in modern society: An empirical test of a model. *Journal of Leisure Research, 19,* 35–40.

Williams, J. (1998, August 2). Ballpark ins and outs. *Houston Chronicle,* pp. A37, A42.

Winkler, J. D., & Taylor, S. E. (1979). Preference, expectations, and attributional bias: Two field studies. *Journal of Applied Social Psychology, 9,* 183–197.

Wolfe, J., Martinez, R., & Scott, W. A. (1998). Baseball and beer: An analysis of alcohol consumption patterns among male spectators at Major-League sporting events. *Annals of Emergency Medicine, 31,* 629–632.

Wolff, A., & O'Brien, R. (1994, December 19). Thrown out. *Sports Illustrated,* p. 19.

Work and play (1996, January 29). *Democrat and Chronicle,* p. 7B.

World gone mad (1998, June 22). *Sports Illustrated,* pp. 24–25.

Wright, S. (1978). *Crowds and riots.* Beverly Hills, CA: Sage.

Yergin, M. L. (1986). Who goes to the game? *American Demographics, 8,* 42–43.

Yonda, A. J. (1998, June 24). Fathers needed if sons are to control their aggression. *Democrat and Chronicle,* p. A15.

Zani, B., & Kirchler, E. (1991). When violence overshadows the spirit of sporting competition: Italian football fans and their clubs. *Journal of Community and Applied Social Psychology, 1,* 5–21.

Zhang, J. J., Pease, D. G., & Hui, S. C. (1996). Value dimensions of professional sport as viewed by spectators. *Journal of Sport & Social Issues, 21,* 78–94.

Zhang, J. J., Pease, D. G., Hui, S. C., & Michaud, T. J. (1995). Variables affecting the spectator decision to attend NBA games. *Sport Marketing Quarterly, 4*(4), 29–39.

Zhang, J. J., Pease, D. G., & Smith, D. W. (1998). Relationship between broadcasting media and minor league hockey game attendance. *Journal of Sport Management, 12,* 103–122.

Zhang, J. J., Pease, D. G., Smith, D. W., Lee, J. L., Lam, E. T. C., & Jambor, E. A. (1997). Factors affecting the decision making of spectators to attend minor league hockey games. *International Sports Journal, 1,* 39–54.

Zhang, J. J., & Smith, D. W. (1997). Impact of broadcasting on the attendance of professional basketball games. *Sport Marketing Quarterly, 6*(1), 23–29.

Zhang, J. J., Smith, D. W., Pease, D. G., & Lam, E. T. C. (1998). Dimensions of spectator satisfaction toward support programs of professional hockey games. *International Sports Journal, 2,* 1–17.

Zillmann, D., Baron, R., & Tamborini, R. (1981). Social costs of smoking: Effects of tobacco smoke on hostile behavior. *Journal of Applied Social Psychology, 11,* 548–561.

Zillmann, D., Bryant, J., & Sapolsky, B. S. (1989). Enjoyment from sports spectatorship. In J. H. Goldstein (Ed.), *Sports, games, and play: Social and psychological viewpoints* (2nd ed., pp. 241–278). Hillsdale, NJ: Erlbaum.

Zillmann, D., & Paulas, P. B. (1993). Spectators: Reactions to sports events and effects on athletic performance. In R. N. Singer, M. Murphey, & L. K. Tennant (Eds.), *Handbook of research on sport psychology* (pp. 600–619). New York: Macmillan.

Zimet, G. D., Lazebnik, R., DiClemente, R. J., Anglin, T. M., Williams, P., & Ellick, E. M. (1993). The relationship of Magic Johnson's announcement of HIV infection to the AIDS attitudes of junior high school students. *The Journal of Sex Research, 38,* 129–134.

Zuckerman, D. M., Singer, D. G., & Singer, J. L. (1980). Children's television viewing, racial and sex-role attitudes. *Journal of Applied Social Psychology, 10,* 281–294.

Zuckerman, M. (1979). *Sensation-seeking: Beyond the optimal level of arousal.* Hillsdale, NJ: Erlbaum.

Zuckerman, M. (1984). Sensation seeking: A comparative approach to a human behavior. *The Behavioral and Brain Sciences, 7,* 413–471.

Zurcher, L. A, & Meadow, A. (1967). On bullfights and baseball: An example of interaction of social institutions. *The International Journal of Comparative Sociology, 8,* 99–117

SUBJECT INDEX

AUTHOR INDEX

Aberle, D. F., 180, 182, 189
Adamson, D., R. 4
Adcock, M. L., 4, 184
Ager, J., 48
Alderfer, C. P., 32
Alker, H. A., 116
Allen, K., 187
Allison, J. A., 4, 167
Alvarez, J., 16
Anderson, C. A., 113
Anderson, D., 9–10, 23, 26
Anderson, D. F., 53, 59
Anglin, T. M., 82
Apter, M. J., 110–111
Arms, R. L., 62, 113, 115–116, 118–119,
    140–146
Armstrong, G., 148
Aveni, A. F., 32
Averill, L. A., 75
Baade, R. A., 57, 62
Babbage, S. B., 205
Bailey, C. I., 190
Bairner, A., 186
Baker, J. A., 47, 64
Balswick, J., 78
Bandura, A., 79, 94, 109
Baranowski, M. D., 83
Barney, R. K., 70–71, 90
Baron, R. A., 94, 112–114, 126
Barry, T., 112
Beasley, F. M., 9
Beck, J., 206
Beisser, A. R., 155
Benedetto, W., 126

Benedict, J., 86
Berkowitz, L., 94, 109, 124, 126, 134
Berman, M., 129
Bernhardt, P. C., 167
Bibby, R. W., 73, 115
Bilyeu, J. K., 45, 47–48, 50
Bird, P. J., 57
Bjorkqvist, K., 146
Blakenhorn, D., 125
Bloss, H., 9
Boldt, D., 125
Bonney, N., 148
Borden, R. J., 36, 170
Brady, E., 187, 193
Bragg, R., 193
Branscombe, N. R., 4–6, 49, 52–53, 56,
    59, 63–64, 67, 111, 115, 164–165,
    171–172, 174–175, 177
Branvold, S. E., 8–9, 32, 36, 58, 64,
    164
Braskamp, L. A., 54, 56, 58, 60, 66–67
Bredemeier, B. J., 76, 86
Brennan, K., 45, 47–48, 50
Brewer, K. R., 49
Brewer, M. B., 176
Briere, N. M. 48–49
Brill, A. A., 38, 155, 164
Brissett, D., 187
Brohm, J. M., 160
Brooks, C. M., 62
Brown, B. R. Jr., 83
Brown, D., 41
Brummett, B. 3, 35
Bryan, C., 101

240